BELTWAY
BOYS

BELTWAY BOYS

Stephen Strasburg, Bryce Harper,
and the Rise of the Nationals

Elliott Smith

TRIUMPH
BOOKS

Library of Congress Cataloging-in-Publication Data

Smith, Elliott, 1976–
  Beltway boys : Stephen Strasburg, Bryce Harper and the rise of the Nationals / Elliott Smith.
    pages cm
  ISBN 978-1-60078-803-1
  1. Washington Nationals (Baseball team) 2. Strasburg, Stephen, 1988– 3. Harper, Bryce, 1992– I. Title.
  GV875.W27S55 2013
  796.357'6409753—dc23
                                     2012046532

This book is available in quantity at special discounts for your group or organization. For further information, contact:

Triumph Books LLC
814 North Franklin Street
Chicago, Illinois 60610
(312) 337–0747
www.triumphbooks.com

Printed in U.S.A.
ISBN: 978-1-60078-803-1
Design by Patricia Frey
Photos courtesy of AP Images unless otherwise indicated

To Denise, Ava, and Xavier—You guys are my No. 1 picks.
To Mom—Thanks for helping to raise a big sports fan.
To Dad—I hope you get to read this up there.

———————————————

CONTENTS

FOREWORD

The remarkable rise of the Washington Nationals has been the most fascinating thing I've watched in three decades of Major League Baseball broadcasting. Hard times, trial and error, and going to war with lineups and pitching staffs overmatched against better opponents were obstacles impossible to overcome in those early years. During many evenings in the broadcast booth, we would look at the matchups and know there was no way the Nats could win that night. Now Charlie Slowes, Dave Jageler, F.P. Santangelo, and I know, even before we get to the park, that we have a chance to win because of the amazing pitching staff and lineup Mike Rizzo and Davey Johnson can put on that field on a daily basis. And this team may have only scratched the surface of what it is capable of!

Everything about this club and nearly everyone on it came from somewhere else, except for the Lerner family that coveted the opportunity to own a major league team and then realized that dream right in their own backyard. Clubhouse man Mike Wallace, media relations guru John Dever, and travel expert Rob McDonald accompanied the team from Montreal as did then-minor leaguers Roger Bernadina and Ian Desmond. Mike Rizzo came from Arizona and Davey Johnson from several stops on his way to Cooperstown, New York, along with player personnel geniuses Bob Boone and Roy Clark, who had made their marks elsewhere. Even the broadcasters came from coast to coast; Charlie from Tampa Bay, Dave from Pawtucket, Rhode Island, F.P. from San Francisco, and myself from St. Louis. I would say none of us were sure what we were getting ourselves into, and those early years were rough, but the rewards of a division title in 2012 made it all worthwhile.

Along with our owners, the uniquely local thing about our team is our knowledgeable and loyal Nats fans, many long-suffering since two versions of the Senators left in the '60s and '70s. After three decades of reluctantly looking 45 miles to the northeast for their baseball, they now have a team—a winning team—to call their own, and we couldn't be happier for them. They didn't fill RFK Stadium every night, and they don't fill Nationals Park every night, but we're getting there. Every season there are more big crowds and sellouts than the year before, and soon Nationals baseball will be a tough ticket. The ones who have faithfully supported this team from Day One in 2005 are a special breed indeed.

There are several young men who are, and will continue to be, the reasons for that. The foundation is made up of Ryan Zimmerman, the Nationals' first homegrown star; Jayson Werth and Adam LaRoche, established veterans who brought their talents and leadership here; organization guys Jordan Zimmermann, Ian Desmond, Danny Espinosa, Ross Detwiler, and Drew Storen; players who came in important deals like Gio Gonzalez, Tyler Clippard, Craig Stammen, and Ryan Mattheus; and the soon-to-be-seen Denard Span and Rafael Soriano. Werth changed the culture of the clubhouse and helped convince this bunch they could win. His epic at-bat in Game 4 of the 2012 NLDS is one for the ages.

To look forward one has to look back a bit, and contributions from Livan Hernandez, Brian Schneider, Chad Cordero, Alfonso Soriano, Pudge Rodriguez, and Michael Morse can't be overlooked. They were excellent Nats and will not be forgotten. Tony Tavares, Kevin Uhlich, Frank Robinson, and Jim Bowden—all instrumental in the move from Montreal to Washington—were organization anchors early in the Nationals' history.

Having listed all these, two very young men have helped take this organization to another level—Stephen Strasburg and Bryce Harper. They share several traits. Both want to win *badly*. Both have God-given talent that is so special, and at times breathtaking, that watching them (and broadcasting their exploits) makes you feel different, as though you're watching the potential for history every time they take the field. They are mature beyond their years, especially Bryce, and they handled the pressure of great, even unfair, expectations so well that one could only sit back and marvel at their poise and serenity on the big stage. From Strasburg's debut in 2010 to being shut down in '12, I am amazed at how he handled everything. From Harper's debut at Dodger Stadium last spring to playoff baseball, I'm amazed at what he did before age 20.

The pages you are about to read will take you on a journey from the nearly contracted, National League doormat to division champion, from 59 wins (twice) to 98, from a team laughed at to one greatly respected, even feared. These are the new Washington Nationals; read about them and know that what they have already accomplished, and what lies ahead is indeed impressive.

—Bob Carpenter,
Washington Nationals television broadcaster

PROLOGUE

AT 9:45 PM ON A COOL NIGHT WITH RAIN HEAVY IN THE AIR, THE
Washington Nationals received a fantastic piece of news from Pittsburgh
of all places.

It was there, at PNC Park, where a ragtag group of Pirates had
recorded the final out against the Atlanta Braves—an out that would make
Washington the National League East champions.

When that final batter was recorded and registered for the books up the
road, a roar, unlike any other, rose from the bowels of sold-out Nationals
Park and crested to the top of the venue, which overlooks the U.S. Capitol
building. You could be forgiven for perhaps thinking this was a movie
set. After all, the Nationals had been a terrible team since moving to the
nation's capital from Montreal, and only the active mind of a screenwriter
would dare give the hapless Nats a division title.

Yet this was real, even though for many it remained mind-boggling.
The Nats, once a ward of the MLB state and a baseball punch line,
were champions, sitting atop the division and the baseball world with a
staggering 96 victories.

Washington had three final outs to make before losing to the
Philadelphia Phillies, but that was a mere formality. When Danny Espinosa
tapped weakly to his counterpart at second base, the celebration began.
The Nationals had stunned the baseball establishment by essentially going
wire-to-wire to win the East, vaulting established powers like the Braves
and Phillies to herald a new arrival at the top of the heap.

Fireworks shot from the façade, and the players raced to the clubhouse
to grab the nearest bottle of bubbly. For the first time in 69 years, a Major

League Baseball team in Washington, D.C. had reason to celebrate. "They stuck with us, and we gave them something to cheer for, finally," said third baseman Ryan Zimmerman, the first-ever pick by the Nationals and the face of the franchise.

Amid the throng of sopping wet players, tykes holding champagne bottles, and savvy reporters wearing ponchos, the Nationals returned to the field to celebrate with the fans, who had wondered if D.C. would ever field a competitive team.

Over the years baseball has been home to several rags-to-riches squads, but you'd be hard-pressed to find a more systematic revamp of an entire franchise than the one the Nationals pulled off. "We were given this team below zero," Washington principal owner Mark Lerner said. "We have rebuilt it from scratch; we've always wanted to do it the right way and build from within. We've done that."

The smiling, soaked faces—from baseball lifer, general manager Mike Rizzo, to steely veteran Adam LaRoche, to chatterbox hurler Gio Gonzalez—said this was a moment to cherish, a night to savior, a culmination of hard work and dogged determination that caught even the sharpest of observers off guard.

As the Nationals players took laps around the field, spraying champagne into the stands and sharing high fives with any hands they could touch, it took the youngest player on Washington's roster to put things in perspective. "It's unbelievable," Bryce Harper said. "It's great to enjoy this with these fans and this city. They've been waiting for it. I want to win. I don't like losing. I want to celebrate like this."

Another crucial member of the Nationals joined in the celebration with what had to be a twinge of sadness. "This is a dream come true," star pitcher Stephen Strasburg said amid the madness. The ace right-hander was shut down just a few weeks earlier to aid in his recovery from Tommy John surgery in 2010, a scrutinized decision that turned into a national (or Nationals) debate. On this night, however, Strasburg celebrated like another one of the guys. "It's great to be winners," he said. "I'm happy to be a part of it."

This October night forever will be remembered by the Nationals franchise, but it was two days in the recent past that helped lay the groundwork for this celebration under the stars.

June 7-8, 2010

With the thousands of moving parts that comprise a Major League Baseball organization, it's nearly impossible to pinpoint the success or failure of a team on any particular time frame, but in the case of the Washington Nationals, the dramatic turnaround of one of MLB's most feckless franchises can be directly traced to two days.

On June 7, 2010, general manager Mike Rizzo once again held the No. 1 pick in the MLB Draft, and once again had a choice that was so simple to make, he could have turned the duties over to one of the tourists strolling the National Mall.

After selecting Stephen Strasburg, a once-in-a-generation pitcher, with the No. 1 pick in the 2009 Draft, Rizzo and the Nationals had another rare prospect at the top of their board—17-year-old phenom Bryce Harper.

Harper first came to national attention as a 16-year-old *Sports Illustrated* cover boy. The magazine detailed his ridiculously talented exploits, monstrous home run balls, and cocksure attitude regarding his seemingly preordained future success. He was a prodigious, precocious talent who earned a GED instead of finishing his last two years of high school so that he could play for the College of Southern Nevada, a junior college that plays in a wood bat conference.

While there, Harper hit .443 with 31 home runs, 98 RBIs, and 20 steals in 66 games, numbers that would seem shocking for a player his age, but they were in line with the expectations placed on Harper by himself and the media. Harper was the easy choice at No. 1 for the Nationals, who immediately announced he would switch positions from catcher to outfielder to reduce the wear and tear on his legs. "We believe that he could pull off being a major league catcher, but his bat is well ahead of his defense as a catcher," Rizzo said. "With the rigors of catching, we think it is going to accelerate his development and extend his career as a major leaguer." Harper, the first junior college player ever selected No. 1, was sanguine about the move, saying, "Anywhere they want me, I'll play."

Under normal circumstances, the drafting of a No. 1 pick would be met with a flurry of activity, but Harper wouldn't be making the traditional appearance at Nationals Park the next day for a news conference. There was something more important on the docket.

THERE WAS A BUZZ IN THE AIR on June 8, 2010 unlike any that had been felt since baseball returned to the nation's capital. The Nationals rarely made headlines, had sellout crowds, or drew the attention of media from across the country, but this day was different. Stephen Strasburg was making his major league debut for the Nationals, and everyone wanted to see if the hype was real.

The lanky fireballer had been attracting crowds ever since his college days at San Diego State, and after tearing through the minor leagues, anticipation had reached a fever pitch for his debut with the Nationals. As soon as the 2010 Nationals schedule was released, the media speculated when he would make his debut. Initially, it was thought that Strasburg would start June 4 against the Cincinnati Reds, leading fans to snap up thousands of tickets. But the Nationals pushed the start to June 8 against the lowly Pittsburgh Pirates, perhaps giving Strasburg a soft landing against one of the worst hitting teams in the majors.

Whatever the rationale, the atmosphere was electric when Strasburg took the hill, as a standing-room-only crowd watched every warm-up toss with giddy anticipation. When Strasburg uncorked his first pitch—a blazing fastball to Pirates outfielder Andrew McCutchen—the flashbulbs went off as if it was Game 7 of the World Series.

When it was all over, Strasburg had struck out 14 Pirates in one of the most dominating debuts ever, stunning everyone with his poise, power, and precision. "He pitched probably the best game I've ever seen pitched," said Adam Dunn, who was then a Nationals first baseman/outfielder.

It may be reductive, but just like that, over the course of two days, a franchise that had fought off contraction, only to drift along in irrelevance, suddenly had a future—and a bright one at that—thanks to two transcendent talents. "It's a lucky time to have two No. 1 picks," Rizzo said.

This is the story of how the quiet, determined Stephen Strasburg and the brash, bold Bryce Harper, along with a host of young talent and a renewed dedication to winning by the ownership and front office, helped turn the Washington Nationals from a laughingstock to a potential powerhouse.

BELTWAY
BOYS

1

THE RED-HATTED
STEPCHILDREN

THE STORY OF THE WASHINGTON NATIONALS BEGINS WITH THE demise of the Montreal Expos, a once proud franchise left in tatters due to contraction rumors, poor ownership, small-market economics, and fan frustration. Montreal had a long and storied baseball history as the Royals, a minor league affiliate of the Brooklyn/Los Angeles Dodgers. Jackie Robinson even played there before becoming the first African American player in the majors, but after the Dodgers moved the Royals closer to L.A., the city was without a team.

After considerable efforts from political figures in Montreal and the support of several key votes in Major League Baseball, including Dodgers owner Walter O'Malley, the Expos were founded in 1969 as part of MLB's expansion efforts.

Named after the 1967 International and Universal Exposition, or Expo '67 as most people referred to it, the Expos played their games at Jarry Park, a makeshift stadium boosted to MLB capability at the 11th hour. The facility, though, still proved substandard due to its exposure to the elements and its orientation, which often placed the sun directly in the vision of the first baseman. Still, the Expos proved to be a success with the people of Montreal despite a decade of losing teams. Rusty Staub became a cult hero of sorts, earning the nickname "Le Grand Orange" for his red hair.

In 1981, now playing at Olympic Stadium and with a corps of young players, including Gary Carter, Andre Dawson, and Tim Wallach, the Expos broke through and earned a playoff berth in the strike-shortened season, only to fall in the National League Championship Series to the Dodgers.

After another fallow period, the Expos of the mid-1990s had some of the best players of the era on their rosters, as Larry Walker, Pedro Martinez, Marquis Grissom, and Moises Alou became stars. But another strike would prove to be the downfall of the franchise. When the 1994 season ended abruptly, the Expos had the best record in baseball at 74–40 and were in line for their first playoff appearance since 1981. But just like that, the season was over, and when baseball started up again, the Expos began jettisoning their best players, much to the dismay of their once-loyal fan base. "They got frustrated with their favorite players leaving every year," Nationals broadcaster and former Expo F.P. Santangelo said. "People didn't want to spend their precious summer days in a decaying stadium."

The team was sold to art dealer Jeffrey Loria in 1999, and after the ownership group failed to replace crumbling Olympic Stadium or negotiate English language TV and radio contracts, the Expos played the majority of their games in a hermetically sealed, increasingly empty dome, becoming an afterthought to most baseball fans.

Baseball's attempts to rectify this increasingly grim situation came in the form of contraction, as the owners voted 28–2 in November 2001 to eliminate two teams: the Expos and the Minnesota Twins. In a fit of fortuitous chair shuffling, John Henry sold the Florida Marlins to Loria, so Henry could acquire the Boston Red Sox, leaving the Expos ownerless until MLB agreed to buy the team for $120 million. But in the case of the Expos, the damage had been done. Loria had moved the entire Montreal front office down to Miami, leaving the Expos with nothing on the verge of the upcoming season.

At this point, contraction would have been a more humane option, but the Metropolitan Sports Facilities Commission, operator of the Metrodome, won an injunction for the Twins to play there in 2002, forcing the owners to abandon their contraction plans for both teams.

During 2002, the Expos' last full season in Montreal, they drew 812,536 — an average of 10,031 fans per game — to Olympic Stadium. Most games, though, looked to have far fewer spectators than those figures, and the team lost approximately $30 million.

A month before the July 31 trading deadline of that 2002 season, general manager Omar Minaya traded prospects Cliff Lee, Grady

Sizemore, and Brandon Phillips to the Cleveland Indians to acquire pitcher Bartolo Colon in an ill-fated attempt to snag a wild-card berth. Although Colon pitched well in his three-month rental, Montreal didn't come close to reaching the playoffs. Each of the players given up by the Expos would become All-Stars, making this one of the most lopsided trades in recent baseball history and crippling the franchise's farm system for years to come, which would have a profound effect on the team's first few years in D.C.

With the growing movement to find the Expos a new home—and Washington, D.C. and the surrounding suburbs becoming a clear favorite—MLB commissioner Bud Selig came up with a new plan. The Expos would play 22 games in 2003 and 2004 in San Juan, Puerto Rico, which had hosted MLB's season-opening game in 2001. Hiram Bithorn Stadium, with a capacity of just 20,000, would be the "Los Expos" home venue for select series, as MLB looked to capitalize on the fervent Caribbean baseball audience to help the Expos stay afloat. "We believe these games will generate considerable excitement in Puerto Rico and throughout the Caribbean region," Selig said. "We have attempted to balance the need for home schedule certainty with this opportunity to stage attractive games in a city and region renowned for its production of players and the enthusiasm of its fans."

While it was clear that time was running out on the Expos in Montreal, Washington, D.C. was building steam to get back into the nation's pastime.

THE STORY OF THE WASHINGTON NATIONALS must also encompass the oft-inglorious history of D.C. baseball, which primarily brought misery to the residents of the nation's capital during the off-and-on dalliances the sport had with the city. The first iteration of the Washington Senators, originally known as the Statesmen, formed in 1891 in the American Association before moving to the National League the next season. But when the NL went about its own contraction plans, the hapless Senators were among four teams trimmed from the ledger.

The Senators were back in 1901, becoming one of the American League's charter franchises. But the Senators were uniformly bad.

Columnist Charles Dryden perfectly encapsulated the Senators in the classic, withering statement: "Washington: first in war, first in peace, and last in the American League."

In 1924, however, the Senators—in a strange turn, the team's owners had changed the name of the franchise to "Nationals" in 1905, but most people still referred to the team as the Senators or "Nats"—won the only World Series in the history of the franchise behind Hall of Fame pitcher Walter "Big Train" Johnson.

In 1933, the Senators captured the AL pennant once again, but lost to the New York Giants in the World Series, beginning a long and dark age for Major League Baseball in D.C. The Senators foundered and became fodder for laughs thanks to their losing way. Case in point: the musical *Damn Yankees* features the sad sack Senators as the team for which Joe Boyd/Joe Hardy sells his soul. There, however, was good baseball being played in the District.

The Homestead Grays were a flagship franchise in the Negro Leagues, filled with some of the brightest stars of the day, including Josh Gibson, Cool Papa Bell, and Buck Leonard. From 1940 until the franchise folded in 1950, it adopted the name of either the Washington Grays or the Washington Homestead Grays and played at Griffith Stadium when the Senators were on road trips, providing a much better brand of baseball and often drawing better crowds than the regular home tenants. The Grays appeared in the Negro League World Series five times, and their 1948 World Series victory would be the last official appearance by a D.C. franchise in the postseason.

On the MLB level, the original Senators began looking for greener pastures, and in 1960, they agreed to move to Minneapolis to become the Minnesota Twins. "Calvin Griffith didn't like the site D.C. picked for the new stadium, because it was in a black neighborhood," said D.C. baseball historian Phil Wood. As the Senators were dragging their feet in adding a black player, so were the Washington Redskins. Griffith had been courted for a number of years by the West Coast. "San Francisco went after the Senators in the early 1950s," Wood said. "They made an overture. But all Calvin could think of was the big earthquake they had 50 years earlier. Minneapolis-St. Paul, which also had gone after the [New York] Giants, put together a sweetheart deal. He left because he could leave, and Minneapolis offered him pretty much anything he wanted."

It didn't hurt that the Twin Cities had a largely white demographic. "I'll tell you why we came to Minnesota," Griffith said. "It was when I found out you only had 15,000 blacks here. Black people don't go to ball games, but they'll fill up a rassling ring and put up such a chant it'll scare you to death. It's unbelievable. We came here because you've got good, hardworking, white people here."

That move, however, also ensured that D.C. would receive an expansion team, and so, the 1961 season kicked off with the "new" Washington Senators, an entirely different franchise from the previous one. According to Wood, MLB was concerned about the Continental League, a new baseball league being formed under the aegis of former Brooklyn Dodgers president Branch Rickey. The goal of the Continental League was to get another team back in New York, though the powers behind the league also wanted to establish teams in territories without an MLB presence. Minneapolis-St. Paul was one of those locations, but when the Senators moved there, MLB acted quickly to quash the threat by announcing two expansion teams in each league. Those teams would become the New York Mets, Houston Colt .45s, Los Angeles Angels, and Senators.

It's hard to imagine, but the new Senators were worse than their predecessor. Shaky ownership plagued the franchise from the very beginning, and the team never acquired the necessary players to even come close to contending.

Slugger Frank Howard did his best to entertain the rapidly dwindling fans at Robert F. Kennedy Stadium, launching mammoth home runs into the empty upper deck, but there was very little else to cheer about. "They'd tease you a little bit," Wood said. "In 1967 after 116 games, they'd won and were 58–58. They came home, and it was variously described as hundreds of people waiting to greet them at the airport. It was a defining moment. What would we do if we had a contender? By end of the season, they were nine games under and tied for sixth place with the Orioles."

There were only a couple of brief highlights during the Senators' second run in D.C., one being Hall of Fame hitter Ted Williams taking over as manager in 1969. "Teddy Ballgame," the last man to hit .400 and a Boston Red Sox legend, was an inspired but surprising choice to be named skipper, given that he had shown no inclination to return to baseball since he retired in 1960.

Senators owner Bob Short, however, sensing an opportunity to get *any* kind of publicity for his ragtag squad, made Williams an offer he couldn't refuse—a five-year contract package worth more than $1.5 million. That kind of money was unheard of at the time. Williams also received a stock option and a chance to purchase more—up to 10 percent—of the club. He was named vice president and had a clause in his contract that he could quit but not be fired.

The hiring of the game's best hitter put a spotlight on the Senators that had never been as bright, and even the publicity-averse Williams handled his new role as ambassador/coach with aplomb. "He brought a lot of attention to the club, nationally," Wood said. "There were always network sportscasting crews in spring training. Williams had been out of the game for a number of years and didn't really know any of the players of the team. He could be irascible. But there was something about when he walked into the room. There was an aura about him. It was a daily thrill just to see him in a uniform with 'Senators' across the front."

Although the talent Williams had on hand as a rookie skipper was downright anemic, he somehow wrangled the wretched Senators to respectability, leading the squad to an 86–76 mark—the only winning record during the franchise's time in D.C. "The players had great things to say about Williams as a hitting instructor," Wood said. "In terms of strategy, however, it was Nellie Fox who was in charge of that. He knew when to play small ball, what to do when a power hitter was at bat."

Williams also inadvertently changed an important part of the baseball process, requiring that his team get a brief respite before reporters could enter the clubhouse after a game. "It used to be as soon as game ended, reporters could go right into the clubhouse. Williams said, 'We need a 15-minute cooling off period.' Now, that's standard," Wood said. "You can't get right in. So he was maybe a little ahead of his time.

"I think he enjoyed being in the limelight a little bit, but he would never would tip his cap or acknowledge any applause. That wore off after 1969. After that first year, he lost interest and the players kind of reverted to form."

With the Baltimore Orioles blossoming into a perennial playoff and World Series contender, the Senators drifted into irrelevance, and Short fell deeper into debt, making him increasingly receptive to the siren call of other cities looking to poach an MLB team. And on September 21, 1971, owners agreed to let Short move the team to Arlington, Texas, where they would become the Texas Rangers. "It was a great deal," Wood said. "[Dallas-Fort Worth was] offering [Short] 10 years of broadcast revenue up front—roughly $7.5 million. The money would be his to keep, so he moved to Texas, and about three years later, he sold the team. He made out real well."

But D.C. fans had the last word, turning the Senators' last game at RFK into a near riot by storming the field in the ninth inning and stealing souvenirs. The umpires were forced to award the New York Yankees the game in a forfeit, an inglorious—but perhaps fitting—end to baseball's turbulent and unsuccessful years in the nation's capital.

The ensuing years were relatively quiet, with dissatisfied teams occasionally using D.C. to gain leverage in their stadium talks. Most fans in the D.C. and Virginia area drifted to the Orioles, who slowly took over the market. "In 1972 the Orioles bought a few billboards around D.C. that showed Boog Powell following through on his swing that said, 'Take a short drive to see a long drive.' But in '72 with no team in Washington, the Orioles' attendance went down," Wood said. "It didn't catch on. Part of the reason, from my perspective, was that O's used to come to D.C. and beat our brains out.

"It took until 1979, when Edward Bennett Williams bought the O's, for it to click in. Fans in D.C. thought Williams was going to move the team here. Fans in Baltimore thought the same thing, but they were drawing more fans from Baltimore. The Orioles had never drawn more than 2 million, but it took 10 years after Senators left to do so."

So when Selig posited moving the Expos to Washington, there was one man standing in the way of making the move happen—Orioles owner Peter Angelos.

Since 1972, Angelos' Orioles held the Baltimore-Washington market to themselves, and he considered a new team in D.C. a major affront to his domain, despite the fact that the Senators and Orioles had shared the population just fine in the past. "It was a situation where [MLB] had no place else to go, where there was a park that had 40,000 seats, parking, and people clamoring to write them big checks," Wood said. "So they worked out a deal with Angelos, where he would own no less than 67

The Soriano Situation

Although many of the Nationals teams in the early days were bereft of talent, Washington did have a superstar—albeit a mercurial one—for a brief spell. Alfonso Soriano was a five-tool player for the first part of his career with the New York Yankees, becoming the second player in franchise history to hit 30 homers and steal 30 bases. One of the brightest young talents in the game, Soriano was the centerpiece of the deal that brought Alex Rodriguez to the Yankees.

The move to Texas did little to slow Soriano's ascent, as he continued to rack up All-Star appearances and Silver Slugger Awards. In 2005 Soriano hit .268 with 36 homers, 104 RBIs, and 30 stolen bases, so when the Nationals pulled off a stunning winter deal that landed them the slugging second baseman, it seemed like a steal, especially given they only sent Brad Wilkerson, Terrmel Sledge, and a minor leaguer (Armando Galarraga) to the Rangers.

But the deal came with a cost. Soriano was due for salary arbitration and, even though he lost, he was awarded $10 million, the highest figure gained in arbitration to date. Soriano turned down the Nationals' contract extension, making him eligible to become a free agent after the season and positioning him, essentially, as a one-year rental.

Washington already had Jose Vidro at second base, Soriano's preferred position, so the Nationals planned to have the slugger move to left field, a shift that immediately caused bad feelings between the player and his new team. Soriano refused to take the field in the Nationals' first spring training game, leaving the team and fans stunned and general manager Jim Bowden little option but to threaten to disqualify Soriano's deal. "If he's going to play here, he's going to have to be out in left field," Nationals manager Frank Robinson said. "He said he's ready to play. He needs to play. He's ready for the season, and I penciled him in the lineup in left field."

Soriano would return to the field for the Nationals next spring training contest and would go on to play left with little consequence the rest of the way. In fact, Soriano would go about putting up one of the best statistical seasons ever seen in D.C. He would become the fourth player in baseball history—along with Jose Canseco, Barry Bonds, and Alex Rodriguez—to join the 40-40 club and later in the season became the first player to add 40 doubles to make him a 40-40-40 player. "Honestly, he wasn't that big of a headache, at least not once he agreed to move to left field. The situation that spring was pretty bizarre, but he agreed to go to left field the next day and was never a problem after that. He was one of the hardest-working players I've ever covered and was a great teammate," said longtime Nationals reporter Mark Zuckerman. "The other guys absolutely loved him. And there was some angst in some corners when they didn't re-sign him after the season. More specifically, there were those, myself included, who thought Jim Bowden made a mistake not trading him at the July 31 deadline and instead letting him walk as a free agent."

Yet Soriano's contract situation hung over the team like a dead albatross. Having refused to negotiate during the season, the July 31 trading deadline became a flashpoint for the team. Would they take a half-baked offer from a team looking for a three-month rental, wait until the end of the season and try to work out a deal with the player, or have Soriano leave and receive compensatory picks in return?

In the end, despite saying that he wanted to stay with the Nationals, Soriano summarily rejected the team's $70 million deal, signing with the Chicago Cubs for eight years and $136 million, a stunning outlay of cash for a perfidious talent. "I waited for those guys to call me," Soriano said of the Nationals. "They never called."

Although it was a painful loss at the time, the Nationals came out on top in the end. "As it turned out, Bowden knew exactly what he was doing," Zuckerman said. "He felt that two draft picks were more valuable than whatever was being offered in a trade."

After Soriano departed D.C., his body began to slowly give out on him. Hampered by hamstring, quadriceps, and knee injuries, Soriano's speed disappeared. After swiping 41 bases with the Nationals, he's never stolen more than 19 in a season and over the past three years he's stolen just 13 bases.

Never a great defender, Soriano also labored in the outfield with the Cubs, and the team in 2008 even instructed him to stop doing his trademark hop after catching fly balls. The Cubs are still on hook for his salary through 2014 and have spent most of the past few seasons trying to find a willing trade partner to help remove some of Soriano's hefty salary from their payroll.

The Nationals received two picks from the Cubs. Although one didn't pan out, the other turned out to be Jordan Zimmermann, the right-handed starter who played a huge role on the 2012 division champions. In this case patience—and overpayment—paid off in the Nationals' favor.

percent of the TV rights. They gave him $75 million to get it started. Those were the roots of [Mid-Atlantic Sports Network] MASN. People thought it was, 'I'll do this and I won't sue you.' That's not true, but Angelos was a litigious guy, and he wouldn't have hesitated to get a temporary restraining order."

On September 29, 2004, despite Angelos' objections, MLB announced the Expos would be moving to D.C. to start the 2005 season. "This is another important step in finalizing the relocation of the Montreal Expos to Washington, D.C.," Selig said. "We are looking forward to finishing the last few steps, including the sale of the ballclub, and the rebirth of the club as the Washington Nationals." The team would start play in venerable (to put it kindly) RFK Stadium, while a new home for the team was found and built. On December 3, 2004, the owners approved the move by a 28–1 vote. (Guess who was the lone dissenting voice.) And baseball was officially back in the nation's capital.

Of course, it wouldn't be that easy. The Nationals still had to navigate through the sordid realm of D.C. politics, Angelos' desire to control Washington's TV rights, and myriad other issues before actually taking the field. And, in reality, the Nationals were in tatters, a shell of an organization given short shrift by the owners, who didn't want to invest any of their money in a team that could potentially cost their own franchises revenues. "By the time they reached the end of their rope in Montreal, they were viewed basically as an orphan of Major League Baseball," said CBSSports. com baseball columnist Scott Miller. "They were the poor street kid that was bruised, and dirty, and taken in off the street, and plopped down in a new home. The first couple of years it was clear it was going to take a long time for them to become relevant."

But on April 4, 2005, those matters were secondary, as the Washington Nationals played their first game, against the Philadelphia Phillies, an 8–4 loss. The Nats would pick up their first win, a 7–3 victory on April 6, in the season's second game behind Brad Wilkerson, who hit for the cycle.

That set the stage for baseball's return to D.C. on April 14, when the Nationals hosted the Arizona Diamondbacks. With more than 45,000 fans in attendance, president George W. Bush throwing out the first pitch, and a feeling of optimism surging through ancient RFK, the Nats earned a 5–3 victory. "In the pageantry and excitement, there was all kinds of hope and promise," Miller said. "But also that sobering reality that it was going to take a while to turn that hope and promise into the kind of baseball that fans were hoping to one day see."

In fact, under the steely tutelage of Hall of Famer Frank Robinson, the team's manager, the Nats overachieved their first season in D.C., tallying a 50–31 mark through their first 81 games and finishing the year a surprising 81–81, a feat that was truly smoke and mirrors. "The first year, there was a lot of attention on them, because it was a brand-new thing," said Mark Zuckerman, who has covered the team since its inception, first for the *Washington Times* and now for Comcast SportsNet and his own blog, Nats Insider. "The fans were into it, but the organization was not built up at all. There was a barebones staff at RFK Stadium. They all worked out of these trailers and they didn't have a whole lot of prep time. Everyone was kind of overwhelmed by all this. But I don't think anyone understood what was going on. They were just going with the flow. If anything, it made people assume, 'Oh, this team should be good again soon.'"

But that was not the case. In the aftermath of their exciting D.C. debut, the Nationals were a terrible team. Featuring such unimpressive names as Terrmel Sledge, Deivi Cruz, J.J. Davis, Sunny Kim, Junior Spivey, Nook Logan and a host of other players whose careers came to an end after they washed out of Washington, the Nationals didn't even have the promise of a bright future. "When I first came here, all of us realized the situation the team was in, having been owned by MLB," said Nationals play-by-play man Bob Carpenter, who started broadcasting for the team's Mid-Atlantic Sports Network in 2006. "In Montreal, there was no stadium, low attendance, payroll limitations, and there was no way they were going to survive, so they bring the team here, and a lot of those problems just followed the team.

"We didn't have the scouting system or minor league people at that time. As a broadcaster you go on the air every night and try to put the best foot forward. We weren't hired to worry about where the organization was at. We were hired to announce games, and that's what we did."

Carpenter's job was even more difficult, considering the sweetheart deal that Angelos made with MLB made it practically impossible to find the Nationals on TV. For the team's first two seasons, as cable providers dragged their feet on adding another channel, most fans missed out on following Washington's on-field exploits. The Nationals are still the only team in Major League Baseball not to own their broadcast rights. "At the beginning the TV games were going virtually nowhere outside the production truck," Carpenter said. "In the latter part of the 2006 season, my friends in Arlington [a suburb of D.C.] could finally see the Nationals. Right now, as you look back, it seems a little bit absurd, given the circumstances and situation the organization was in."

Aside from on-field struggles, the other major problems for the Nationals revolved around finding ownership and the construction of a new stadium, both of which were tied to each other.

The Expos' move to Washington was contingent on the team building a new stadium, but that plan relied on the notoriously murky D.C. City Council pushing through a plan for a $581 million stadium that most residents were against, since it was lacking financial support from Virginia and Maryland whose residents would account for a large percentage of the stadium's attendance. After much back and forth between the city and MLB, however, the plans for the $611 million stadium, located near the Anacostia River in the city's southeast district, were finalized on March 7, 2006.

MLB agreed to contribute $20 million toward the stadium's construction but pointedly did not agree to cover cost overruns on the park, which had been one of the primary debates leading up to the agreement. (This would prove to be a win for the league, as the final cost of the stadium came in at an estimated $693 million.)

That set the stage for MLB to finally find an owner for its wayward franchise, which loomed over the team for nearly four years.

The selection came down to three groups of finalists: one led by billionaire developer Theodore "Ted" Lerner, another by former Seattle Mariners owner Jeff Smulyan, and one by Fred Malek and Jeffrey Zients, the leaders of the Washington Baseball Club. In the end Selig chose the Lerner group, who bought the Nationals off MLB's hands for $450 million and gave the team either the richest or second-richest owner in the league, depending on how you slice the investment pies. "This has been a long journey," commissioner Bud Selig said. "While I do apologize for the time, I think history will prove it maybe was time well spent."

Lerner, who was born in Washington, D.C., made his fortune in real estate, and his Lerner Enterprises was the largest private owner of property in the city. Given his background, it was only fitting that this scion would be the franchise's savior. "Wow, it's been some kind of day," Lerner said during a press conference announcing the sale. "It's something I've been thinking about all my life, from the time I used to pay 25 cents to sit in the bleachers at Griffith Stadium."

While Ted Lerner was the figurehead, his sons would run the day-to-day ownership roles, with Mark Lerner, a jovial man who sometimes put on a uniform and shagged fly balls in the outfield, becoming the primary face of the organization. "When Commissioner Selig gave us a team, it was a big decision on his part," Mark Lerner said. "First of all my family wants to thank him for having the trust for us to do it the right way. I hope he is proud of what we have become."

Although acquiring stable ownership who were willing to spend money was a huge step, the damage had already been done. The Nationals, who would go on to lose 91 games in 2006 and 89 games in 2007 before Nationals Park opened in 2008, already had earned the wrong kind of reputation in baseball both on and off the field. For the most part, Washington played in relative obscurity, only coming to national attention once or twice a year, such as when Nationals pitcher Mike Bascik gave up Barry Bonds' record-breaking 756th home run on August 7, 2007.

But a major blow for the franchise revolved around the heralded signing of Dominican Republic prospect Esmailyn "Smiley" Gonzalez, who was listed as 19 when the team inked him to a $1.4 million deal in 2006, but actually turned out to be a 23-year-old named Carlos Alvarez. The deal raised eyebrows around baseball because the Nationals seemed to have overpaid for an average prospect and circumvented an agent to work with Gonzalez/Alvarez's personal *buscon* or handler, Basilo Vizcaino.

Vizcaino was a childhood friend of then-Nationals general manager Jim Bowden's special assistant, former major league pitcher Jose Rijo. Vizcaino was also connected to Jose Baez, then the Nationals director of operations in the Dominican. The disparity of the bonus—the Texas Rangers were the next highest bidder for the player's services, at $700,000—and the connections between Vizcaino, Rijo, and Baez drew the attention of the FBI and MLB's investigative arm.

(Alvarez still remains in the Nationals' farm system. In 2012 he was promoted to Single A Hagerstown, Maryland, but at 26, he is not considered a prospect.)

But during 2009 spring training and in large part because of the Alvarez controversy, Bowden stepped down, though he continues to deny any involvement in the wrongdoing. The Nationals had to start from scratch in the fertile Dominican Republic, hurting their player development for several years. All in all, it was another black eye for a franchise struggling to right the ship. "They were a laughingstock around baseball," Zuckerman said. "If you asked people around baseball what they knew about the Nationals, it would be Jim Bowden, their GM, who was not very well respected around the game. You had the Smiley Gonzalez fiasco, which did not speak highly of the organization. You had ownership that was new at this and didn't always know how to go about things and wasn't getting a lot of positive reaction.

"They had really small payrolls, which didn't sit well with people. They had a first-round draft pick, Aaron Crow, that didn't sign with them. You had some bad signings. You put that all together, and it was a low point. I distinctly remember feeling like, in looking around the rest of the game, players wouldn't even think of coming to Washington. That was your last chance. That's where Ronnie Belliard would go, or Dmitri Young would go, or Elijah Dukes would go, when they had no other options."

Aside from finally getting out from under the thumb of MLB and acquiring stable ownership, there was another bright spot for the Nationals as they prepared to open the 2008 campaign. Third baseman Ryan Zimmerman was the fourth overall pick by the Nationals in the 2005 Draft, and by the end of that season, he was up in the big leagues. Born and raised in the Tidewater area of Virginia and a collegiate star at the University of Virginia, Zimmerman was a local product. His talents were undeniable, even on dreadful teams, and he was the only reason that anyone would have paid attention to the team during its first few years of existence. "Well, I knew one thing about the Nationals," said F.P. Santangelo, who started his broadcasting career as the in-game reporter with the San Francisco Giants before moving on to Washington. "They had a good third baseman. Every time he came out West, this was the guy who people said, 'Hey, he could play.'"

2

THE RACE FOR AN ACE

With the Lerners on board and Zimmerman on the field, the 2008 season appeared to be another step in the right direction. Other positives included the opening of Nationals Park and a manager in Manny Acta, who seemed comfortable with the challenge of rebuilding the team. But it was a disaster in every way...except one.

THE FINAL WEEK OF THE BASEBALL SEASON, FOR THOSE NOT involved in a pennant race, is a desultory affair filled with newcomers getting a taste of the big leagues, veterans playing out the string, and teams trying to wrap up a lost year as quickly as possible. While the haves battled for playoff position and home-field advantage, the have-nots generally went about their business in quiet stadiums, occasionally playing spoiler, but more often than not, marking off the days until they could pack up and head home.

By this time, the optimism found at the beginning of the campaign had given way to the reality of failure, setting the stage for the inevitable house cleaning and personnel shuffling done once Game 162 has been recorded. Rarely is there ever any intrigue at the bottom of the standings, but the 2008 season was quite different, because there was a once-in-a-lifetime prize waiting for the worst team in baseball.

After a dominating junior season in which he had compiled a 13–1 record and 1.45 ERA, San Diego State pitcher Stephen Strasburg had emerged as the clear No. 1 pick in the upcoming draft. Pitchers with his skill set and comport come along once every decade, so it was a no-brainer that Strasburg would be the top choice of the team with the worst record in baseball. Although everyone would have loved to have been in the Strasburg discussion, there were two main candidates in the race for an ace—the Washington Nationals and Seattle Mariners.

The 2008 season got started in stirring fashion for Washington, who opened Nationals Park with a nationally televised ESPN Sunday night game against the Atlanta Braves. Ryan Zimmerman hit a two-out, walk-off home run in the bottom of the ninth to give the Nationals a dramatic victory in the showcase of their new home. After defeating the Philadelphia

Phillies in their next two games, the Nats would start the year 3–0. But any hopes that this would be a different and more successful Washington team were quickly erased by a 6–16 skid, which set the tone for the remainder of the year.

The Nationals did not give fans much to cheer about at their new stadium. The team was assembled with a variety of spare parts and has-been veterans, including Paul Lo Duca, Aaron Boone, Wily Mo Pena, Lastings Milledge, Shawn Hill, Odalis Perez, Jason Bergmann, and other forgettable names. Washington had two nine-game losing streaks and one 12-game losing streak during the season.

Even Zimmerman, the cornerstone of the franchise, played in just 106 games after suffering a labral tear in his left shoulder. The Nationals couldn't hit, couldn't field, and couldn't stay healthy—a recipe for impending doom. "It was a total collapse," manager Manny Acta said.

On the other side of the country, it was a similar nightmare scenario for the Mariners. Seattle was expected to contend in 2008. After all, the team played very well during 2007, earning its first winning record since 2003, the halcyon days of the franchise. And the 2008 squad looked even stronger on paper than its predecessor. During the offseason, the Mariners acquired pitchers Erik Bedard and Carlos Silva to further bolster a staff anchored by young stud Felix Hernandez.

But things quickly went south in the Emerald City. Sidelined with a variety of maladies and ineffective on the hill, Bedard was a dud. From the start, though, he was in a bad situation. The Mariners named Bedard as the No. 1 starter in the 2008 season over Hernandez, which all parties said was fine at the time. Later, however, it was discovered that Hernandez was irked with the decision, and Bedard was uncomfortable with the label of "ace."

In the first month of the season, Bedard went on the disabled list with a sore hip. During May he forced the team's hand and made them use Jamie Burke as his own personal catcher. All the while, he wasn't delivering on the hill, laboring through starts, often lasting five innings before running out of gas.

In the offseason, Bedard would claim to need shoulder surgery, but once doctors explored the area, they found nothing more than minor fraying. Perhaps appropriately, Bedard missed several days of the 2009 season with a strained gluteus maximus. Mariners beat reporters had a good laugh, considering that Bedard had been a pain in the ass during his entire tenure with Seattle. The lefty would miss a majority of that season with more shoulder issues and finish his Seattle tenure with a 15–14 mark in 46 starts.

The deal the Mariners made with the Orioles for Bedard now ranks as one of the worst in team history given the development of outfielder Adam Jones for Baltimore. Jones, a five-tool player whom the Mariners carefully nurtured through their farm system, went to Baltimore and became an All-Star and the centerpiece of the Orioles resurgence, signing a six-year, $85 million contract extension in May 2012. (And Jones continues to terrorize his former team, with a .314 batting average, .350 slugging percentage, and .450 on-base plus slugging percentage in 42 games against the Mariners.)

During midseason and shortly after the Nationals swept the M's in Seattle, the Mariners fired general manager Bill Bavasi and manager John McLaren, naming Jim Riggleman, who would ironically manage the Nationals the next season, as interim manager. Seattle released overpaid and underperforming slugger Richie Sexson in July and Jose Vidro (a former National) in August.

That set the stage for a September that would permanently shape both franchises. "At some point late in '08, when you knew the Nationals were going to be around the worst in the league, and you started to hear more about this kid from San Diego State that was almost certainly going to be the No. 1 pick," said longtime Nationals writer Mark Zuckerman, "there was an understanding that it was going to be an interesting competition to finish for the worst record [with the Mariners], and that it wouldn't be the worst thing in the world if they did."

The Nationals entered the final month of the season sporting a garish 52–85 record, while the Mariners were 53–83. The glow of a new stadium had already faded from the minds of most Washington fans, as the Nats were down to an average daily attendance of about 25,000 people. In the final month, they would play 22 of 25 games against NL East foes, with three games against the San Diego Padres (also an outside contender for Strasburg) mixed in. The Mariners would counter with 26 games, the majority of which were against AL West opponents, with series against the New York Yankees and Kansas City Royals thrown in.

As expected, both teams struggled mightily during the month. Washington lost 11 of 14 games going into the final series of the season, giving them a 59–99 record with three games remaining at the Philadelphia Phillies. Seattle topped that, dropping 14 of 15 heading into its final series at home against the Oakland A's, putting them ahead in the Strasburg race at 58–101.

And make no mistake, it was a freefall to the bottom. The Nats' September series against the Padres even earned a special designation. "We were calling it the Strasburg series," Zuckerman said. "And [then GM Jim] Bowden wouldn't come all the way out and say they were trying to lose the games, but he was kind of jokingly talking about that sort of thing, and I don't think it upset him at all that they got swept by the Padres."

While Bowden took a slightly facetious tone regarding the prize for the worst record in the majors, the Mariners took a more serious approach. "There were never any conversations about the No. 1 draft pick," said then-Mariners manager Riggleman. "It was understood you just go out and try to win the games...There were a lot of things to play for. We had such a bad September. Just to win a couple of games felt good. We weren't really thinking in terms of the No. 1 pick. The feeling was, if we're picking one through five, we're going to get an exceptional athlete."

The Mariners needed to lose two of their final three to lock up Strasburg; the Nationals needed to lose all three. With the Phillies fighting to earn an NL East crown, the Nationals were facing a motivated opponent, who had no trouble sweeping away weary Washington, even with backups playing in the final game of the season.

The Phillies celebrated a division crown while the Nationals staggered to a 100-loss season. The gulf between the two teams never seemed larger.

Meanwhile, the Mariners woke up and played three solid games against the A's, sweeping Oakland to essentially remove themselves from the No. 1 pick. Instead they earned the inglorious distinction of becoming the first team with a $100 million payroll to lose 100 games and earn the No. 2 pick, which they used to select second baseman Dustin Ackley.

That's not to say there was celebration in the Nationals dugout. This was a team that cratered to a 59–102 mark, and most of the principals would not be involved with the team going forward. "Not one of those guys was trying to lose 100 games," Zuckerman said. "Except for Zimmerman and maybe a couple of guys, who felt like they could be part of the team down the road, they all knew they weren't going to be part of it."

Riggleman, who lit just enough of a fire underneath the Mariners to prevent them from finishing with the worst record in baseball, would be named Nationals bench coach prior to the 2009 season and take over the managerial reins in July when Acta was fired, giving him the opportunity to be Strasburg's first big league skipper.

The Nationals had won the losers race to the bottom of the Major League Baseball standings, and their reward—Stephen Strasburg—awaited.

3

THE PHENOM, PART I

"THE SCOUTS WOULD CALL, AND THEY'D ASK ME, 'WHO DO YOU have?'" recalls longtime high school baseball coach Scott "Hoppy" Hopgood of his days at West Hills High School just outside of San Diego in the suburb of Santee, California. "I'd tell them I had a kid named Aaron Richardson. And then, I've got this other kid, Strasburg."

Not exactly the story of legend. But Stephen Strasburg wasn't a phenomenon from the first time he stepped foot on a baseball field. He was just a kid, struggling to find his way in the game he loved but couldn't master. "The thing, I think, people forget about Strasburg is that he didn't become Stephen Strasburg, the Phenom, until his last two years or so of college," said former *Washington Times* and current NatsInsider.com writer Mark Zuckerman.

Born July 20, 1988 in San Diego, Strasburg was a tall, powerful kid who blazed through little league competition with a live arm and raw power. By the time he reached Hopgood in high school, Strasburg had the build but little else. "He was a big kid—6'4", 255 pounds," Hopgood said. "He was throwing 90 [miles per hour] as a junior."

But Strasburg's conditioning was terrible. He ate fast food and hung out instead of working out, and so the teenager would often struggle to get through practices. His fragile knees often couldn't bear the weight of his upper body, and he would collapse on the mound. "He would just go out and throw," Hopgood said. "There was no effort from Stephen; he was just cruising. I figured he would take care of it, but he wouldn't. He didn't know how to run. Running is not fun. It's going to hurt, and you're going to puke. But I just wanted to make sure he was ready to go for his next start. There wasn't much discipline on my part, because it was my first head coaching job."

The West Hills team was a ragtag bunch, and they struggled mightily during Strasburg's first year. Snapping at his teammates after they made errors and barking at umpires for missed calls, Strasburg didn't help the cause. The righty was 0–10 going into his last start of the season, which just so happened to be against the team that had set the state record for consecutive losses, and Hopgood knew it. "He was pitching well, but we didn't do much as a team," he said. "It was a real frustrating year for him. That's where he got a lot of the labels that he was aggressive toward teammates and yelling at umps. But that was because he wanted to win. He had the raw talent, but he was easy to rattle. But we got him a start on three days rest against the worst team in the state and beat them 3–0."

So how did Stephen Strasburg go from a 1–10 high school pitcher to *the* Stephen Strasburg? Hopgood credits the pitcher's determination. "I never had an issue with him," Hopgood said. "I knew he wanted to win. There were a few things he needed to change mechanically and mentally. But when you're talking to a 16, 17-year-old kid about being professional, some of that goes right over his head. He really improved on the basis of getting in shape and the mental aspect of the game—the mentality of pitching. He started learning how to pitch. I always made sure my guys got the right coaching, and he really bought into it."

In his senior year, Strasburg posted a 1.36 ERA, 74 strikeouts in 62 innings, and seven complete games to go along with a 7–2 record. And he played a major role in helping West Hills turn from one of the conference's bottom feeders into a playoff contender. "We were like the Bad News Bears," Hopgood said. "By Strasburg's senior year, we were playing great baseball and had earned a lot of respect. Before, we were the stomping ground for the other teams in our league, but then we went further than anyone had ever gone. It's a totally different atmosphere [at West Hills] because of what that team started, and I feel like we all had a part in it somehow."

Still, there was no chance that he would be drafted by a major league team, and there weren't many college coaches knocking down Hopgood's door either. "He said, 'I'm going to Stanford,' so I never called any colleges," Hopgood said. "People would say, 'What are you doing with Strasburg?' and I said, 'He's going to Stanford.' I said, 'Give him three years in a college weight room.' I thought the college game would mature him."

And while Strasburg may have wanted to join the powerhouse Cardinal team, another door opened much closer to home when Tony Gwynn, one of the best baseball hitters of his generation, offered him a spot on the San Diego State team at the urging of Aztecs pitching coach Rusty Filter.

But college life—and the rigors of preseason conditioning—didn't immediately suit Strasburg, who came close to calling it quits. "I was going to find a job," he said of his early college days. "We [had] a Home Depot and a Lowe's near our house." But with the help of Gwynn and the tough love of Aztecs strength coach Dave Ohton, Strasburg began to reshape his body, which also would reshape his mind.

Ohton took one look at his burly new charge and balked, rechristening Strasburg as "Slothburg," which later became shortened to "Sloth." Strasburg couldn't even make it through an off-season conditioning session. "I had never seen a college athlete as far behind as he was," Ohton said. "I didn't think it was possible to be that bad. I asked him if he had a medical condition."

Ohton put Strasburg through the wringer, teaching the pitcher the proper techniques for weightlifting and conditioning. To his credit, Strasburg responded. He cut out fast foods and began to drop pounds, eventually shedding more than 30 pounds under Ohton's watch. "I had to get tougher both mentally and physically," he said. "It came down to, if you want something bad enough, you have to go out and get it. I just never really understood what I needed to do personally to be successful. That's what I really learned at San Diego State. I came in at 250 pounds, pretty overweight, and I was able to shed all that and get a lot stronger from it."

Strasburg immediately began to reap the dividends of his renewed focus, seeing his fastball leap from the low to mid-90s while working as a relief pitcher during his freshman year. Strasburg was 1–3 with a 2.43 ERA and seven saves—fine numbers for a mid-major college program, but nothing that signaled what he would become in the future. "He didn't understand what he had to do when he came here," said Gwynn, a Hall of Famer with the San Diego Padres. "He didn't understand that to be one of the best, you have to roll up your sleeves and work. He got to work, and his fastball went from 90 to 97 miles an hour [as a sophomore]. That's when the lightbulb came on. He said, 'I think I can do this.'"

After his freshman season, thanks to the help of Filter, Strasburg joined the Torrington (Connecticut) Twisters of the New England Collegiate Baseball League, a summer league that doesn't have the cache of the more-storied Cape Cod League, but does have a history of nurturing solid players. There, Strasburg dominated good competition, impressing scouts. "He was in my mix as someone who I thought could be a closer for us," Twisters general manager Kirk Fredriksson said. "But when Stephen threw that first day for us, he was lights out. It was a noticeable difference between him and everyone else. We knew we had someone special."

Strasburg hit triple digits on the radar gun not long after that and immediately leapt to the forefront of Major League Baseball scouting reports as well as turning San Diego State games into destination events. "When I first saw him pitch for State, it was at Petco [Park] against Michigan," Hopgood said. "They zoomed in on his face, and I saw him and went, 'Oh, he's going to have a great year.' And he just dominated. This was sophomore year. He was ridiculous in college. And it was as big a minor league feel you could get in college. You could not get in when he pitched. It was standing room only for Strasburg."

During that sophomore season, Strasburg went 8–3 with a 1.58 ERA and 133 strikeouts in 98⅓ innings of work, including striking out 23 batters, a Mountain West Conference record, during a game against Utah in April. That was the third most strikeouts ever in a college game. Strasburg finished second in the nation in strikeouts (133) and was named first team All-America after his dominating year.

"I've had numerous requests for his workout program," Filter said. "It's incredible. I've probably had 50 of them this year—grandmas for their grandsons, from parents, from kids. It's been an array of people. I'm not going to do that. It's the same program for every pitcher on the team. He has some things he does, but it's baseball. There are no secrets."

But 2008 would only get better for Strasburg. After a stint on Team USA's collegiate national squad, he was selected for the U.S. Olympic team, the lone college player who went to Beijing. "He was on our radar before this summer," said USA manager Davey Johnson, now Strasburg's current skipper, at the time of Strasburg's selection. "He throws high 90s and he throws strikes. He pounds the strike zone awfully good and he was lights out in the tournament. He's one of my starters."

Strasburg held his own against the international competition on a team that was littered with future MLB players, including pitchers Clayton Richard (Padres) and Jake Arrieta (Baltimore Orioles) and position players Dexter Fowler (Colorado Rockies), Colby Rasmus (Toronto Blue Jays), and Taylor Teagarden (Orioles). Strasburg went 1–1 in the Olympic tournament, earning a bronze medal and the confidence that his career was headed in the right direction. "I knew I was ready. I knew I was there when I was playing in the Olympics in '08," Strasburg said. "I mean, look at that roster. All those guys went to the big leagues in September right after that. I knew that if I was able to play with them, all I had to do was keep working and keep focused."

Only one thing stood in the way of Strasburg's MLB dreams, and that was the 2009 season at San Diego State, which was arguably the most anticipated collegiate season ever for a pitcher. "Going into that year, I'd heard the buzz that, 'Hey, San Diego State has a kid that could be the No. 1 pick,'" said CBSSports.com national baseball columnist Scott Miller. "I went to watch him pitch, and Tony [Gwynn] told me that when Strasburg first came on, nobody knew what they had was a future No. 1 pick. He reported to the team overweight, and his work ethic wasn't that great. But they all put their heads together and told Stephen that if he wanted to play at this level, you have to get serious about things. From his freshman year to where he ended up, talk about three years making a difference. I don't think anybody, anywhere had such a transition from point A to point B."

A preseason All-America selection, Strasburg was the focus of intense media scrutiny as the surefire No. 1 pick. Gwynn moved his ace to once-a-week starts—on Fridays—and began to limit access to Strasburg once the media crush began to wear on his young pitcher. "It's been a strain," Gwynn said at the time. "He's only 20, and the guy can't even get a burger. The guy can't sit in the library. He's got collectors hanging outside the ballpark, trying to get his autograph so they can put it on eBay. People are building him up to be this Messiah, but in this game they love to build you up just so they can tear you down. Can't we just let him enjoy his junior year here before everyone gets their piece of him?"

By this point, Strasburg was regularly throwing over 100 mph, even touching 102 on the gun at times. Mix in a filthy slurve (slider/curve) and debilitating change-up, and college hitters had no chance. "He reminds me of Mark Prior in college," Gwynn said, "the way he dominates the game. He locates, changes speeds, his angles. He's got tilt to his pitches."

Strasburg still carried himself as a regular guy, spending time with his teammates and enjoying the life of a college student—albeit one with a rocket arm. "I'm just going to out there and do my best," Strasburg told the Aztecs' website prior to his junior year. "Whatever happens, happens."

Strasburg's junior season was one for the record books, with dominating performance after dominating performance littering his ledger. But one effort stood above the rest. On May 8, 2009, Strasburg took the hill for his final home start at State and delivered one more masterpiece. Before a record crowd at Aztec Stadium, Strasburg mowed down the overmatched Air Force Falcons one by one, throwing the first no-hitter of his career while striking out 17 Falcons.

Amazingly, as the game progressed, Strasburg's stuff improved; he only needed 116 pitches to complete the no-hitter. "I was giving everything I had left," Strasburg said. "In that last inning, I think my stuff was the best it was all game. It was great to see a bunch of fans come out again, especially possibly for my last home night. To finish it like that was very memorable." Acting GM Mike Rizzo and scouting director Dana Brown were in the stands, representing the Nationals, and were no doubt fantasizing about seeing Strasburg wearing the curly W.

The win improved Strasburg's record to an unthinkable 11–0 and helped San Diego State reach the NCAA tournament for the first time in 18 years. It was there that Strasburg finally proved fallible. On May 29, 2009 against the Virginia Cavaliers in an NCAA regional game, Strasburg's season came to a close, as Virginia stung Strasburg for eight hits and two runs in seven innings, offsetting 15 strikeouts. "I was pretty excited to be out there, but it's pretty tough to pitch against a team that you've never really heard of. You don't really have a good scouting report on them," Strasburg said after the loss. "They put a good bat on the ball."

Strasburg finished his junior campaign 13–1 with a 1.32 ERA. He allowed just 59 hits in 109 innings pitched, giving up a mere 19 walks and 16 earned runs, leaving no doubt that he was worthy of the Nationals' selection. "That's how you go from a question mark in high school to the No. 1 draft pick," Hopgood said. "He became a damn good baseball player."

Back in Santee, Hopgood would continue to watch his prize pupil grow with pride. "He's kind of the face of an organization now," said Hopgood, who now coaches at Junipero Serra High in San Diego. "He's the next era. You had Nolan Ryan, Randy Johnson, Curt Schilling, Cliff Lee. Now you have Stephen Strasburg. He really put in the work."

Hopgood doesn't have much contact with Strasburg these days but knows that his ace has other responsibilities. "I wish he'd drop a line every once in a while," he said. "But he's the face of an organization. He's married. He's got to take care of business. I'm still waiting on an autographed ball, and it'd be great if he could call, but everyone knows that I'm his coach."

Gwynn has continued to build the San Diego State program with some assistance from his former pupil, who donated nearly $150,000 to the baseball program and sponsors an annual 5-kilometer race. The former Padres great said Strasburg deserves the accolades he has achieved in his young career. "I didn't do much to make him what he became," Gwynn said. "The athlete puts the work in. To see him now, what he's doing—it's a great feeling."

Strasburg wasn't a born star, but he put in the work to become one, and when his college career was over, his next destination was clear. "Washington is going to draft Strasburg," ousted GM Jim Bowden told a radio station in April, midway through Strasburg's junior year. "The decision has already been made. It was made when I was there. That is who they are going to take...This is the best amateur pitcher since I was born. He is that good—his delivery, his stuff, 100 miles an hour in the eighth inning, his makeup. He's got the entire package."

Bowden was right. Strasburg was a pitching prospect unlike any other. The Nationals knew it. And so did Scott Boras.

4

THE HYPE IS REAL

THE SELECTION OF STEPHEN STRASBURG BY THE WASHINGTON Nationals, which took place on June 9, 2009, was something of an afterthought. Everyone knew the talent-starved Nats would not pass on one of the best arms of the last 20 years, and so, when commissioner Bud Selig announced the pick live on the MLB Network, it was a mere formality. Strasburg wasn't even in attendance, preferring (possibly under agent's orders) to stay at home.

No one saw Strasburg and his nearest and dearest celebrating. No one saw the tears flowing from a dream realized. No one saw him shake Selig's hand. Instead Strasburg was at home with his family, and, even though he would later describe his excitement during a conference call with the media, his deadpan delivery did little to suggest the significance of the moment for the young pitcher.

The Nationals, on the other hand, were elated. "We are thrilled to select someone with the special talents that Stephen possesses," said Mike Rizzo, then the Nats acting general manager. "Those talents have long been on our radar and Stephen's domination at San Diego State and vast experiences gained with Team USA last summer have done nothing to change our thoughts about his abilities."

For Strasburg, getting selected No. 1 did have a bittersweet tinge, as it closed the door on a time of his life that was very important to him. "It was an amazing feeling," he said. "I had so many different emotions. I was so happy, but at the same time, I was kind of sad that the three years that I've had [in college], that were absolutely amazing, have come to an end. It just goes to show the last three years how hard I worked to where I am today. I'm so thankful to the coaches and players that helped me along the way."

Since everyone knew Washington would pick Strasburg, it allowed the negotiation process to get off to an early start, which played right into Scott Boras' hands. The mega-agent, who had worked with Strasburg during college as his advisor, now represented the pitcher as a professional. Reports emerged that Boras would look to shatter the record book for a rookie contract, with some claiming that the agent would ask for a $50 million deal.

This was in line with Boras' reputation as a ruthless negotiator for his clients, which had earned him the enmity of both baseball front offices and their fan bases. They viewed him as a mercenary out to extract the most money from team coffers, while forcing players to turn a blind eye to franchise loyalty in favor of the almighty dollar.

Boras was a former minor league player who had logged time with the St. Louis Cardinals and Chicago Cubs organizations before a knee injury sidelined his career. After earning his law degree from the University of the Pacific, Boras got his start representing his former high school teammate Mike Fischlin and former minor league teammate Bill Caudill. Before long, Boras started his namesake corporation, and the players, in search of big-time contracts constructed by this hard-charging agent, were lining up to join the fold. "The best thing to understand about me is that, being a former ballplayer, I have a different way of looking at things when you do things for your clients," Boras told *The New York Times*. "I love the game of baseball. Seventy percent of what I do is not related to money. It's related to the game."

Boras' tactics—the attention to detail, the tome-like statistical notebooks, the flashy offices, the sports psychologists—and eye-opening results were like catnip to players, who often had wound up with the short end of the stick during contract negotiations. The agent's ledger is filled with firsts and record-breaking deals, starting with the $7.5 million deal from the Seattle Mariners he landed for Caudill in 1983, one of the largest contracts to that date. He is responsible for the first $50 million (pitcher Greg Maddux), $100 million (pitcher Kevin Brown), and $200 million (shortstop Alex Rodriguez) deals.

Boras also pushed the envelope in what he argued was an unjust draft salary scale, with deals for pitcher Ben McDonald, pitcher Todd Van Poppel, pitcher Brien Taylor, outfielder J.D. Drew, and first baseman

Mark Teixeira all leading to a more reasonable compensation scheme in the mind of his clients.

A Google search for "Scott Boras hate" yields more than 700,000 results and includes defaced pictures of the agent wearing devil horns. Teams are often leery of dealing with Boras, given his sometimes astronomical contract demands and hard-line stance, though very few make those feelings public for fear of missing out on his top free agents and draft prospects.

Former Major League Baseball standout Gary Sheffield, however, cut ties with the agent when he couldn't negotiate a deal for the disgruntled slugger to leave the Los Angeles Dodgers. "I fired Scott Boras because he made a promise to me, and the organization made a promise to me, and they lied," he said. "If you break a promise, you get fired."

In the 2012 Draft, Stanford pitcher Mark Appel was considered by many scouts to be the No. 1 prospect in the draft, but by the time draft day came around, it was clear that he was slipping. It wasn't because of a late revelation about his talent or character. Instead, with Boras as Appel's agent, teams feared they would not be able to meet his pricey demands.

Appel slid all the way to the No. 8 pick, where the Pittsburgh Pirates took a flier on the pitcher. But the Pirates didn't reach an agreement with the pitcher before the signing deadline, and Appel headed back to Stanford for his senior season. "Selecting Mark was a calculated risk, as we knew he would be a difficult sign," Pirates GM Neal Huntington said. "We drafted Mark Appel to sign Mark Appel. We were excited about the opportunity to add him to a plethora of quality, young arms. It didn't happen. So, now we turn the corner. This, too, shall pass. We move forward."

Boras blamed the Pirates' inability to reach a deal with Appel on MLB's new slotting system for draft picks, which taxed teams for going over their pool of money, eventually leading to the loss of future draft picks, calling the process a "mockery." "We have shattered the productivity of many teams by putting an artificial cap on their decision making," Boras said. "It's horrible for baseball and illustrates a real failure in the system."

Boras certainly had the upper hand in the Strasburg negotiations, given that the Nationals were a laughingstock franchise that *needed* to get a deal done, even if it meant breaking the record contract of $10.5 million handed out to Mark Prior by the Cubs in 2001.

Then-team president Stan Kasten and the Nationals, however, opened with a hard-line stance, two months before the August 15 deadline. "We intend to be aggressive and we have every intention of signing the pick," said Kasten, the former front man for the Nationals' contract negotiations. "We know what [top picks] have made [in the past]. We know the risks associated with any draft pick, much less a pitcher. It's why they get what they get. And we're going to be consistent with that. And if [a contract agreement] doesn't happen, and we have to take the second pick next year [as compensation], so be it."

That line of reasoning did not sit well with Nationals fans desperate to make sure Strasburg would be in the fold, especially after the team had failed to sign 2008's No. 1 pick, pitcher Aaron Crow. He was a hard-throwing right-hander out of the University of Missouri that the team selected with the ninth pick of the draft. Then-Nationals GM Jim Bowden said he did not hear from Crow's agents, Alan and Randy Hendricks, until the 11th hour, when they requested a $9 million deal and a major league contract, staggering requests that the Nationals turned down.

According to reports, the Nationals made Crow a last-ditch offer of $3.5 million, more than the Baltimore Orioles gave their No. 4 pick, pitcher Brian Matusz. Washington even had the major league contract as part of the negotiations for Crow. That incentive, which the Nationals had used on top draft picks like Ryan Zimmerman, would have placed Crow on the team's 40-man roster and given him a greater potential for future salaries and made his path to the major leagues that much easier. Washington pulled the offer at the end because an MRI on Crow's shoulder was not performed. "We offered Crow more than any other pitcher got in this draft," Bowden said. "That's how we value the player."

Crow and his agents refused the Nats' offer, and the pitcher signed with the Fort Worth Cats of the Independent League. For a team that was awful, losing out on a top 10 pick was seen as a black eye. (The compensatory pick the Nationals would get for failing to sign Crow, though, would turn out to be eventual closer Drew Storen, so the end result actually worked out fine.)

But the entire Crow fiasco put immense pressure on the Nationals to get the Strasburg deal done, no matter how much it might take. And as time dragged on, there was a palpable sense that the pitcher might not sign before the deadline. "The negotiations were entirely posturing on Boras' part," said longtime Nationals reporter Mark Zuckerman. "The first time around with Strasburg, we all worried because we hadn't been through it before. But this is just what Boras does—wait until the last minute to start negotiating."

Indeed, as the deadline loomed, negotiations ramped up, and on August 15, shortly before the deadline, Strasburg signed a record deal with Washington worth $15.1 million over four years. Strasburg received a $7.5 million signing bonus and yearly salaries of $400,000 in 2009, $2 million in 2010, $2.5 million in 2011, and $3 million in 2012. Kasten said the deal was signed just prior to 11:59 PM. He joked, "We didn't even need that last minute."

For Strasburg, who had been under the radar—per Boras' instructions— for most of the summer, the end of the contract talk was a relief. "It feels awesome. I got a little nervous there for a while that it might not happen, but I feel very blessed," Strasburg told ESPN's Pedro Gomez. "I'm not sure of the plan right now…It's an amazing feeling. I really wasn't sure if it was going to happen, but I'm glad it did."

With the money out of the way, the Nationals and Strasburg could turn their attention to more important matters—baseball. On August 21, 2009, the Nationals introduced Strasburg at a press conference at Nationals Park. Joined by third baseman Ryan Zimmerman and team officials, Strasburg gave fans and the media an initial glimpse at his low-key demeanor. "When I first met him, it was at the press conference, which we carried live on TV," Nationals broadcaster Bob Carpenter said. "He handled it very well. Stephen tends to be kind of a quiet, soft-spoken guy. He carried himself well, and my impression was, 'Here's somebody who is in control of himself and his surroundings.' Nothing seems to bother this guy."

Although the knee-jerk reaction to Strasburg's raw talent was to place him on the big league squad, the Nationals were preaching patience. Strasburg was assigned to the Arizona Fall League's Phoenix Desert Dogs, where his debut on October 16, 2009 was covered by numerous media outlets, an indication of the madness to come. After being out of action for several months, the stint in the AFL was critical not only for Strasburg to begin regaining his strength, but also to get accustomed to the notion of pitching every five days.

But the time in the desert almost resulted in a disaster. Prior to the team's final game of the season, Strasburg hurt his knee during a long toss session. The injury left him crumpled on the ground, and witnesses reported hearing a pop. But upon further examination, the injury was revealed to be a dislocated kneecap, a painful injury for sure, but one that would not require surgery, threaten his career, or even delay his schedule for the 2010 season.

In 19 innings with the Desert Dogs, Strasburg struck out 26 and walked seven but also was tagged for three homers and posted a 4.26 ERA. Still, the Nationals saw plenty to demonstrate their investment was a wise one, as the command on his fastball and change-up were impressive. "I went out there and saw him pitch [in Arizona]," Zuckerman said. "You'd heard about him. I'd seen video and stuff, but when you see him in person, you realize just what a talent he was. I remember seeing the curveball the first couple of times and thinking, 'Man, I've never seen break like that.' He was fooling these elite minor league hitters that were several levels above him—in theory. I realized pretty quickly that this guy was the real deal, and that it wasn't going to take long before we'd see him in D.C."

As the Nationals entered spring training in 2010, the buzz was that Strasburg would likely be heading north with the team to open the season. But the ever-patient Mike Rizzo, now officially the team's GM, would adhere to the organization's philosophy of not rushing its prized prospects. "I believe Stephen Strasburg needs some seasoning in the minor leagues," Rizzo told Comcast SportsNet. "He hasn't thrown a minor league pitch for us yet. He hasn't pitched in professional baseball yet. The difference between college baseball and professional baseball is huge. The everyday-ness of it alone is something to be adapted to. It's a different process. He needs to face professional hitters. We're going to put him at a pace that's good for his development. When we see him in Washington, D.C., it should be for good."

Each one of Strasburg's spring training starts became an event. His debut—against the Detroit Tigers—drew a host of curious onlookers, eager to see Strasburg toe the bump. He did not disappoint, allowing two strikeouts and two singles during an economical two innings of work.

In his three starts during spring training, Strasburg went 1–0 with a 2.00 ERA, surrendering eight hits, walking one, and striking out 12 over the course of nine innings. But on March 20, the team delivered the news that he was heading to minor league camp and that he would be opening the season with the Double A Harrisburg, Pennsylvania Senators.

To this day, Strasburg remains fine with the team's decision to send him down. "[The Nationals] like to have guys go to Double A or Triple A," Strasburg said. "If you're ready, you're ready. That's the bottom line. I think having a manager like Davey [Johnson] and a GM like Rizz, they aren't going to waste all your years and at-bats in the minors. If they think you're ready, they're going to give you an opportunity and stick with you."

Strasburg's quest to prove that he was ready began in Altoona, Pennsylvania, on April 11, 2010, as the Senators met the Altoona Curve, the Double A affiliate of the Pittsburgh Pirates. With nearly 8,000 fans, more than 70 credentialed media in attendance, and portions of the game broadcast live on ESPN, this was no ordinary debut.

An anxious Strasburg threw 24 first-inning pitches, giving up an RBI single before settling down. When his five-inning stint was complete after 82 pitches, he had allowed four hits and four runs—just one earned—with eight strikeouts and two walks, as Harrisburg pulled out a 6–4 victory, giving the No. 1 pick win No. 1. "I definitely was super excited," Strasburg said. "There was a lot of anticipation for this outing." And it would only grow from there. The frenzy had begun, and there was nothing Strasburg could do about it. "The hype and everything, I don't put that out there," he said. "It's just part of the game."

Strasburg's first home start for Harrisburg occurred on April 16 against New Britain, Connecticut, where a standing room only crowd waited through a two-hour rain delay to see him pitch 2⅓ impressive innings before another rain delay ended his night.

He would make five starts with Harrisburg in all, with his final Double A appearance coming on May 2 and drawing a robust crowd of 7,619 to Metro Bank Park to see the Senators take on the Curve once again. This time, the Curve sent Strasburg to his first Double A defeat, but no matter. Strasburg's first stop in the minors was an overwhelming success: 3–1 record, 1.64 ERA, 27 strikeouts, six walks, 13 hits allowed, and a booming box office. "It was an interesting experience," Harrisburg GM Randy Whitaker said. "I can't imagine that we will go through something like that again. It was a circus."

The big top moved on to Syracuse, New York, the Triple A affiliate for the Nationals, as Strasburg was scheduled to make his debut May 7 against the Gwinnett Braves. By this point, speculation was running rampant about when the ace would make his debut for the Nationals, with the likely date pointing toward June, so the team would avoid an earlier bout with free agency.

The media scrum and fan attention grew with the Syracuse Chiefs, as a crowd of more than 13,000 filled the stadium and saw Strasburg cruise through his first Triple A start. Against the overmatched Braves, Strasburg gave up just one hit during six innings of scoreless work, throwing 45 strikes and striking out six. He faced just 20 batters in what was his most impressive minor league start to date. "I'm just trying to get my feet wet," Strasburg said. "I've got six starts under my belt. I'm starting to get comfortable." That spelled trouble for the rest of the International League. Strasburg made six starts at Triple A, showing poise that belied his 21 years every time he took the hill.

After spring training, the slight mechanical tweaks the Nationals wanted him to work on—slowing down his delivery with runners on base—were easily rectified. The command of his pitches, save for a hitter or two, was pinpoint. The minor league lifestyle—grinding through bus rides and playing in small parks against up-and-comers and journeymen—was duly experienced.

And so, when Strasburg went out for his sixth start with the Chiefs on June 3, his days in the minors were numbered. Strasburg knew he was ready, and if he had not proven it already, he certainly showed it to everyone during his last start. During the young pitcher's minor league swan song, Strasburg shut down the Buffalo Bisons with a five-inning scoreless appearance. "Why is he here?" Bisons manager Ken Oberkfell said. "I'm impressed, very impressed. He's major league."

In six Triple A appearances, Strasburg went 4–1 with a 1.08 ERA. In 33⅓ innings, he struck out a ridiculous 38 batters while walking just seven. Overall, his minor league numbers were 7–2 with a 1.30 ERA and 65 total strikeouts. "He's exceptionally prepared," then-Syracuse manager Trent Jewett said. "I think everyone in the organization feels that way. And was he not prepared, I don't think he'd be going. He's a well-armed young man."

The Nationals, who had monitored Strasburg's starts in the minors like a watchful mother guarding her offspring, had been tinkering with their call-up date to ensure that their ace would have the best possible situation. Initially, the team suggested that Strasburg would make his debut against the Cincinnati Reds on June 4, which immediately turned that game into the hottest ticket in town. The team, however, adjusted its plans, and just as quickly, the secondary market was flooded with tickets for just another meaningless Nationals game.

On June 1 Washington officially announced Strasburg's major league debut would occur on June 8 against the lowly Pittsburgh Pirates. "We believe he is ready to go," said Rizzo upon announcing the start, which the team immediately began hyping. The timing and opponent, the struggling Bucs, had been carefully selected. "It set itself up very well," Zuckerman said. "It helped that it was at home. That was the biggest thing. I think they preferred it come against a team that wasn't as good. There was a little bit of calculation there."

The wait was over. The big leagues had called. And Stephen Strasburg would answer with a resounding performance, one that would send the baseball world—and the nation's capital—into a frenzy.

5

STRASMAS

NATIONALS PARK WAS BUILT ALONG THE ANACOSTIA RIVER IN Southeast D.C., the crown jewel in a plan to revitalize a neighborhood that, while in the shadow of the U.S. Capitol, had become a largely forgotten stretch of land rarely trod upon other than by those who lived there.

Southeast D.C. had earned a reputation as a hardscrabble area, filled with the kind of crime that gave the District its shaky reputation. In Anacostia, the population was 92 percent African American, according to the 2000 census. Although pockets of larger Southeast encompassed middle class black neighborhoods, Anacostia was hit particularly hard by the drug blight, with large swaths of the neighborhood essentially off-limits to tourists and locals, who rarely ventured there.

In 1993, the Seventh District Metropolitan Police statistics showed that there were 133 homicides in the area; by 2005, that number was down to 62. By 2011, the number had dropped to 20. Still, putting a stadium in the heart of what was perceived to be one of the most dangerous areas in the U.S. was a risky move.

Many wondered why the Nationals would build in an area with an overwhelmingly black population when baseball was considered a "white" sport. But D.C. Mayor Anthony Williams, who was the driving force behind building the stadium and locating it in Southeast, knew the stadium would spur economic growth and help revitalize the surrounding area. "It was an uphill slog all the way," Williams said. "I'd say, 'People, we're gonna get there,' but there were a lot of naysayers. We had to convince Major League Baseball, we had to get everyone to work together as a region, and we had to convince the city it was a worthwhile investment. We always believed D.C. was a different economy—that it could support a team—and it has turned out that way."

But the stadium was built in the middle of the country's biggest financial crisis since the Great Depression, and the lofty goals of new housing and gameday amenities, which would turn the area around the ballpark into a destination, had gone largely unrealized. The banners that promised exciting new developments grew more hollow with each passing day, as the empty lots remained devoid of activity.

Most fans arrived at Nationals Park by the Metro subway system, which deposited them directly outside the center-field gate. They filed in, and trudged back out when the game was over, in a perfunctory manner. The stadium was fine, in a modern sort of way, but lacked the charm of the retro parks that had sprung up in the wake of Camden Yards in Baltimore and instead felt more similar to the sterile new stadiums like the Mets' Citi Field and new Yankee Stadium.

One nagging feature about the stadium is that one can only see the majestic Capitol building from the upper reaches of the ballpark, with most of the views blocked by a parking garage. If the building had been oriented just slightly to the left, one of the most prominent symbols of the United States would have provided a dramatic backdrop beyond the outfield walls.

The consensus for most seemed to be that, though it was good to have baseball back in D.C., it was nothing to get too excited about. It was one more activity in a town filled with them, and it didn't promise anything more than the opportunity to watch a bad baseball team (or cheer for the opposition, which many fans who attended games at Nationals Park eagerly did). "Over the years, people would say D.C. isn't a good baseball town," historian Phil Wood said. "No one wanted to bring up the fact that there's a correlation between winning and attendance. When they went 50–31 the first half of the season in 2005, people showed up. They drew 2.7 million fans. After that, things fell off, because MLB gutted their system."

And still the history (or absence) of baseball in the District hangs over the proceedings. After years of going to games in Baltimore, fans found habits hard to break. "The Orioles did a good job of marketing in D.C. The games were on Home Team Sports, then Comcast SportsNet. They had marketed well. If you went to a Nationals game during the first few years, people were still yelling 'O's' during the National Anthem," Wood said, referring to a Baltimore tradition in which fans yelled during the "Oh, say does that star-spangled banner," section of the anthem. "They had convinced themselves that people yelled 'O' in every ballpark. It's a

Baltimore thing. Now, if you go to Nats game, there only will be a few people who do it."

The most embarrassing instance of opposing fan invasion occurred earlier in 2010, when busloads of Philadelphia Phillies fans made their way to Nationals Park for Opening Day and essentially took over the stadium, booing vociferously during Nationals player introductions and cheering the Phillies so vehemently, it felt like Philadelphia's Citizens Bank Ballpark had somehow been transported due south. It turned out that Philadelphia fans had taken advantage of Washington's group sales policy and bought huge blocks of tickets before the general public had a chance, and hordes of well-organized Phillies fanatics descended upon D.C. in buses—complete with their own Philadelphia-centric pre and postgame parties.

Making matters worse, the Nats got smacked around 11–1 by the Phillies to kick off the 2010 campaign. Often cited as symbolizing ownership's short-sighted approach to filling the stadium, the cheers of Philly fans still sting many to this day. Late in the 2009 season, president Stan Kasten went on a Philadelphia radio show and practically begged Phillies fans, who were unable to purchase tickets at their own sold-out stadium, to buy tickets for a series in D.C. Those remarks left a bad taste in the mouth of many Nats fans in the aftermath of the Philly takeover. (The Nationals would try to correct the folly of their ways in 2012, when they staged a "Take Back The Park" campaign, setting up a presale for residents of D.C., Maryland, and Virginia to buy tickets for the team's first series against the Phillies.)

It also didn't help matters that President Barack Obama, on hand during April of 2010 to throw out the first pitch per tradition, pulled a Chicago White Sox hat out of his pocket before firing a strike, another slap in the face to long-suffering D.C. baseball fans.

JUNE 8, 2010 WAS DIFFERENT.

As the day dawned on Stephen Strasburg's MLB debut against the Pittsburgh Pirates, the city crackled with the kind of anticipation and energy usually reserved for the Washington Redskins. The holiday fans declared "Strasmas" had finally arrived, and they were eager to take the wrapping paper off their shiny new toy.

The Nationals were expecting a rare sellout crowd, the game was being broadcast nationally on the MLB network, and the team had issued more than 200 media credentials. "The attention rivals anything I've ever seen in sports," Kasten said. "For us, this is as big as it gets. We've got a World Series-sized media contingent here for a Tuesday game against the Pirates."

The buzz built throughout the day. Radio stations fielded calls about Strasburg's debut, and tickets were sold at astronomical markups, considering the two teams playing. The website, SeatGeek.com, calculated that the average price for a Nationals ticket on May 8 against the Marlins was $41.90. For the June 8 game against the Pirates, the price had shot up to an average of $103.28.

Strasburg arrived at Nationals Park with his wife, Rachel, and when he went inside the clubhouse, he came face-to-face with a media horde, and every TV inside the room blared wall-to-wall coverage about his start later that evening. But if Strasburg felt any butterflies about the moment, he didn't show it, going about his business with the kind of clear-eyed intensity that would become his calling card.

Outside, the scene was unbelievable. Fans milled about the stadium, creating an audible hum that had rarely been heard since baseball had returned to D.C. This was an *event*, and even those without tickets showed up so that they could be within striking distance of what was unfolding.

The Nationals set up merchandise shops all around the stadium, selling official No. 37 shirts, jerseys, hats, and anything else that could be produced to commemorate the start. Fans poured into the building, holding home-made signs that read "Baseball Jesus," "Strasburg is Our Savior," "Strasmas is Here!" Using San Diego State associate dean of the college of business Jim Lackritz to help with the numbers, sports business reporter Darren Rovell estimated that the Nationals took in more than $1.5 million from the debut.

When Strasburg emerged from the dugout about 30 minutes before the game to warm up, fans along the outfield wall roared, cheering every stride and stretch. By the time he ran in from the bullpen, the crowd had worked itself into a fervor. Before one pitch had been thrown, the night was unlike any other that had been seen in D.C. in several years.

As Strasburg took the hill in preparation for his first major league pitch, flashbulbs popped and exploded, as if this was Game 7 of the World Series. The hype, expectation, anticipation, whatever you wanted to call it, had grown to intoxicating levels. It almost seemed unfair to expect the young pitcher to live up to what was expected of him on this day.

But he did.

From the opening pitch, a high, blazing fastball that just missed the strike zone, to the Pirates' Andrew McCutchen, Strasburg had the capacity crowd of 40,315 and the Pirates eating out of his hand. It was a surreal experience, even for those on the field. "I just remember missing probably four or five pitches, at least, from just watching him," said Adam Dunn, who was the Nationals starting first baseman in that game. "Just catching myself going, 'I know he ain't hitting the ball here. I don't have to worry about it. I just want to see how bad they look.'"

Strasburg went 1–2–3 on the Pirates in the first inning, recording his first MLB strikeout by punching out former National Lastings Milledge on a 0–2 pitch. Any chance that Strasburg was merely running on adrenaline passed in the second inning, when he struck out the side, signaling it was clear that this night was going to be something special. "I remember that there were almost 100 people in San Francisco who were gathered around TV screens 'Oohing' and 'Aahing,'" said Nats broadcaster F.P. Santangelo, who was working television for the Giants at the time. "Very rarely does one player live up to the hype, and he captivated us where we were working. We were high fiving like little kids."

For Strasburg's high school coach Scott Hopgood, it was a proud moment to see his former student on the hill. Hopgood wanted to attend the game in person, but settled for watching it with several of Strasburg's high school teammates. "I did take a bunch of the West Hills team out. We all went to sports bar in Santee, [California], and the owner called the TV station," Hopgood said. "The TV station came and interviewed us. Well, [former high school teammate] Aaron Richardson had called in sick, and the next thing you know, his boss is watching the news, and Richardson ends up getting fired. It's like, 'C'mon, this is once in a lifetime.' He got fired to watch Strasburg in his debut...A player's success is the coach's ultimate reward. That's my high five—that he's gone on and done everything that he's supposed to do and more."

Strasburg's only hiccup on the night occurred during the fourth inning. He gave up back-to-back singles to Neil Walker and Milledge but erased one runner, when Garrett Jones grounded into a double play. With a runner on third, Delwyn Young lifted a 90 mph change-up out of the park, putting the only blemish on Strasburg's ledger.

After that, it was back to dominating Pittsburgh's lineup. "After the first couple of innings, I think, as I threw to break, I said something like,

'He can't be this good,'" Nats play-by-play man Bob Carpenter said. "It was just shocking how dominant he was, how unhittable he was. It was truly a revelation."

In the top of the seventh inning, with relievers in the bullpen warming up and Strasburg's night coming to a close, it was only fitting that the phenom finished with a flourish, striking out the side yet again and leaving the mound to delirious cheers from a flabbergasted crowd. "The most amazing thing is that he was around the plate and threw strikes. He is always in the strike zone," Nationals catcher Ivan "Pudge" Rodriguez said. "Guys that are young are always behind in the count. Stephen didn't do that today. He just attacked the strike zone. He was tremendous. He was unbelievable."

In his MLB debut, Stephen Strasburg had pitched seven innings, struck out 14 batters and walked none, making him the first pitcher to ever record more than 10 strikeouts without a walk in his big league debut. Though the actual score was an afterthought, the Nationals would go on to win the game 5–2. "This was the first time I felt like everyone at the ballpark was just happy," longtime Nationals writer Mark Zuckerman said. "It wasn't even so much about the result of the game. It was just marveling in amazement of what this kid was doing and that, 'He's ours. And he's going to be ours for a long time.' And that was the moment—when whatever skeptics there were about 'the plan' or the future of the organization—I think that was the moment when people could envision however many years down the road, this guy is going to be at the center of it all."

More than two years later, Dunn remains impressed about how Strasburg kept everything under control. "You know he has great stuff, but in that atmosphere, you never know what you're going to get," he said. "First start in the big leagues, and everybody from ESPN to freakin' TV Tokyo is there, and he didn't disappoint. He was incredible." In the postgame press conference, Strasburg was his normal, unflappable self. "The only thing I really remember was the first pitch," he said. "It was a ball inside. Everything else was kind of a blur."

In the speed of a Strasburg fastball, the Nationals had taken a huge step toward legitimacy. "It was one of the few cases when a guy not only lives up to the hype but exceeds it," said CBSSports.com columnist Scott Miller. "From Day One, they viewed him as a guy who could change a franchise, no question. Once the Nationals were in position to pick him, it was a case where this was the guy who could take us to heights that were unimaginable before."

IN THE AFTERMATH OF STRASMAS, the Nationals tried to keep their reticent young star under wraps. It didn't work. In a manner of hours, a lanky 21-year-old with a rocket arm suddenly made every start going forward must-see TV. Two days after his breakthrough debut, Strasburg would even read the Top 10 list on *The Late Show with David Letterman.* Thanks to the rookie's deadpan delivery, it was quite funny, and Strasburg flashed the kind of personality that many weren't sure he possessed.

All jokes aside, the Strasburg business was a good one to be in. Hours of discussion were afforded to Strasburg on ESPN's various shows. Before his second start against the Cleveland Indians, TBS switched its regularly scheduled broadcast between the Boston Red Sox and Philadelphia Phillies to the Nationals-Indians game, a contest matching two last-place teams. In the 24 hours after Strasburg worked his magic against the Pirates, the Indians had seen a spike in ticket sales at Progressive Field in Cleveland, assuring one of the largest crowds there since Opening Day.

Strasburg's second start didn't go quite as smoothly as his first, partially because he had trouble with the pitching mound all day, but he certainly didn't disappoint the more than 30,000 who came out to see him or the national TV audience. He threw the kind of gas the spectators had hoped to see, hitting 100 mph on the radar gun twice in the first inning and striking out two of the first three Cleveland hitters he faced. Though less spectacular than his debut, it made for another impressive outing—5⅓ innings pitched, eight strikeouts, two hits, and just one run, as the Nationals picked up a 9–4 victory.

Two starts and two knockout performances for Washington's savior landed Strasburg on the cover of *Sports Illustrated* just days later with the headline "National Treasure." The eyes of the baseball world were focused on the young pitcher, which didn't sit well with a kid who tried to avoid the spotlight as much as possible. "Whenever anyone used the word 'hype,' you could almost see him tense up," Zuckerman said. "He hated talking about that, because he felt like, 'What have I done? I'm no different.' But at the same time, the Nationals were treating him differently than everyone else. They were being very protective of him. It was very coordinated and very structured, and I don't think that always sits well with everyone else in the clubhouse. But at the same time, I think they understood how this kid was thrown into the firestorm. And after that first game, everyone realized this is never going to be the same anymore. Every single start is going to be

Late Show with David Letterman's Top 10 Little Known Facts About Stephen Strasburg

No. 10: To keep my focus on pitching, I sleep on a mound of dirt.

No. 9: Every morning I spread Icy Hot on my toast.

No. 8: Got three of my 14 strikeouts while Twittering.

No. 7: To celebrate my first big-league win I bought a hot tub time machine.

No. 6: I wasn't really good till I got bitten by that radioactive spider.

No. 5: Dumb guys think I directed *E.T.*

No. 4: I also scored the winning goal for the Blackhawks in the Stanley Cup finals.

No. 3: I blew my signing bonus on laser back hair removal.

No. 2: Don't even try to talk to me before I start, or while I'm watching *Glee*.

No. 1: If I would have known I'd be on *Letterman*, I wouldn't have pitched so well.

an event. A lot of people in a lot of cities were paying really close attention to that, because they wanted to see him."

For his third start, Strasburg returned home to face the Chicago White Sox on June 18 before another packed house (that once again included die-hard Sox fan Obama) at Nationals Park. He earned a no-decision, despite allowing just one run and striking out 10 batters in seven innings of impressive work. "He's good. He's the real deal," then-White Sox outfielder Juan Pierre said. "You've got to throw all techniques out the window, pitches to look for, none of that. You see something decent—you put a good swing on it. He's got a bright future. I don't know how they sent that guy to the minor leagues. If I got a team, he's on the roster from Day One." Then-White Sox manager Ozzie Guillen called him, "maybe the best pitcher I've seen in the National League."

Strasburg hadn't experienced much losing since his sophomore season at San Diego State, but in his fourth start, despite a nine-strikeout, one-run effort in six innings on a sweltering afternoon against the Kansas City Royals, he earned his first major league defeat in a tough 1–0 loss. "Things didn't go our way today," Strasburg said. "I know there's going to be times when it's going to be like this in the future. And there's going to be times when I'm not pitching well, and they'll just go out there and score a ton of runs and save me. It's baseball."

Strasburg was still pitching at an insanely high level. It was to the point where teams felt thrilled to get anything off the young pitcher. He was pitching so well that there was talk the rookie should be named to the All-Star team, an almost-unheard of scenario, given the paucity of starts he had under his belt. On one hand, no pitcher had single-handedly electrified baseball since the days of Doc Gooden and Fernandomania. On the other hand, had Strasburg proved himself yet? Were six or seven starts enough to designate him an All-Star? "He's very talented," said Phillies and NL All-Star manager Charlie Manuel. "I have a very open mind about it."

In the end, Strasburg wasn't picked for the National League squad, a decision that made sense to the young pitcher. "I really didn't feel like I was qualified to make the team, No. 1, based on how much experience I have," he said. "I'm sure I'll have opportunities somewhere down the road."

Strasburg followed that loss with another defeat in his fifth start, but at this point, he had fallen into a nice rhythm, with the Nationals carefully monitoring his inning totals to make sure their prized investment stayed healthy. The plan was to have Strasburg throw 160 innings in 2010, counting his minor league starts. And midway through his major league season, things were looking up for a franchise that had spent so much time trending down. "You had a feeling that we are really on to something," Carpenter said. "You got a glimpse into the future of the franchise."

Coming on the heels of the team drafting Bryce Harper, the impressive beginning to Strasburg's rookie campaign made the Nationals relevant, a rare feat during their time in the District. "All of a sudden, they were at the center of attention and for positive reasons," Zuckerman said. "That was a turning point."

The Nationals were riding the right arm of their young stud to respectability. Washington had gained something more powerful than wins and losses. It had hope. But would that optimism last or would bad luck—and injuries—derail it?

6

THEY'RE NO. 1…AGAIN

ALTHOUGH THE NATIONALS WERE ABLE TO REAP THE BENEFITS of a horrible 2008 season, when Stephen Strasburg electrified the baseball world two years later, the 2009 campaign would play an equally important role in shaping the franchise, albeit after another painful season.

After the disaster that was Washington's 59–102 season in 2008, there wasn't much optimism regarding the 2009 campaign. Manager Manny Acta returned to lead the team, but the cupboard wasn't exactly stocked, as many of the same on-field principals from 2008 returned. (However, the entire coaching staff, save for pitching coach Randy St. Claire, had been let go after 2008.)

The season got off to an inauspicious start when general manager Jim Bowden resigned on March 1 under pressure due to the Smiley Gonzalez scandal that embroiled the club and its operations in the Dominican Republic. With evidence of wrongdoing mounting in the signing of the player, who had falsified his identity, Bowden stepped aside to prevent further distractions. "It's an emotional decision," Bowden said at a press conference during spring training, while also steadfastly maintaining his innocence in the matter. "It saddens me. But I feel it's in the best interest of two of the things I love the most, and that's the Washington Nationals and baseball." With the Alfonso Soriano deal, the signing of veterans past their prime, and the failure to develop the team's farm system as his legacy, Bowden's regime could not be considered a success. Bowden's resignation, however, did open the door for his protégé, Mike Rizzo, to be named interim GM by team president Stan Kasten—a move that would reap benefits down the road.

In 2009, however, there weren't many benefits in sight.

One of Bowden's final moves was bringing in slugger Adam Dunn, arguably one of the best players ever imported into Washington to that date. Acta claimed that the 2009 Nats were the best team he'd ever had,

but the results did not bear that out in any way. Washington got off to an
0–7 start and spiraled out of control from there. Adding insult to the on-
field performance, Dunn and Ryan Zimmerman took the field on April
17 wearing jerseys that read "Natinals," turning the team into a national
joke that only seemed fitting, given the awful way the year was unfolding.
(From Teddy "Rossevelt" bobblehead doll night to the scoreboard misiden-
tifying starting pitcher John Lannan as John "Lannon," the Nationals have
a strange, unfortunate history with misspellings.)

When Washington's hitters got off to a fast start, the Nationals pitching
staff was putrid. When the Nats' rotation and bullpen finally stabilized,
the bats went cold. It didn't take long for a Fire Manny Acta blog to get
started, as the placid manager drew the ire of many fans for his seemingly
laid-back nature and relentless optimism in the face of failure. The losses
continued to mount, and the team looked adrift, forcing Rizzo to make the
first major decision of his tenure.

After a loss to the Houston Astros sent the Nationals into the All-
Star break at a major league-worst 26–61, Rizzo fired Acta, replacing him
with bench coach Jim Riggleman, the veteran skipper who had previously
managed the San Diego Padres, Chicago Cubs, and Seattle Mariners. "I
thank the Nationals for giving me this opportunity, and I'm sorry that
things didn't work out as expected," Acta said. "It's normal for the manager
to pay the price when the team is not doing well."

While the Nationals' situation was indeed dour, there were several
critical seeds being planted that would help shape the team in the years
to come. On June 28 Washington traded outfielder Ryan Langerhans to
Seattle for Michael Morse, an oversized shortstop whom the Mariners tried
to turn into an outfielder with less than successful results. The Mariners
were enamored with Morse's offensive potential but grew tired of waiting
for the physically gifted player to figure it out. The deal was met with a
collective shrug by both fan bases but with excitement by the Nationals
front office. "We had recently scouted him," Rizzo said. "I had seen him
in the past when I was scouting. I'd always liked his athleticism, his size,
his strength component. We always thought he looked out of place playing
shortstop in Triple A and Seattle. So we thought a position change was
inevitable. But we liked the way he swung the bat."

The move would change Morse's career, turning a lost prospect into a
fun-loving guy who helped energize the clubhouse with his "Beast Mode"

T-shirts and give the Nationals another legitimate power source in the middle of the order. "I told Rizzo—he probably didn't hear me—but I said, 'Thank you.' I was in Seattle, and he got me here, and it's been a blessing ever since," Morse said in the aftermath of the Nats' clinching celebration three years later. Morse became the victim of a crowded outfield, however, and was dealt back to Seattle in January 2013.

Later during the 2009 year, young shortstop Ian Desmond earned a promotion to the big leagues. A third-round pick by the Expos in 2004, he was considered a raw but talented player with a rocket arm but iffy offensive skills.

On the hill 2007 second-round draft pick Jordan Zimmermann made his debut at the start of the season, and the Nationals' top prospect flashed plenty of promise in his 16 starts. But he went on the disabled list in July and was forced to have Tommy John surgery in August to repair a torn ulnar collateral ligament, a harbinger of things to come. Ross Detwiler, the No. 6 overall pick in 2007, made 14 starts. Reliever Tyler Clippard made 41 appearances, and after a June trade, Sean Burnett joined the Nationals bullpen.

These are names that would have a big impact as the Nationals made their remarkable run to respectability, but in 2009 they were just young players, trying to make it in the big leagues on a team staggering to the finish line. "We stuck by it. I'm sure there were many times where people said, 'Why don't they go get this guy or get that guy,' but there is a time and place for everything," Nationals principal owner Mark Lerner said. "I think most of the moves that we have made over the last few years have been the right ones. Most importantly you can see this product on the field, and the fact that these guys are locked in for a long time. We're going to continue to do that. We're going to continue to try and keep our young players as part of the organization hopefully for their entire careers."

Not only were the pieces in place for the future, but the Nationals were once again in the mix for the No. 1 pick in the MLB Draft, and once again, the target seemed clear. It was a known commodity by the name of Bryce Harper. "We were aware of Harper earlier than we were with Stephen Strasburg," said longtime Nationals reporter Mark Zuckerman. "There was a lot of talk about would he be eligible for the draft. I think having been through the Strasburg thing the year before, you were a little bit more aware of who was out there."

Ready for Their Close-Up

When legendary writer-director James L. Brooks decided to set his 2010 comedy, *How Do You Know,* in the world of professional baseball, he surprisingly chose the downtrodden Washington Nationals, one of MLB's most obscure teams. "They wanted to go after the Nationals," said the film's location manager, Carol Flaisher. "They didn't want to go to Yankee Stadium and do the same old thing. And everyone knows what Dodger Stadium looks like. Nobody knows what Nationals Stadium looks like."

And so began the process of transforming the ugly duckling Nats—the orphans of the league for several years—into glamorous movie stars. *How Do You Know* marks the first time the Nationals franchise has been on the silver screen, but 2010 actually was a banner year for Washington, as it was also featured in an episode of the hit TV show, *Top Chef,* that summer.

How does a team that even people in D.C. treat as an afterthought suddenly land two high-profile entertainment appearances in a year?

Catherine Silver is the Nationals' executive director of ballpark enterprises and guest services. Normally her job involves the logistics of bar mitzvahs and weddings at the stadium, so when Hollywood comes calling, it's a big deal. "We are contacting people, and then we go after stuff filming in the area," Silver said. "It's extremely beneficial to us. The audience for *Top Chef* was enormous, and all over the world people found out who we were because of it. The movie was something that was very fun, but it required a little more work."

In *How Do You Know,* Owen Wilson starred as Nationals closer Matty Reynolds, and several scenes were filmed in the three-year-old park during a 36-hour stretch. "James is known for being a stickler, and he

Washington played better under Riggleman, posting a 33–42 record, but even a seven-game winning streak at the end of the season—making the Nationals the first team in MLB history to lose their first seven games and win their last seven—couldn't prevent them from finishing one loss worse than in 2008. Their record was a ghastly 59–103. "This franchise was at a low point," Zuckerman said.

But with the philosophy put into place by ownership and Rizzo, there wasn't any panic after the dreadful 2009 campaign. They were past rebuilding. They just wanted to augment the building blocks on the roster filmed one scene 75 times," Silver said. "It was extraordinary to watch. He worked with us hand in hand, so the film looked very authentic right down to the bullpen. We even helped him find the extras so that they looked like real players."

In typical Hollywood style, some artistic liberties were taken. For example, the Nationals bullpen in the film is actually the visitors bullpen, and references to Reynolds' $14 million salary stretch the boundaries of belief, but all parties worked to ensure the process was smooth. "They let us go into places that a normal person would not be able to," Flaisher said. "They made it easier. It was a win-win for everybody. I'm a Washington girl. I'm trying to push the stadium, and any kind of exposure helps."

During the *Top Chef* episode, former Nationals Adam Dunn and Matt Capps joined starter John Lannan during the tasting, and in *How Do You Know*, the game footage was shot during a Lannan start. Nationals reliever Drew Storen was invited to the Hollywood premiere, and he walked the red carpet among Wilson, Reese Witherspoon, and Paul Rudd. Given that he was a Nat, Storen went unnoticed. "I don't think anybody really recognizes me. I'm not a physical specimen," Storen said. "But seeing the curly W on the big screen was good. That will help us. Hopefully, [in 2011] we can win some more ballgames and get some more attention. There wasn't too much baseball in the movie, but anything helps. It's just so funny to see our clubhouse on the big screen."

Befitting the struggling nature of the Nats, the film, which cost approximately $120 million, was a box office bomb, pulling in just under $50 million.

and in the farm system. "I don't see a mass blowing up of the ballclub," Rizzo said. "I think we have a lot of good, core pieces in place. I'm excited about the youth and the players we can control over a long period of time who are going to be on the team in 2010. I think a few shrewd, strategic moves in some key areas will improve the ballclub for 2010."

The biggest offseason move would not be a deft free agent signing or trade. But it would come via a brash, bold jolt of precocious energy. It would come via Bryce Harper.

7

THE PHENOM, PART II

THE STORIES OF BRYCE ARON MAX HARPER SOUND APOCRYPHAL. As a three-year-old, he played T-ball games against six-year-olds. By nine years old, he became a hired gun, traveling to baseball tournaments. At 16 he was on the cover of *Sports Illustrated*. At 17 he was featured in *The New York Times*. During a high school showcase, he hit a 500-foot home run at Tropicana Field. Although those anecdotes sound like they were scripted by a Hollywood screenwriter, those episodes all played out along the young athlete's timeline.

Harper's story begins out in the desert, where the glitz and glamour of Las Vegas gradually gives way to the dusty roads and Spanish-style houses of the workers, who help make this desert oasis the place where anything can happen. It was where steelworker Ron Harper taught his sons the game that would change all of their lives, throwing them sunflower seeds and other tiny objects to hone their batting eyes. But Harper was no Stefano Capriati, Earl Woods, or Marv Marinovich—fathers who relentlessly pushed their child prodigies by orchestrating every move, berating coaches and officials, and stifling their adolescence. Harper gave Bryce and his brother, Bryan, room to play other sports and enjoy growing up. "His parents are good people. The only vibe I got from the father-son relationship was that it was all positive," said *Las Vegas Review-Journal* reporter Matt Youmans, who covered Bryce Harper. "There were no Marv Marinovich comparisons to be drawn. Ron is a blue-collar guy. He had the full respect of his kids. He was not an overbearing parent. He was like the perfect baseball dad from my view."

Believe it or not, Bryce Harper said he was more focused on being an all-around athlete than becoming a baseball prodigy. "I don't know if I was ever a fan," he said. "I just tried to play the game and take different parts

59

of everyone's game. My dad installed in my head to play the game the right way every day, and you have to look at these guys [old players]. Once he said a name, I'd be like, 'Click, I want to look this guy up.' But I liked to play football, baseball, basketball, everything."

As Harper grew up, it became clear that he was no ordinary player, blossoming into a 6'3" man-child capable of dominating opposition several years older than he. The stories of Harper blasting his way through tournaments from coast to coast became the stuff of legend. *Baseball America* named Harper "possibly the country's best 12-year-old hitter" in 2005, but you could argue that only die-hards were aware of him at that point. It wasn't until Harper took the field for Las Vegas High that his work became official, so to speak, legitimized through the media and the structure with which most fans were familiar.

The catcher and occasional outfielder took the field for the Wildcats and immediately looked like an old pro, hitting 11 homers and driving in 67 RBIs. After that year Harper participated in the Area Code Games and the Aflac All-American Game, as the exploits of the 15-year-old began to grow. That set the stage for an amazing sophomore season, where Harper exploded into the record books, hitting .626 with 14 homers, 22 doubles, nine triples, 36 steals, and 55 RBIs, earning *Baseball America's* High School Player of the Year honors. Not only was Harper a statistically good player, but he also showed the kind of passion that was rare for high school players, attacking every pitch, grounder, at-bat, and game with a maniacal intensity that bordered on over the top.

"When he was on the cover of *SI* before his junior year of high school," Youmans said, "I had heard about him a year before that. I had no idea how good he was. I had just heard stories. Two months before the *SI* story, I went out to see him play. You never know how good a player is at that age. I had seen a lot of guys get a lot of hype. What Bryce looked like was a surefire baseball prospect, if there is a thing. He had power, speed, and a love for the game. The guy is one of the most determined players I've ever seen. I was confident he was going to succeed."

Harper appeared on the cover of the June 8, 2009 issue of *Sports Illustrated* under the headline "Baseball's Chosen One," where he declared his goal of playing in the majors at "18 or 19" and outlined his ideal professional career. "Be in the Hall of Fame, definitely. Play in Yankee

Stadium. Play in the pinstripes. Be considered the greatest baseball player who ever lived," Harper told writer Tom Verducci. "I can't wait." The fact that the story was on the cover of the world's most famous sports magazine even caught the precocious teenager off guard. "I was in shock," Harper told the *Las Vegas Review-Journal*. "I couldn't believe it. I didn't think some 16-year-old kid would be on the cover. It's something you dream about."

It was a bold introduction to a player whom many sports fans and media members had never heard of, and some weren't ready for the Harper experience. "I'd heard vaguely about some phenom kid," CBSSports.com baseball columnist Scott Miller said. "But then he pops up on the *Sports Illustrated* cover, and it was like, 'Whoa!' I'll tell you what, my initial reaction was negative, and I kind of had a chip on my shoulder against him because I get so tired of the hype in today's world. I get tired of people going out and finding some eighth grader or whatever and blowing him up as the next big thing. I've always believed that as kids grow, they ought to be able to prove a few things before we worship at their altar."

The cocksure Harper did not worry about impressing anyone or living up to his growing reputation. He was simply focused on getting better each day, a trait that would serve him well as his career progressed. "I love the pressure," he said. "That's why you play the game—to be in pressure situations. If you don't want pressure, you shouldn't be playing."

It was also in the *SI* piece where Ron and Sheri Harper detailed plans to advance Bryce into better competition, moving him to junior college two years early by allowing him to get his GED. By mid-June Harper's time at Las Vegas High was over, as he enrolled at the College of Southern Nevada, a JUCO powerhouse in the wooden bat Scenic West Athletic Conference (SWAC). Harper obtained his GED in October, which made him eligible to play for Southern Nevada in the spring and—more importantly—eligible for the 2010 Major League Baseball Draft.

It was an unprecedented gamble in a city known for them. "There was some backlash to it. There were some people in Las Vegas who felt like Harper's parents weren't doing the right thing," Youmans said. "And some people said, 'He's a special talent and he should be put on a faster track.' Anybody who disapproves of what they did is being short-sighted. When you look at all the athletes who leave school early—tennis players, golf players—because they are ready to jump ahead of their peers, it's really idiotic to criticize this move."

Making the transition to junior college easier was the fact that Southern Nevada's coach, Tim Chambers, was a friend of the Harper family. "He made sure that Bryce had good guidance while going through college," Youmans said. In addition, Bryce's brother, Bryan, was a pitcher on the Coyotes.

If Harper's high school days were a show, his time with the Coyotes was the equivalent of a Vegas extravaganza. Crowds flocked to the previously sparse stadium to see the man-child boom towering batting practice home runs and fire the ball at ridiculous speeds from behind the plate. Scouts littered the stands, charting the kid's every swing and drooling over his five-tool skills. And opponents did their best to knock the No. 1 prospect in the country off his pedestal.

Harper, perhaps for the first time in his life, had a brief period of self-doubt at the beginning of his unique odyssey, when the hits were not dropping and the reality of being in college truly hit him. "I had a transition from high school to college, and it was pretty hard at the beginning," he said. "I was second-guessing myself and thinking, *maybe I shouldn't have done this*. There were times, when I was in my room or with my family or something, and it was pretty hard, because everybody was out there saying stuff: 'I can't live up to all the hype' and everything like that."

But that brief moment of doubt crept away with the crack of each successive hit. College of Southern Nevada games were can't-miss affairs, and Harper made sure they stayed that way. With his signature swath of eye black, his cocksure manner at the plate and in the field, and the aura that being a teenage prodigy afforded him, Harper was the center of attention each time the Coyotes took the field. "I was surprised that he wasn't cockier," Youmans said. "All of us, when we were teens, talked trash when we played sports. He earned the right to be cocky. But there was nothing where he crossed the line. There were a lot of guys on other teams looking to take their best shots. Of course he wants to respond."

For the most part, Harper let his bat do the talking. In 66 games with College of Southern Nevada, he put up astonishing numbers, hitting .443 and slugging to the tune of .987. He crushed 31 home runs (with a wood

bat), obliterating the school record of 12, and added 98 RBIs to earn SWAC
Player of the Year honors. He also became only the second junior college
player to ever win the Golden Spikes Award as the top amateur in the
country.

But with his team on the brink of elimination and his college career
winding down, Harper saved his best performance for last. At the NJCAA
Western District Tournament in Lamar, Colorado, Harper and the Coyotes
faced a must-win game against Central Arizona in order to advance to the
Junior College World Series. The 17-year-old put together the game of a
lifetime, crushing four home runs and adding a double and a triple to finish
6–for–6 with 10 RBIs, as the Coyotes rolled to a 25–11 victory and a spot
in the World Series. "Bryce had a great day," said Chambers, offering the
understatement of the century.

Harper had extended his college career with a heroic effort, but it
would all come undone two weeks later. At the National Junior College
World Series, Harper tried to ensure the focus was not solely on him but
on the rest of his CSN teammates. That strategy, though, backfired in a
winner's bracket game against San Jacinto on June 2.

After a questionable strike three call in the fifth inning by home plate
umpire Don Gilmore, Harper drew a line in the dirt with his bat as he left
the plate, and Gilmore quickly responded, delivering an emphatic ejection
that drew cheers from San Jacinto's players and fans. "The ump was trying
to grandstand. It was completely ridiculous," said Youmans, who covered
the game for the *Review-Journal*. "He was looking to ring up Harper on a
dramatic third strike. The pitch was clearly outside—a good six inches off
the plate—and he did this dramatic strike call. He wanted to strike out the
phenom, no question."

Harper was escorted from the ballpark. Under NJCAA rules, he was
deemed ineligible for the Coyotes' next two games and banned from the
stadium. (Harper had been ejected earlier in the season after taking a bow
after a right-field throw, thus earning the two-game ban.) It proved to be
the end of Harper's collegiate career, as CSN lost its next World Series
game to abruptly finish one of the most unique journeys in sports history.
"He felt terrible. I know it was killing him not to be out there," Ron Harper
said. "I told him, 'You've got to forgive, you've got to ask for forgiveness,
and move on.'"

It wouldn't take long for that to happen. Five days after Harper's ejection, he was back in Las Vegas with advisor Scott Boras at his side. The MLB Draft was June 7, and with the Washington Nationals picking first, it was all but assured that Harper would join fellow phenom Stephen Strasburg as the Nats' back-to-back No. 1 picks.

When MLB commissioner Bud Selig read the selection, applause rang out through the MLB Network studios, though, as was the case with Strasburg, Boras kept Harper's family and friends off the TV screens. It was up to Selig to deliver a bit of emotion, as he cracked after the cheers, "Thank you. I didn't think it was that much of a surprise."

Harper was announced as an outfielder rather than catcher, a move that most baseball analysts expected the Nationals to make, allowing the youngster to focus on his hitting and not worry about the rigors of working behind the plate. "This is the way I've understood it all along," analyst Peter Gammons said during the draft broadcast. "They don't want to risk the injury. They don't want to take away…from the bat in any way. He's a tremendous athlete—a Larry Walker type of athlete. And when you take that immense power—as one general manager said, 'He's a lock for 500 home runs.'—you don't put that behind the plate."

The draft signaled that one journey had ended for the precocious teen with the powerful swing, and another had just begun. Bryce Harper, all of 17 years old, was a professional baseball player. "It's what I've wanted since I was seven years old," he said.

8

LEARNING THE ROPES

FROM DAY ONE THE KNOCK ON BRYCE HARPER WAS THAT HE WAS a self-absorbed prima donna, more in tune with his own stats than winning or his teammates. He would have to disprove that label every step along the way.

As expected, with Boras—who also represents Edwin Jackson, Stephen Strasburg, and Jayson Werth—calling the shots now as Harper's agent, the negotiations were protracted, with the kind of posturing and jockeying that had become all too familiar for Nationals fans, who went through the same scenario with Strasburg. "The charade, the kabuki dance, the nature of all of this, is just kind of silly," Nationals president Stan Kasten told *The Washington Post*. "We can do better as an industry, and I think both sides recognize that."

Strasburg raised some eyebrows when he chimed in on Harper's iffy contract status, saying, "If he doesn't want to play here, then we don't want him here," on the eve of the deadline. But it was clear that the Nationals, Boras, and Harper would come to an accord. The parties had worked together to sign Strasburg last season, and while Harper posed his own set of challenges as a fellow No. 1 pick, it would make no sense for the youngster to have jumped through all the hoops he did in order to get drafted, only to return back to CSN for another season of college baseball. "They had been through this before," Zuckerman said. "There was less drama about the situation."

All the pointed words and speculation proved to be for naught, when minutes before the midnight deadline on August 16, 2010, Boras reached an agreement with Mike Rizzo and the Nationals on a five-year, $9.9 million contract that included a $6.25 million signing bonus, the richest draft package ever given to a position player. "He deserves it, because he really is that gifted," Boras said.

After Harper had gone through one of the longest baseball breaks of his young life, the Nationals planned to get him in their system quickly, but first he had to meet the media in D.C., many of whom were eager to catch their first glimpse of the prodigy. Harper didn't disappoint, showing up in a stylish black suit with a subtle Mohawk haircut styled by his sister, Brittany, and turning on the charm in his introduction to the larger baseball world.

Nationals broadcaster Bob Carpenter emceed the press conference. Third baseman Ryan Zimmerman, in his duties as the face of the Nationals, presented Harper with a "34" jersey and curly W hat. From there Harper opined about his baseball idols ("I love Mickey Mantle."); playing at Nationals Park ("I feel like a kid in a candy store."); the media scrutiny ("I am really used to it now."); and his trademark touch of style to ward off glare ("I love wearing the eye black.") It was a smashing performance that revealed Harper not to be an egomaniacal lout, but a relaxed, self-aware teenager handling his unique situation with aplomb. "I thought, 'Wow, this guy is pretty cool for his age,'" Carpenter said. "This was a family that was in control. They were excited but not blown away. They were glad to be in D.C., but they weren't goo-goo, ga-ga over the whole thing. Bryce handled himself very coolly in the press conference and said all the right things. It wasn't just about 'me' and 'what I want to do.'"

At the press conference, Rizzo indicated that Harper would go to the Florida Instructional League to get his first taste of professional experience before spring training in 2011. As expected there were ups and downs during Harper's time in Florida, but his .319 average, four homers, and 12 RBIs in 47 at-bats earned him a trip to the Arizona Fall League, where he would make his debut as a taxi squad player, eligible to play only Wednesday and Saturday.

Harper once again hit well over .300, though at times he appeared to be too eager at the plate. "When I'm only playing twice a week, I'm going to go up there and swing as much as I can," Harper said. "Sometimes I look stupid and sometimes I look good. Hopefully, I look good more than I look stupid."

With his first series of professional tests under his belt, Harper was ready for the next step—spring training and his eventual stint in the minors, where he would be tested with every pitch.

WASHINGTON'S SPRING TRAINING HOME IN VIERA, FLORIDA, grew up around, well…nothing. When the Nats first started playing there, there was very little to offer outside of Space Coast Stadium, and the desultory action on the field didn't make spring training games much of a destination for fans. But with the arrival of Stephen Strasburg in 2010 and now Harper in 2011, Space Coast was bubbling with excitement, as Nationals fans and Grapefruit League foes wanted to get a look at Washington's bonus babies. Heading into spring training, *Baseball America* ranked Harper as the No. 1 prospect in the sport—just ahead of Angels outfielder Mike Trout.

Harper arrived at Nationals camp with little to no chance of making the major league roster, but that wasn't going to prevent the 18-year-old from going all out to make the show. "Why can't it be realistic?" he said. "Why can't I come in here and think that I can make this team? I've exceeded expectations my whole life. Everybody said I couldn't do it last year at [the College of Southern Nevada]. I know this is a totally different level, totally different people, and I respect that. But I'm going to make their decision hard. I'm going to come out here every day and play like I can, and until they send me down to minor league camp, I'm going to try to make it hard."

Although Harper's veteran teammates could have treated the brash youngster in a frosty manner, it didn't take long for the rookie to feel at home. "Everybody took me under their wing," Harper said. "They really helped me out every single day."

But in reality, Harper was different, a raw teenager in the province of salty veterans who were either secure in their spot on the team or unnerved by this brash, young pup unabashedly trying to make the roster. "He stood out like a sore thumb," longtime Nationals reporter Mark Zuckerman said. "He's this 18-year-old kid who's all his life owned the world. It's not that he was disrespectful or anything of the guys in the clubhouse, but you noticed him a lot more. His presence was there. He had a little air of superiority, maybe, to him."

Harper made his spring training debut on February 28, 2011 against the New York Mets. Although no one had really seen Harper on this stage, the best way to baffle a young hitter is to feed him a steady diet of off-speed pitches, which is exactly what the Mets did, striking out Harper twice. But like the professional hitter he was, it didn't take him long to find his swing, and before the inevitable assignment to minor league camp, he had picked up seven hits in 18 at-bats.

The Nationals had no intention of throwing Harper to the wolves, and so, on March 12, they sent the youngster to Single A Hagerstown, Pennsylvania, where he would get the experience of the game's daily grind without quite as much attention tied to his performance. Later that spring, Harper's minor league debut was not met with much fanfare in Rome, Georgia, home of the Rome Braves of the South Atlantic League. There were a few curious onlookers, but it otherwise lacked the electricity of Strasburg's first minor league start. Harper went 2–for–4, dropping down a perfect bunt that fooled the Braves and showing that he wasn't all about power.

But the low Single A lifestyle wasn't exactly the stuff of memory. Harper and the Suns slogged through the early part of the season, logging countless miles on their bus. The prodigy wasn't exactly lighting the world on fire at Hagerstown either in the early going, but one adjustment helped make a world of difference. Harper felt as if he wasn't seeing the ball that well, which for a hitter is of the utmost importance.

So, the Nationals sent the rookie to see their team optometrist, Dr. Keith Smithson, a Northern Virginia-based specialist in the field of sports vision, having worked with former D.C.-based athletes like Redskins RB Clinton Portis, Wizards guard Kirk Hinrich, Washington Freedom forward Mia Hamm, and Nationals infielder Cristian Guzman.

Smithson asked Harper to check out his eye chart, and the results were shocking. "I don't know how you ever hit before. You have some of the worst eyes I've ever seen," Harper said the doctor told him. Harper acknowledged that his vision wasn't good, but that he had trouble with contacts before. "I needed [the contacts] in college," he said. "But I tried them for a while in high school, and they gave me headaches really bad. So, I just got by without them. But these are a new kind [of lenses], and they really help. The difference [in vision] is huge."

After getting some visual clarity, Harper's bat exploded as he went on an offensive tear, which put him near the top of the South Atlantic League leaderboard in nearly every category. More than anything Harper's time with the Suns would be remembered for two instances that showed the youngster still had a ways to go before being ready to handle the high-pressure life of the major leagues.

On April 27 he was involved in a bench-clearing incident against the West Virginia Power. After Harper hit a first-inning home run, power pitcher Tyler Waldron struck him out in the third. Harper took off his batting gloves while in the box and then turned to have a few words with Waldron, while both benches ran on to the field.

Then, on June 6 against the Greensboro Grasshoppers, Harper blasted a home run off Zachary Neal, his 14th of the season, and took his time admiring the shot. While Neal and the Grasshoppers squawked at him during his home run trot, Harper blew a kiss toward the pitcher. That gesture set off a firestorm of controversy, with talking heads across the country decrying the 18-year-old's actions. "I hate to bring this into it, but I would think at some point, the game itself, the competition on the field, is going to have to figure out a way to police this young man," Hall of Famer Mike Schmidt said on ESPN. "If indeed his manager won't, the game will end up taking care of it."

"When you get to the major league level, blowing kisses won't be tolerated. He'll see a high frequency of 95 mph fastballs that could put him on the disabled list," former Nats general manager Jim Bowden wrote in his ESPN column. "Like Barry Bonds in his prime, Harper needs to learn now that his response to taunting or comments from opposing players must be made with his bat, not with gestures."

What everyone didn't realize about "the kiss" was that Harper was sticking up for his teammates, who had been shown up by Neal earlier. After recording strikeouts, the Grasshoppers pitcher glowered into the Suns' dugout, seemingly daring Hagerstown's hitters to do something about it. Well, Harper did just that. "A lot of people were looking to make more out of that than what it was," Carpenter said. "When Harper came to the bigs, we found out that the same pitcher had shown up some of his teammates. He was responding to that. Once you hear that, it's pretty impressive. He was protecting his guys."

Within the Nationals organization, these blips were met with little more than a shrug, as they understood there would be some growing pains from a teenager thrust into the spotlight. "There was an understanding with everyone in the organization that this is an 18-year-old," said Mark Zuckerman of Nats Insider. "The thought was, 'He's going to have these moments, and we're going to watch him carefully. We don't want him to change his personality and who he's always been, but there are some maturity things along the way that he will have to learn.' And that's why he was in the minors from the start and starting at low A. They wanted him to experience that."

After Harper's 72 games in Hagerstown, the Nationals announced on July 4 that Harper was being promoted to Double A Harrisburg, Pennsylvania. While with the Suns, he hit .318 with 14 homers, 46 RBIs, and a .977 OPS (on-base plus slugging percentage). The numbers meant little to the Nationals brass. The real goal was to get Harper acclimated to the daily grind, playing outfield, and the lack of trappings at the minor league level. It worked, even though Harper didn't exactly love his time in A ball. "Those last 20 games, I was really, you know, really not too focused," Harper told Comcast SportsNet Washington. "I was wanting to get out of there, doing things that I shouldn't have been doing. And once I got [to Harrisburg], baseball was fun again. It was a lot of fun being out here, being in this kind of crowd, this type of atmosphere. You know, that's what you live for."

At Harrisburg, Harper's Independence Day debut drew 8,092, the largest attendance in Senators history. Harper didn't let the crowd down, going 2–for–3, while also displaying some of the flash that rubs people the wrong way, using his blazing speed to go from first to third on a groundout.

Shortly after his Double A career kicked off, Harper headed to the MLB Futures Game in Arizona, a place where his panache would be seen by a national television audience. Harper was the second youngest player on the USA squad, and it would be a litmus test for the teenager against some of the best young talent in baseball. This was one of the rare instances where Harper didn't deliver while on center stage, going 0–for–4 with two strikeouts, drawing boos from the crowd at Phoenix's Chase Field. "I'm terrible at All-Star Games," he said.

Being selected to the squad, though, was its own distinction as was the chance to head home to Las Vegas for a bit. Back in Harrisburg, he didn't put up great numbers. Harper hit .256 with a .329 on-base percentage and .395 slugging percentage, but he was doing a good job of fitting in and getting comfortable in the outfield, when on August 18, he strained his left hamstring while running the bases and had to be carted off the field.

Like Strasburg's injury in the Arizona Fall League, the Nationals would dodge a bullet. The team decided to shut Harper down with only a few weeks remaining in the season to prepare him for his own trip to the AFL.

WHEN HARPER, FULLY HEALED, ARRIVED IN ARIZONA to play with the Scottsdale Scorpions in the AFL, little did he know he would become teammates with a player with whom he will be inevitably linked years into the future.

Harper had already bested Mike Trout before the 2011 season in *Baseball America*'s rankings, and now they were teammates on a loaded Scorpions squad that also featured Red Sox third baseman Will Middlebrooks, and Giants prospects Gary Brown and shortstop Brandon Crawford. "It was a great mix of guys who all loved to play," Harper said.

After a slow start, Harper thrived in Arizona despite being the youngest player in the league. Playing among some of the brightest young stars in the game, Harper seemed energized and had plenty of fun out in the desert, even pulling a Ruthian move to help the Scorpions win a game. "We were playing a kid from the White Sox, and he kept hanging his changeup," Harper said. "So Crawford was sitting in the dugout and he goes, 'Well, what are you going to do?' I go, 'Well, first two guys get on, I'm going to drop a bomb and walk off this field, telling them we own this place.' I was just kidding but serious at the same time.

"He goes, 'Yeah, right.' I go, 'I promise you, I'm going to hit a jack right here. I swear on everything.' And Trout was there and he says, 'Yeah, okay.' I was like, 'All right.' So the first two guys get on, and I'm standing in the on-deck circle laughing. I get him to a 3–2 count, and he throws me a change-up and I hit it out to center. Everybody ran inside the clubhouse. It was a great moment. I had a blast out there. We had a little too much fun."

When it was all over, Harper made such an impression there was talk he'd go straight to the Nationals after spring training in 2012. Harper turned 19 in the middle of the Scorpions' season—they would go on to win the AFL championship—and finished with a .333 average with six home runs in 93 at-bats and a strong 1.084 OPS. "I think Bryce made a lot of progress," GM Mike Rizzo said. "He's got a unique skill set. He's got a unique talent base. He's going to be a terrific player for us in the near future."

The very near future.

9

DISASTER

ALTHOUGH THE GIDDY DELIRIUM OF STRASMAS HAD WORN OFF slightly with each successive 2010 start, the Nationals pitcher had given the team a signature player—not to mention a top-flight starter—who appeared to have the stuff of a No. 1 ace for years to come. Cracks, though, were starting to show in the façade.

After Stephen Strasburg improved to 5–2, following a seven-strikeout performance against the Cincinnati Reds on July 21, he would miss his next start with a sore arm. Miguel Batista was forced to make an emergency start when Strasburg's warm-up session didn't meet expectations. (Batista, an erudite guy and aspiring author, had perhaps the quote of the year upon hearing boos from fans who expected to see Strasburg on the hill and got him instead: "Imagine if you go to see Miss Universe, then you end up having Miss Iowa," he said. "You might get those kind of boos.")

The Nationals immediately put Strasburg on the 15-day disabled list despite no evidence of a tear in his shoulder and the fact that the pitcher felt like he was doing better. "They're taking every precaution with me," Strasburg said. "It's feeling great already. I'm making big strides. I'm just going to keep getting better, keep getting stronger, and when the time comes, I'm going to be ready to go."

There had been grumblings about Strasburg's pitching mechanics for several years, even dating back to high school. In the wake of his stint on the disabled list, those arguments flared up. "He does something with his arm action that is difficult, in my mind, to pitch a whole lot of innings on," White Sox pitching coach Don Cooper told MLB Radio in July, shortly after Chicago faced Strasburg.

After the scare with Strasburg's "shoulder inflammation," as the team called it, the young pitcher returned to the hill on August 10 for one of the worst performances of his career, as the Florida Marlins knocked him around for six runs in 4⅓ innings, the shortest outing of his 10 starts. Strasburg then muddled through a five-inning, 85-pitch effort against the Arizona Diamondbacks on August 15, setting the stage for a nightmare scenario for the Nationals and baseball.

On August 21 Strasburg took the hill against the Philadelphia Phillies at Citizens Bank Ballpark and came out flying, dominating a very strong Phillies lineup, which would help propel the team toward the National League East title. Through 4⅓ innings Strasburg had six strikeouts, no walks, and had allowed just one run on two hits.

On the 56th pitch of his night, however, Strasburg winced in pain after throwing a change-up to Phillies outfielder Domonic Brown. Immediately, catcher Ivan Rodriguez, manager Jim Riggleman, pitching coach Steve McCatty, and trainer Lee Kuntz came out to the mound. Strasburg lobbied to remain in the game, but the team pulled him right then and there. The official postgame word was that the injury was a strained flexor tendon in his right forearm. "The night it happened, everybody saw it, saw him wince, and your first thought is, *Oh God, this is not going to be good*," longtime Nationals reporter Mark Zuckerman said. "And then they gave him the tests, and by all accounts they said he's going to be fine. It's nothing major. And I think people were breathing a sigh of relief for a couple of days."

The brief window of silence between the injury and the official diagnosis led to all manner of speculation and worry. Rob Dibble, a SiriusXM radio host who also worked as the Nationals' color commentator at the time, went on his radio show on August 23 and excoriated Strasburg for what he perceived as a lack of toughness. "Suck it up, kid. This is your profession," Dibble said. "You chose to be a baseball player. You can't have the cavalry come in and save your butt every time you feel a little stiff shoulder, sore elbow."

But it was much more than that. The results of an enhanced MRI revealed a significant tear of the ulnar collateral ligament of his elbow, which would require season-ending and career-jeopardizing Tommy John surgery and a 12-to-18 month recovery time—essentially, the worst possible scenario. "It was a punch to the gut," Zuckerman said.

The team found out the results of the MRI on a Thursday but held off announcing it to the press because that was the day Bryce Harper was scheduled for his initial meeting with the D.C. media. In this case the baseball gods giveth and taketh away.

A somber Strasburg sat with general manager Mike Rizzo on August 27 and reflected on the injury and the end of a remarkable run in his rookie season. "It was kind of a shock to me, because I didn't really feel anything. It is what it is. In a way, it's good that it happened now, instead of when we're going to the postseason or getting ready for a World Series," Strasburg said. "This is a new challenge. I want to be the best at everything. Right now, I'm going to be the best at rehabbing and getting back out here.

"It kind of sucks to have it end like this. I've gotten a lot of great experience when I was up here. The weird thing about it, that last game— that was when everything started to click. That was when I had that feeling. That was a packed house with some rowdy fans, and I didn't feel like they were there. I was just so locked in, and everything was working. Sure enough, something happened. But that's something to build on."

This was a crushing blow to the Nationals' short and long-term plans, but the organization did its best not to let it show. "We're going to take this news and we're going to persevere," Rizzo said. "We're going to move and we're going to get our rotation intact. And when Stephen Strasburg returns, along with Jordan Zimmermann, and the rest of our good young rotation, we'll be prepared to take on the 2011 season and beyond."

Zuckerman added: "Whatever vision they had, this was going to delay it a year. It was going to have to be pushed back another year. Despite whatever talent they had on their roster, there was no way they were going to win without him."

An outpouring of support came to the injured young pitcher, including the namesake of the surgery he was about to undergo. Tommy John offered to help the pitcher through this difficult time. "I would be honored, I really would. I don't care how strong of a person you say you are, when you have to enter into a wilderness, you're scared," John said in an interview with D.C. sports talk station 106.7 The Fan. "Fear is of the unknown, and you don't know what it's gonna be. And the more people you can talk to—to allay those fears, the better off you'll be. I would love to. I would love to talk to Stephen. Give him my cell number, and maybe I can help him to come back."

John was also confident that Strasburg would bounce back from the procedure, just as he did in 1974. "He already throws the ball 96 to 101 mph," John said. "How could he be better? If he comes back the same or slightly worse, he's still going to throw the ball harder than 90 percent of the guys in the major leagues."

Bolstered by a strong foundation, Strasburg remained on an even keel. "I've got great support all around me, and they reminded me of everything I should be thankful for, and they put everything in perspective for me," Strasburg said. "Bottom line, this is a game. I'm very blessed to play this game for a living. It's a minor setback, but in the grand scheme of things it's just a blip on the radar screen."

The number of pitchers who had the procedure done only to bounce back with strong seasons—St. Louis Cardinals right-handers Chris Carpenter and Adam Wainwright, Atlanta Braves right-hander John Smoltz, and the Nationals' own Zimmermann, for example—was another silver lining in what appeared to be a very dark cloud. "The injury, as tragic as it was, is a blessing in disguise," Nationals broadcaster F.P. Santangelo said. "You have to get in serious shape to go 30 starts. From that regard, he realized, 'Hey, this is the big leagues, and I'm going to have to get in shape to get back and if I'm going to be the best, I'm going to work real hard at it.' It was a blessing in disguise for the longevity of his career."

On September 3, under the care of noted surgeon Dr. Lewis Yocum, Strasburg underwent the Tommy John procedure, where a piece of ligament was taken from Strasburg's leg and transplanted into his right elbow. "Everything went very smoothly, and the reports were very good," Rizzo said. "He'll start his rehab in a couple of days, and we're very confident he will come back strong from this surgery. I really feel this is just a blip in what is going to be an outstanding career for Stephen."

Losing Strasburg was a crushing blow. Slowly but surely, however, the Nationals were putting together a team that would be able to persevere and thrive despite missing one of its stalwarts. Thanks to the efforts of Rizzo and his staff, Washington wasn't a one-man show. Once the laughingstock of the league, the Nationals were developing a fertile farm system and making the necessary moves to contend in the near future.

10

PUTTING THE PIECES TOGETHER

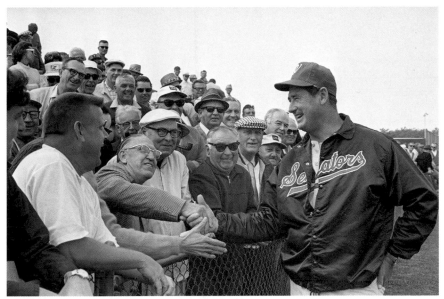

To spur interest in their team, the Washington Senators turned to Ted Williams in 1969 as their manager and vice president.

Expos manager Frank Robinson leaves the field on September 29, 2004 after Montreal's last home game at Olympic Stadium. The hapless organization would play its next season in Washington, D.C. (Getty Images)

After signing a record $15.1 million deal, Stephen Strasburg (left) poses with third baseman Ryan Zimmerman, general manager Mike Rizzo, and former team president Stan Kasten (far right) during August of 2009.

With Strasmas, the mania surrounding Stephen Strasburg, hitting Washington, D.C., sports business experts estimate that the Nats took in $1.5 million during Strasburg's major league debut.

Stephen Strasburg, the first pitcher to ever strike out more than 10 players without a walk in his initial big league start, throws against the Pittsburgh Pirates during that June 8, 2010 debut.

Sporting his trademark eye black, 17-year-old Bryce Harper hit .443 and crushed 31 home runs during his lone season with the College of Southern Nevada.

Seated next to agent Scott Boras, Bryce Harper is introduced to the media during August of 2010. Boras also represents Stephen Strasburg. (Getty Images)

Scout-turned-general manager Mike Rizzo (left) and veteran manager Davey Johnson, who has led the New York Mets, Cincinnati Reds, Baltimore Orioles, and Los Angeles Dodgers, are two of the architects behind the Nats' turnaround.

The brash Bryce Harper often sports odd haircuts and slathers eye black on his face. (Getty Images)

Known for his hustle and aggressiveness on the base path, Bryce Harper races to third base during a May 6, 2012 game.
(Getty Images)

During a game broadcast on ESPN, Bryce Harper gets intentionally plunked by Philadelphia Phillies pitcher Cole Hamels. Harper, though, would respond by stealing home.

Bryce Harper's answer to a media question about drinking Canadian beer has spawned a popular catchphrase that even U.S. senator Harry Reid referenced.
(Getty Images)

Players douse general manager Mike Rizzo with beer and champagne on October 1, 2012 as the Nationals celebrate their National League East title. (Getty Images)

Outfielder Jayson Werth rejoices after his walk-off homer, which forced a Game 5 in the 2012 NLDS against the St. Louis Cardinals. His epic at-bat against Lance Lynn has earned a permanent place in Nationals lore. (Getty Images)

After reaching his predetermined innings limit, Stephen Strasburg is reduced to watching his teammates during the 2012 NLDS. The Nationals' decision to shut down their ace triggered a firestorm of controversy.

MIKE RIZZO WAS A FORMER PLAYER, THE KIND OF GRITTY KID THAT a scout observes during his days traversing the road before convincing his bosses to take a chance on the grinder. In Rizzo's case, it was the California Angels, who drafted him in the 22nd round of the 1982 Draft. A baseball nut, Rizzo was perfectly content to kick around the minors, holding on to his slim chance of making it to the show.

From 1982 to 1984, Rizzo played with the short-season Single A Salem (Oregon) Angels, the Single A Peoria (Illinois) Suns, and the high Single A Redwood (Oregon) Pioneers, playing first, second, and third base. In his three years as a player, Rizzo hit .247 with five home runs and 44 RBIs. In 1984, the Angels released him. "Greatest years of my life," Rizzo told Adam Kilgore of *The Washington Post*. "Every day you get to play baseball, then stay up late, sleep in late, get up, and do it again. The camaraderie of the guys and the friends that you make—those minor league dog days, they weren't dog days to me."

After his playing career ended, Rizzo took a graduate assistant job at the University of Illinois and was then hired by the White Sox as an area scout—the beginning of a long and winding journey that would prove Rizzo was a true baseball lifer. Those among the baseball hierarchy would notice his dedication to the craft of scouting. Rizzo joined the nascent Arizona Diamondbacks in 1998 and served as the director of scouting for the Diamondbacks from 2000–2006. He was credited with building one of the best farm systems in the majors, drafting and acquiring players like outfielder Justin Upton, third baseman Mark Reynolds, and outfielder Carlos Quentin.

But when Arizona replaced general manager Joe Garagiola Jr. with Josh Byrnes, Rizzo began looking for a way out of the desert, feeling he had paid his dues and deserved a shot at running his own club. When the opportunity arrived for Rizzo to join the Nationals as an assistant GM, he leapt at the opportunity. "It's a step up, a move forward, something I wanted to do," Rizzo said.

But working under the direction of then-GM Jim Bowden and—after Bowden's resignation—team president Stan Kasten didn't afford Rizzo the true autonomy to make player decisions with the Nationals. Rizzo was named acting GM for the 2009 season, though he didn't have his current powers until after the 2010 campaign. That's when Kasten left the team, and Rizzo was promoted to executive vice president of baseball operations and general manager and given free reign to run the Nationals by his own design. The promotion represented the ultimate job for Rizzo. "For a guy who loves baseball and grew up in it his whole life," Rizzo said, "this is a dream opportunity for me to be able to hone in on a franchise and build it the way I see fit."

Rizzo now had a direct pipeline to ownership, which would conceivably make expenditures to acquire personnel that much easier. "Mike Rizzo is unquestionably one of the best baseball minds in the game," managing principal owner Ted Lerner said in a statement. "He has a unique ability to see player talent for what it is, what it can be, and how it fits into building a team. Mike has been one of the architects of the rebuilding of the entire Nationals player system, from scouting to player development to big league signings. We believe the talent foundation we are establishing on and off the field will make the Nationals one of baseball's most exciting teams over the next several seasons."

Bumping Rizzo up the ladder was a natural fit, and one that gave the Nationals a keen baseball mind at the helm of their operations. His promotion would have immediate repercussions. "There was some thought of whether he was GM material," said longtime Nationals reporter Mark Zuckerman. "He had a long, good career as a scout, but there was a question about his ability to deal with press, deal with agents, deal with other GMs. Did he have that communication side of it that a modern day GM has to have? I give him a lot of credit. He worked his ass off to get better at those things while at the same time staying true to all his principles as a scout. It brought respectability to the organization and it was the first point you realized that the ownership was going to let the person running the baseball operations have control."

Having Rizzo at the top was a boon to Washington's farm system, which continues to flourish under his reign. He made several key moves below the major league squad, dismissing Double A manager John Stearns, Triple A pitching coach Rich Gale, and Gulf Coast Nationals coach Cesar Cedeno, among other hirings and firings. "The biggest name to go was Jose Rijo, who was at the center of the Dominican scandal and was one of Bowden's closest friends," Zuckerman said. "But Rizzo actually retained several guys, including Bob Boone, who still works for the Nationals. More than anything, Rizzo added people to the scouting department, convincing ownership they needed to expand the operation."

In the front office, amateur scouting director Dana Brown departed, and the team cut ties with Moose Stubing, special assistant to the general manager. Rizzo bolstered the team's operations and showed no hesitation in making moves, including removing the interim tag from manager Jim Riggleman's title in 2010. "I do believe that with the new responsibility and the new title and the new job description, I feel it will certainly be my baby," Rizzo said. "My fingerprints will be all over the organization, more so than they are already."

Entering the 2011 season, the Nationals were once again coming off a last-place finish, in which the team finished 69–93 and was left reeling down the stretch by the catastrophic injury to Stephen Strasburg. But there were some indications that things were starting to turn around. The Nationals won 10 more games in 2011 than the year before and posted their first winning record at home (41–40) since 2006. "When I got here, I was pleasantly surprised with how Rizzo had set everything up. The minor leagues were stocked," said Nats broadcaster F.P. Santangelo, who joined the team in 2011. "They were set up to be good for a long time, depending on how they developed. In Montreal, we were voted minor league system of the year, and it was the same kind of setup in D.C. [Rizzo] surrounded himself with wonderful people. And not really knowing any names or faces, I knew they had a chance to win. I felt like I landed on my feet with an organization that was headed north in a hurry."

The face of the organization remained third baseman Ryan Zimmerman, who had maintained a stoic front throughout even the darkest days of the franchise. Zimmerman was coming off his second straight Silver Slugger Award as the best offensive corner man in the National League. But for once, Zimmerman wasn't the sole focus when it came to discussing the Nationals.

In the offseason, Washington made its biggest free agent splash since moving from Montreal, choosing to let slugging first baseman Adam Dunn go to the Chicago White Sox and signing Philadelphia Phillies outfielder Jayson Werth to a staggering, seven-year, $126 million contract on December 5, 2010. That move was greeted with gasps by the baseball community, considering the other teams interested in Werth—the Boston Red Sox and Detroit Tigers—weren't offering numbers close to what the Nationals delivered.

The 31-year-old Werth averaged 29 homers, 84 RBIs, and 18 steals in his last three years with the Phillies but was seen by many as both a complementary player and a benefactor of both the Phillies' hitter-friendly ballpark and potent lineup. In addition, during the final years of the deal when Werth would be pushing 40, the Nationals would be on the hook for $18 million. Still, Rizzo and the organization were thrilled with their coup. "I sleep like a baby," Rizzo said at the press conference introducing the newest Nat to D.C, "knowing that we got Jayson Werth."

But why, aside from the obvious 126 million reasons, would Werth leave a perennial playoff contender to join the cellar-dwelling Nats? "The young talent in this organization is immense. With the length of the contract I got, I felt good about the chances of this organization winning over the course of my contract," Werth said. "That was very important to me. I've been in the postseason a lot the last couple of years. That's what it's all about. That's what you play for. That's what you work out for. That's what you get to spring training early for. I hate to lose. I'm here to win."

Werth's deal, while adding a very good player, was about more than just a personnel move. It was a clear signal to the rest of the baseball world that the Nationals were no longer the indigent, irresponsible pushovers of Major League Baseball. They wanted to make a statement that the organization was for real and to be reckoned with—and they did. "It was looked at as a gamble and frowned upon by a lot of people. I definitely caught a lot of grief for it, but realistically I knew the situation I was going to," Werth said. "I said all along, 'I wanted to go somewhere where I had a chance to win for a long, long time.' And it turned out, this was probably the best place I could've [gone]. I felt good about it when I signed here."

Even Dunn, who had expressed a desire to stay in Washington, couldn't fault the team for its moves. "They've got tremendous people in place," he said. "Ownership is incredible, and they got the right man at GM in Mike Rizzo. He's a good as they get. They did it right. They did it the right way. It's a great, classy organization. They had a plan and they stuck with it."

"The Plan," which had been viewed by fans with skepticism for several years, was actually being implemented, and it seemed to be on the verge of producing results. "Even though the signing was mocked at first, the Werth signing was another step in the respectability of the franchise," Zuckerman said, "and in showing they were serious about spending money, because there was a question of whether this ownership group would spend money. It also brought in a certain attitude that the clubhouse needed, from someone who had been there and won before and wasn't going to accept anything less than their best."

That was important, because the Nationals were going to be counting on a host of young players—shortstop Ian Desmond, second baseman Danny Espinosa, outfielder Roger Bernadina, catcher Wilson Ramos, outfielder Mike Morse, and pitchers Jordan Zimmermann, Drew Storen, Tyler Clippard, and Ryan Mattheus. "It's guys like Ian Desmond, guys like Ryan Zimmerman being here through all the losing streaks and all the losing seasons," Strasburg said. "Guys like Jordan Zimmermann coming off Tommy John and pitching really well, Jayson Werth coming in and really changing the whole image of the clubhouse—getting guys to learn how to win. We've got a lot of young guys who go out there and compete hard."

The 2011 season, however, didn't start with a bang. Washington treaded water for the early part of the year. The Nats were hampered by a torn abdominal muscle to Zimmerman and a painfully slow start from Werth, who clearly was affected by the pressure of being the man after signing his mega-deal. Never the best interview subject, Werth and his prickly nature and plummeting stats made him an easy target for fans and the media. "Everyone would agree that he didn't have a huge, monster season," Nationals play-by-play announcer Bob Carpenter said. "But he instilled some new attitudes in the clubhouse."

Another important free-agent acquisition, first baseman Adam LaRoche, tore his labrum during spring training and attempted to play through the injury, as doctors informed him it would not affect his swing. But LaRoche looked feeble at the plate and would eventually have season-ending surgery in June, taking a .172 batting average with him. Sitting at 20–21 on May 16, the Nationals lost 10 of their next 13 games and seemed, despite the promise of new ways, to be the same old cellar-dwelling Nats.

Washington, though, showed signs of life in June, as Morse turned into a slugging powerhouse, Werth began to produce from the leadoff spot, and Riggleman's unorthodox move of having the pitcher hit eighth in the lineup worked wonders. The Nationals won 10 of 11 games to finally reach the .500 mark at 37–37, heading into a June 23 game against the Seattle Mariners—a contest that, in its aftermath, would have a profound effect on the franchise going forward.

After pulling out a dramatic 1–0 win against the Mariners, which put the team at its highest point in more than six years, Riggleman's postgame press conference was delayed. Many in attendance suspected that something was up. And when Rizzo came out to meet the assembled media, that assumption was revealed to be correct.

Shortly after informing the equally shocked Nationals players, Rizzo told a stunned media contingent that Riggleman, who was guiding the hottest team in baseball, had resigned over a contract dispute. "Jim told me pregame today that, if we wouldn't pick up his option, then he wouldn't get on the team bus today," Rizzo said during the press conference. "I felt that the time wasn't right for me to pick up the option, and certainly today's conversation—put to me in the way it was put to me—you certainly can't make that decision in a knee-jerk reaction. It's too big of a decision."

Riggleman, a native of nearby Rockville, Maryland, was working on a one-year deal, as he had been since taking over for the fired Manny Acta in July 2009. The team had a one-year option for 2012, but Riggleman felt he deserved more job security. In essence, he called the Nationals' bluff and lost. "I tell ya, I've been in this 10 years," Riggleman said. "Maybe I'll never get another opportunity, but I promise you I'll never do it on a one-year deal again…You don't bring people in on a one-year deal. I'm sure they will never do it here. When they get the guy they want, it won't be on a one-year deal."

Riggleman simply felt that he could not effectively manage the team, make tough player decisions, and maintain his credibility in the clubhouse without a contract extension, even though it appeared, by the Nationals' strong play, that he was doing just that. Riggleman's gambit was not without some precedent. In 1991 Chicago Cubs manager Don Zimmer, unsatisfied with his own contract status, quit with the Cubs sitting at 18–19, and despite his constant presence in baseball clubhouses in the ensuing 20 years, he never managed again.

Riding an eight-game winning streak, Seattle Mariners manager Mike Hargrove had his team overachieving at the midway point of the 2007 season when he decided to resign, citing burnout after a career in the sport. His replacement was John McLaren, who—ironically—would also take over for Riggleman on an immediate interim basis.

It was a stunning turn of events for a team that seemed to have finally figured out how to win and how to thrive. "He was going to be one of my coaches for the All-Star Game. I guess I have to pick another one," San Francisco Giants manager Bruce Bochy said. "I feel awful for Jimmy. I knew how hard he worked over there."

Storen spoke to reporters after the stunning announcement. "I see both sides of it. I understand he needs to take care of himself. In the end it's his decision, and I respect him for it," Storen said. "I don't think anything's going to change. We have enough veteran leadership on this team that—a distraction like this—it's going to test us, but I think we're going to get through it, and in the end, might even come out better."

That was an optimistic view, but realistically, could the Nationals bounce back from such a stunning turn of events? "You could see things were on the upswing, and there was a lot of excitement," Zuckerman said. "And then Riggleman does that, and all of a sudden you're thinking, *This could blow up a lot of what they've accomplished.*"

But the Nationals had an ace in the hole and quickly played that card to stabilize the volcanic situation.

OVER THE COURSE OF HIS SIX DECADES IN THE GAME, Davey Johnson has seen just about everything that baseball can throw at a man and he always seems to respond in exactly the right way. Johnson was signed as a free agent by the Baltimore Orioles in 1962 and immediately knocked the cover off the ball.

During his four years of playing in the minors—which included brief cups of coffee at the major league level—Johnson pounded the ball relentlessly, tearing up pitchers at every stop on his winding journey to the bigs. In 1966, the Orioles finally made room for the second baseman, and he responded with a solid campaign that earned him a third-place finish in the Rookie of the Year voting. It also earned Johnson a World Series ring, as the loaded Orioles knocked off the Los Angeles Dodgers for the world championship. (During Game 2 of the World Series, Johnson also earned the distinction of being the last man to get a hit off Hall of Fame pitcher Sandy Koufax, who retired after the Birds' sweep.)

That kicked off a stellar big league career for Johnson, who would win three straight Gold Gloves, appear in three more World Series (winning another championship in 1970), and hit 40-plus home runs (unheard of at the position in those days). He also would spend two seasons in Japan before closing out his playing career with the Phillies in 1978. Along the way Johnson never stopped hitting, always earning the respect of his more decorated teammates. "[He was] a good headsy hitter, a good headsy player, and he was a thinker," said former teammate Frank Robinson, who also managed the Nationals. "And if [Orioles manager] Earl [Weaver] would hold still long enough, he would tell Earl how to do things. Earl wasn't having too much of it, but Davey was a real thinker back then. Sometimes he would think too much, and that's where he got the name, 'Dum Dum,' because he used to get four hits and then go back out working on hitting the next day and think himself into an 0-for. But he was a good teammate and a good player. He knew the game and he played it well."

Johnson's keen mind made him a natural choice to be a skipper one day, and he got his shot in 1979 in a curious collection called the Inter-American League, which featured six Triple A teams in the United States, Dominican Republic, Puerto Rico, Panama, and Venezuela. Johnson took to the job easily, leading his ragtag group of fringe prospects on the Miami Amigos to the best record in the league before the entire operation folded midway through the season.

But a new career had been born, and Johnson was then hired to guide the New York Mets' Double A affiliate in Jackson, Mississippi, in 1981. Two years later Johnson was bumped up to the Mets' Triple A affiliate, the Tidewater (Virginia) Tides.

The New York Mets named Johnson manager in 1984, and the team was a mess at that point. The move, however, paid immediate dividends. Johnson is a no-nonsense sort, but he believes in letting his players play with minimal interference from him off the field, and the young, talented Mets immediately took to their new skipper. "He was able to seemingly see young talent that was on the verge and feel that they could play now, when the minor league development people—and maybe even the general manager—would think, *He needs more time*," said Nats analyst and former Met Ray Knight. "Davey would push young players, talk to them, and tell them: 'I think you can play up here. It's up to you.'"

The 1984 Mets went 90–72, setting the stage for their remarkable World Series run two years later. Of course, it helped that Johnson had players like Darryl Strawberry and Dwight Gooden, phenoms that lit the night sky for several years before flaming out. But Johnson got the most out of everyone on the Mets, and it all came together when New York beat the Boston Red Sox to win the 1986 World Series.

Johnson's famous line, "The bad guys won!" summed up the wild ways of that Mets team, who partied just as hard as they played. But Johnson's light touch and perfectly timed words of wisdom worked wonders for a larger-than-life roster replete with personalities. "His philosophy was basically: 'I'll let the guys play. I've got younger players. I'll let them play, let them learn what this is all about,'" Strawberry wrote in his autobiography *Straw*. "'They're gonna make mistakes, and I'll get on their behind when I need to, but they can only learn by doing.' He didn't hammer us."

Even though Johnson became the first National League manager to win 90 games in his first five seasons, the fact that Johnson was friendly with his charges never sat well with the Mets, especially as the team's stars started to struggle with their own personal demons. When the Mets got off to a slow start in 1990, Johnson was made the scapegoat and fired. "I would have liked to have met with the ballplayers to say good-bye but they [management] didn't want me to stay around," he told the *Orlando Sentinel* after his dismissal. "I knew this was coming since last year. It was just a matter of when. I have no regrets. I'm not comfortable about what happened today. But I am comfortable about coming home. I was beginning to like New York, even though I'm still just a cracker boy."

Johnson is still the most successful manager in Mets history, and the team inducted him, along with Strawberry, Gooden, and Frank Cashen (the man who fired him), into the team's Hall of Fame in 2010.

Johnson's next opportunity came in 1993, when he took over the Cincinnati Reds early in the campaign. He immediately revived the Reds and had them in the NL Central lead when the strike hit in 1994. Cincinnati would go on to win the division in 1995 behind stellar shortstop Barry Larkin. But one person stood in the way of Johnson's success—Reds owner Marge Schott, one of the game's most bizarre and difficult personalities. Schott had many peccadilloes, including treating her dog better than many of her Reds staff, and was none too fond of Johnson living with his then-girlfriend.

"Oh, Marge was something," Johnson told *ESPN The Magazine*. "I used to get these little notes from the St. Bernard before a game: 'Better pull this one out tonight—Woofs and licks, Schottzie.' One night, she invited Sue and I up to her dining room for some wine—screw top Gallo, by the way. All of a sudden, the dog jumps on the table and starts licking the bowl of mayonnaise. Marge just says, 'Oh, that's okay' and stirs the bowl up with a spoon, as if nothing had happened."

Schott handpicked Knight to take over for Johnson and needed to be talked out of firing Johnson after the 1994 season by GM Jim Bowden. But in 1995, the Reds' mercurial owner announced that Knight would be taking over for Johnson in 1996, and once again, Johnson's managerial days were over.

Johnson's dream job, however, was just around the corner, as the Orioles made their former Gold Glover a sweetheart deal to take over the team, and Johnson even was involved in hiring GM Pat Gillick, an old friend. And yet again, Johnson sprinkled some of his managerial magic on his new charges, as Baltimore earned a wild-card berth in 1996 and won the American League East in 1997—the first taste of playoff baseball in the Charm City since the Orioles won the 1983 World Series. "Any player wants to play for a manager like Davey Johnson," Orioles outfielder Eric Davis said.

But the rumors of bad blood between Johnson and acerbic Orioles owner Peter Angelos never subsided. Depending on who you believed, the two men never spoke to each other, and the final straw came down to a fine. The manager fined Orioles star second baseman Roberto Alomar for skipping a team banquet and then later an exhibition game in July against Baltimore's Triple A club. Johnson informed Alomar he could write a check to a charity, for which Johnson's wife was a paid fundraiser. When informed by the MLB Players Association that it might be a conflict of interest, Alomar donated the money to another charity. Johnson was willing to admit he had made a mistake in his handling of the situation, but Angelos apparently wanted the skipper to say he reacted recklessly, and Johnson was not willing to go that far.

So, on the day that Johnson won the AL Manager of the Year award, he was forced to resign "under pressure," meaning that a manager, who had taken two different teams to the playoffs over the last three seasons, was out of a job. "I thought we had a great year. We went wire-to-wire and beat the Yankees [in the standings], who had a heck of a ballclub. [We] didn't get to the dance. I know that didn't please Mr. Angelos, among other things, I guess," Johnson told *The Baltimore Sun*. "They announced I got Manager of the Year [in November 1997] and also announced I was no longer with the Orioles. It was kind of a terrible day. Double your bang for your money for the TV stations. I got fired, or whatever you want to call it."

After another brief period of unemployment, Johnson was back on the scene, hired by the Dodgers in 1999 to be just the fifth manager of the franchise since the team had moved to Los Angeles. Unlike his other reclamation jobs, Johnson wasn't able to turn the Dodgers around and he battled almost daily with GM Kevin Malone. The Dodgers had a collection of expensive pieces, but guys like Gary Sheffield, Kevin Brown, and Shawn Green never came together to produce the kind of loose, well-playing unit that Johnson was able to marshal at his other stops. "For me personally, that Dodger experience was awful—just a bad time to be in that organization. Kevin Malone was over his skis as general manager," said F.P. Santangelo, a member of the 2000 squad. "Davey is just a genuine person, honest, and open, and I don't think Los Angeles is very conducive to people like that. It's pretty pretentious for the most part. It's Hollywood. It just didn't seem like a good fit."

Johnson guided the Dodgers to an 86–76 mark and second-place finish in 2000, but it wasn't enough to save his job, and the news of his firing came out while he was on a fishing trip in Cabo San Lucas, Mexico. "It was quite clear as we talked. Everybody realized it was in the best interests that we should make a change," then-Dodgers chairman Bob Daly said.

Let Teddy Win!

Taking a cue from the minor leagues, where having fun outside the construct of the game seemed to be the primary strategy, MLB teams have incorporated walk-up music, scoreboard games, and mascot races into the fold. The most famous mascot race happens in Milwaukee, where the Sausage Race features bratwurst, Polish sausage, Italian sausage, chorizo, and hot dog characters sprinting around Miller Park. In 2003 Pittsburgh Pirates first baseman Randall Simon struck Guido, the Italian Sausage, in the head with a bat, causing the woman inside, Mandy Block, to fall over and need medical attention, though she was fine afterward. Simon was arrested, fined, and suspended for three games. He later apologized during a press conference and presented Block with an autographed bat. T-shirts sprung up, bearing the slogan: "Don't Whack Our Wieners!"

While teams around MLB raced all kinds of crazy characters, ranging from condiments to pierogies, the Nationals had a built-in hook for their mascot race. With the nation's history tied so closely into D.C., the Nationals' Presidents Race was a hit from the start, as George Washington, Thomas Jefferson, Abraham Lincoln, and Teddy Roosevelt—or rather, the giant head caricatures of those presidents—entertained fans every night. Often the outcome of the race hinged on some sort of interference from an outside source, which allowed one of the presidents to sneak ahead for the win.

All of them, that is, except for Teddy. The Nationals curiously decided that the nation's 26th commander-in-chief and an avid sportsman would become a perennial loser. More than 500 times, Roosevelt would lose in all manner of ways, turning the Rough Rider into a cause célèbre around D.C.

Before long, "Let Teddy Win!" became a rallying cry for Nats fans, and a blog was launched to chronicle the efforts of Teddy and support his chances of pulling off a victory. T-shirts saying, "Abe Cheats" began popping up in the stands, and the Presidents Race became an integral part of the Nationals Park experience. The fervor even touched the Nationals players. Jayson Werth became strangely invested in the race, feeling that Teddy's consistent losing did not match the culture change the team was trying to achieve. "Why doesn't Teddy get to win?" the outfielder said.

When he didn't receive a satisfactory answer, Werth took matters into his own hands late in the 2011 season. During the last homestand of the year, Werth and several relievers tried to run interference on the presidents one night, and the next night, he actually knocked all the runners out of the race, crossing the finish line himself. "Let's say, 'It's Teddy Roosevelt's last stand of the Rough Riders,'" Werth said. "If Teddy can't win, then no one wins in my vote. I must be the last remaining member of the Bull Moose Party, I guess."

Werth continued the cause in 2012, interfering with the race on one occasion before it began by breaking the finish line tape on his way in from the outfield. As the Nationals kept winning, the outcry for Teddy to win his first race grew louder, leading some players to openly lobby on Roosevelt's behalf.

By the time the Nationals clinched the National League East crown in October, many felt that the only thing left to do was let Teddy win. Teddy was on the receiving end of pep talks from Nats players, WWE wrestler John Cena, and even Arizona senator and former Republican presidential candidate John McCain, who spoke during a video displayed on the Nationals Park scoreboard before the Presidents Race. "First of all, Teddy, I am fully aware that you are the victim of a vast left-wing conspiracy by the commie pinko libs in this town," McCain told the crowd. "I got that. And it's tough. And I want to assure you: There's going to be a full investigation by the United States Senate, and you're going to be vindicated. But you can overcome that. You're the Rough Rider at San Juan Hill. You're the man in the arena. You can do it, Teddy. I know you can do it. You are the man who inspired generations like mine."

And during the final game of the season on October 3, Nationals fans got their wish, as Teddy captured his first-ever victory, thanks to some interference from a faux Phillie Phanatic mascot. Ryan Zimmerman, the next Nationals batter after Roosevelt's historic race, followed with a home run to spark Washington to a win that would wrap up baseball's best record, signaling to many that the maybe letting Teddy win isn't a bad idea after all. "I guess it marks the end of an era," Werth said, "and the beginning of a new chapter in Nats baseball."

"Davey said, 'I think it's time for me to move on. I think it's time for the organization to move on.'"

Johnson continued to dabble in baseball after being fired by the Dodgers, managing the Team USA squad in the 2005 World Cup and 2008 Summer Olympics, when one of his charges was a college kid named Stephen Strasburg. "I love baseball," Johnson said. "I mean, I love the game itself. I've had reputations like, 'He's better with older players,' or, 'He's better with younger players.' Well, I just like players. It's fun, with all the experience I've had with great hitters, to pass on some things I've learned from guys like Hank Aaron, Frank Robinson, Ted Williams, and relate them to the current players."

In some ways, Johnson used baseball as a salve after some very emotional, difficult aspects in his personal life. In 2004 Johnson had two surgeries to alleviate chronic abdominal issues, losing part of his stomach and 50 pounds before doctors at the Mayo Clinic figured out that Johnson's appendix had ruptured years ago, filling his body with poisonous toxins. It was a near miracle that he survived. In 2005 Johnson's daughter from his first marriage, Andrea Lyn, a former professional surfer, died at 32 from septic shock after years of battling schizophrenia. Johnson was forced to make the harrowing decision to take his daughter off life support.

Shortly thereafter, Johnson became involved with the Nationals, having been brought on by former GM Jim Bowden, who hired him to manage the Reds in 1993, as a part-time consultant. After the 2009 season, he was named senior advisor to Rizzo. So, Johnson had intimate knowledge of the team and its personnel, which made him a logical choice to take over—despite an 11-year break from managing in the majors—after Riggleman's abrupt departure. "It was not a tough decision for me to step in," he said. "It's really exciting to even have a chance to compete."

It was another coup for Rizzo. His overhaul of the organization and its player development system allowed the team to quickly react in the face of adversity. "Mike Rizzo has done a remarkable job," CBSSports.com baseball columnist Scott Miller said. "The Riggleman thing happened, and even though that was shocking, he had some people in place that could stabilize the thing immediately. When things could have gone south, because of how Rizzo operated, they didn't miss."

Johnson's player-friendly style, folksy rhythms, calming personality, and vast experience was just what the doctor ordered for the callow

Nationals. "He's been around the game for a long, long time. Everybody knows that and everybody's going to listen to him," Bryce Harper said. "That's huge for the whole team."

Johnson was no pushover, but he gave the players the right amount of freedom, both in and out of the clubhouse. And media members loved the new skipper, who was forthright when presented with questions and prone to giving florid responses to even the most banal queries.

Take this Johnson chestnut from a question asked about the upcoming All-Star break: "I welcome it. I get to go home and see my beautiful 12-year-old German shorthair, Savannah. I got a stray cat that my daughter got me 10 years ago that's bigger than a house, named Red. I get to have them in my lap all the time. It will be good for me, too. Not so much physically, I'm already shot physically. And I get to see my wife. I told her, it's not usually your chore over the last 10, 12 years, but can you fill in and go to the grocery store before I get home tonight? I'm looking for a nice relaxing time for a couple, two, or three days—maybe hustling some old cronies on the golf course before I start hustling some guys in the league again."

For those who know Johnson, that's right on line with the kind of person he is—a guy who can diffuse any kind of issue with a laugh or story. "One of the big things that Davey did was he just settled down the whole situation. What he did was—he came in at a troubled time with a team we could see was getting better and stabilized the whole thing," Carpenter said. "The stability was huge. Davey's the kind of guy who knows how to handle young guys and veterans. The Nationals were extremely fortunate to have a guy like that in the organization. He knew all these kids. He knew what they could do. I just think that was another piece of karma that fell into place. I'm not sure someone who came in kicking and screaming or someone who was passive would have helped. He knows how to take charge of a game. He was the right guy, at the right place, at the right time."

The Nationals, 40–38 when Johnson took over, went 40–43 the rest of the season to finish 80–81 and in third place in the NL East. It was the team's second-best record since moving to Washington. "Davey's got that great combination of dad, granddad, older brother, and wizened old baseball man. He combines all of it," Miller said. "He knows as much baseball as anybody, and when you combine the other things, he's got a little something for everybody. The veterans really like to play for him. He handles kids extraordinarily well, and everybody respects him, because the veterans remember what he did as a player, and the kids have no idea, but then they hear the stories. He's something special. He was the perfect man at the perfect time."

The Nationals knew he was a perfect choice, too. During the 2012 offseason, they announced that Johnson, the 2012 National League Manager of the Year, would continue as manager for the 2013 season, when the 70-year-old will be MLB's oldest active manager, before moving into a consulting role for the club in 2014.

But it was during Johnson's initial year managing the Nats in the 2011 season, when the team first showed so much promise. There was a real sense of hope that the Nationals had turned the corner. Zimmerman came back from his injury and was his usual steadying force on the field. Morse had a breakout campaign, in which he hit .303 with 31 home runs and 95 RBIs. Desmond and Espinosa proved to be an electric middle infield combination. Werth changed the clubhouse culture. Zimmermann looked like the pitcher he was before undergoing Tommy John surgery. Storen had emerged as a top-flight closer with Clippard as the rock solid set-up man. And perhaps the biggest lift of all, Strasburg returned during the final month of the 2011 season to prove that he was back and better than ever. "When I got here, this place was upside down," Werth said. "It wasn't until Davey took over, and really when September came around, that this team became the type of team that could really play. It could show up every day and had a lot of heart."

It's hard to pinpoint one series that showed that things were going to be different in the future for the Washington Nationals, but at the tail end of the 2011 campaign, the Nats traveled to Philadelphia for a four-game series against the rival Phillies, a team that had systematically owned Washington over the course of the franchise's time in D.C. The Phillies, five-time National League East champions, were headed to another postseason appearance. The Nationals came in at 72–79 and were simply playing out the string.

But Washington wouldn't be denied. Displaying a harbinger of things to come, it swept the four-game set from Philadelphia. The sweep signaled the Nationals would no longer be a pushover for its more storied NL East foes. With a roster of young, hungry contributors, the Nationals were now in the mix going forward. "For us, there's certainly significance," Rizzo said. "That's probably the best team in the National League. We're showing them that we belong with them and we're going to be a team to be reckoned with in the future."

With Rizzo running the show from upstairs, Johnson providing a critical influence in the dugout, and a host of young players flourishing, the 2011 season was the turning point for the Washington Nationals. "I knew it [in 2011]," Santangelo said. "I was there when they learned to win on the road. They went into Philly and swept the series, which is hard to do. I knew they would be good [in 2012]. I told everybody I knew. I told numerous people they will win the NL East."

THE RETURN

AS ONE MIGHT IMAGINE, WHEN STEPHEN STRASBURG FIRST heard the news that he would need Tommy John surgery to replace a torn ligament in his pitching arm, his first reaction was to feel sorry for himself. But just as quickly, Strasburg's competitiveness took over, and he decided to approach his rehab with same drive that he channeled for his starts. "It's a good measure of character when it happens to a young guy. It's a big test," Strasburg said. "It's make or break sometimes. If you're the type of guy that wants to persevere and prove to everybody that you can overcome anything, you'll be fine. You're going to find a way."

Strasburg underwent his surgery on September 3, 2010. Shortly thereafter, in San Diego, Strasburg would begin the grueling physical therapy sessions, which would take up much of the next year. "You're doing all this shoulder and elbow stuff every day for hours and hours," Strasburg said. "The biggest thing is that you can't get frustrated." From the start, the young pitcher jumped all over the tedious total body workouts that he would need to build not only his elbow, but also his shoulder in order to prevent further injuries once he returned to the mound. "He took that thing by the throat," Nats broadcaster Bob Carpenter said. "He got going on [rehab], and with all the hard work, his timetable was probably shorter than a lot of other guys."

Despite Strasburg's dedication and hard work, he was still months away from being able to throw, and without baseball as a carrot, the time working on his arm seemed to tick even more slowly. "It's hard. It's probably the longest time in my entire baseball career, where I haven't been able to throw a baseball," Strasburg told reporters during December of 2010. "I trust in what Dr. [Lewis] Yocum says and what my physical therapist says and what [Nationals trainer] Lee Kuntz says, because they've been through it before."

For a guy who cringed at the insane media scrutiny during the height of his rookie season, rehab did afford Strasburg a welcome sense of anonymity and quiet. In the relative isolation of San Diego, Strasburg went about his business away from the prying eyes of the media and the speculation of the fans, grinding through his daily workouts with a steely resolve.

After months of working out in California, the next step in Strasburg's recovery was coming back East and working at the Nationals extended spring training camp in Viera, Florida. There, the Nationals brought Strasburg along ever so slowly, because building back his arm strength and flexibility was just one challenge. "It's much more of a mental recovery than a physical one," Strasburg said. "I was in Florida just grinding. It kind of makes you forget why you play. You're not out there competing. You have to keep your head down and think it's all going to pay off. You might not see results the next day or the next month, but at the end of the 12 or 18 months, you're going to be where you want to be."

After throwing off flat ground at less than 100 percent, Strasburg would face the next phase in his recovery on May 23, when he threw a bullpen session in Viera, tossing 30 to 40 fastballs at half speed. After the session the normally Twitter-averse Strasburg tweeted, "First bullpen in the books. Felt great! Hopefully time will speed up now!"

But the Nationals continued to move Strasburg along at a glacial pace, a wise process for their prized investment. "It was tough for him at times," longtime Nationals writer Mark Zuckerman said. "But he's been good all along at listening to what the doctors and coaches told him."

Strasburg cleared another hurdle during July, when he faced real hitters in a live batting practice session, putting him on the outside track to be called up in time for the close of the 2011 season. "He's been champing at the bit, wanting to do more," Nationals manager Davey Johnson said. "He feels like he's on his way back, and that's the good news. And I think he feels good and hasn't had a lot of setbacks. I figure we'll see him sometime in September."

The quest began for real in August, as the Nationals sent Strasburg on a rehab tour of their minor league affiliates. After six long months of rehab in Viera, Strasburg was eager to show the baseball world his stuff, but he knew that the results would reveal he was still a work in progress. "It's an ongoing thing," he said. "It's not as soon as you're ready to start pitching again. You're still working. You can't just say that you're completely back."

Back in Hagerstown, Pennsylvania, Strasburg made his first rehab start on August 7 and immediately hit 98 mph on the radar gun. Using a steady diet of fastballs, Strasburg struck out four and walked none in his brief appearance. "I went out there, and it seemed almost like once they said, 'Play ball,'" Strasburg said, "I got that feeling back real quick." Five nights later, Strasburg was on the hill for the Potomac Nationals before a capacity crowd and blew away the Myrtle Beach Pelicans in three innings of high-caliber work. On a 50-pitch limit, Strasburg mowed down the Pelicans with such ease that he had to throw 17 pitches in the bullpen afterward.

The Nationals had 30 days with which to work on Strasburg's rehab assignment, and the minor league tour would continue unabated for the pitcher. He was back in Hagerstown for his third start, and this time Strasburg finally faced a bit of setback. The Lexington Legends pounded Strasburg to the tune of five runs in 1⅔ innings, as Strasburg did not reach his innings limit. Strangely, though, the Nationals ace was pleased with the way the game turned out, given that he had to battle through a long inning and fight with his command. "It's good to go out there and kind of struggle, because there's going to be some tough innings down the road," he said. "Not every outing is going to be a piece of cake...So I was pretty happy for that. It was something I was a little unsure of."

In front of principal owner Mark Lerner and general manager Mike Rizzo, Strasburg bounced back in his next Hagerstown performance before stepping up in competition for a Triple A Syracuse, New York start against the Rochester Red Wings. Facing more experienced hitters, Strasburg looked on top of his game, not allowing a hit through five innings and leaving in the sixth with seven strikeouts and no walks. "I wasn't surprised," Strasburg said after his penultimate rehab start. "I mean, I've done it before. It's all about going out there...and if it feels good, that's the bottom line."

In his final start, completing his long journey back to the majors, Strasburg tossed six innings of one-hit ball for the Harrisburg Senators, striking out four and walking none, essentially announcing to all that he had conquered Tommy John surgery. "The one thing you notice about Stras is how dedicated he is to getting back to where he was before," Nationals pitching coach Steve McCatty said. "From everything I've seen, from all the doctors and all the things we've gathered, the background, I'm sure that he's fine. I feel he's fine."

In 20⅓ innings scattered across Single A Hagerstown, Single A Potomac, Double A Harrisburg, and Triple A Syracuse, Strasburg struck out 29 batters, walked three, and gave up eight earned runs. Most importantly, he threw with ease and looked comfortable on the mound, as his confidence and rhythm grew with each start. "It felt like it was gonna take forever the first five, six months," Strasburg said after the Harrisburg game. "Then, once I started throwing more, once I started facing hitters, it started to speed up. I kind of got back in the normal swing of things, being healthy. By no means do I think I'm done. I still gotta go up there, keep working hard, doing everything that I've been doing to get to this point. And I'm gonna have to maintain that for the rest of my career."

Did the Nationals even need to bring Strasburg all the way back to the majors for 2011? After all, he had done enough during his rehab to show that he was healthy. But it almost seemed a waste not to give him more action despite the risk involved. "There was some questioning from outside the organization why they would bother bringing Strasburg back for games that were essentially meaningless, since the Nats were out of the race by then. But it was always the plan to have him pitch in September, because it was a necessary part of his rehab," Zuckerman said. "They probably would have kept him in the minors, except the minor league season was over. The only place to pitch against legitimate hitters was in the big leagues. They were careful to treat all of his starts like rehab outings and hold him to a strict pitch count. But it certainly worked out well, just as it did for Zimmermann the previous year. Above all else, the Nats wanted Strasburg to get a few starts under his belt and work out some of the kinks, so he wasn't making his return after 18 months on Opening Day at Wrigley Field."

THE WASHINGTON NATIONALS TEAM to which Stephen Strasburg returned after suffering his elbow injury was much different than the one he left 12½ months earlier. Out was manager Jim Riggleman; in was Davey Johnson. Several familiar faces had left and were replaced with a young group of players. And the Nationals were actually winning, making Strasburg's September starts not just a mere formality, but an important cog in the team's quest to achieve a winning record in 2011 and set the stage going into the 2012 campaign.

Washington had done its best to downplay Strasburg's return, attempting to avoid the kind of Strasmas atmosphere that overwhelmed the pitcher's major league debut. Strasburg would be facing the Los Angeles Dodgers on September 6 under a cloudy sky and the looming threat of rain at Nationals Park—with a crowd that was a far cry from the heyday of 2010.

But those in attendance saw a remarkable performance. Showing an amazing amount of poise and efficiency, Strasburg was lights out in his five scoreless innings of work, striking out four, walking none, and allowing just two hits. His fastball regularly reached the upper 90s, and his breaking pitches seemingly had even more bite than normal. It was if Strasburg had never left. "Obviously, he's projected to be our No. 1, and he showed there why," manager Davey Johnson said. "That was pretty obvious that he was a dominant pitcher. First time out in a year? If you didn't like what you saw tonight, you don't like great pitchers." Added shortstop Ian Desmond: "It looked like he didn't skip a beat. To be able to come back with the adrenaline, with the media, with everything else, and be able to hone in on the strike zone and do your job to that ability? Unbelievable."

When Strasburg first learned he needed Tommy John surgery, he wrote himself a note with a list of objectives to help motivate him during rehab. One of them was to pitch in the majors in 2011. "It's a big milestone that I accomplished here," he said. "Ever since I went under the knife, my goal was to pitch in the big leagues in 2011. I've been able to do that. Now it's all about getting stronger, staying healthy, being better than ever for 2012."

Strict pitch limits would keep Strasburg out of the win column in his next two starts, against the Houston Astros and the Florida (now called Miami) Marlins. Facing the Marlins on September 17, Strasburg looked sharp in a 61-pitch outing, but with a limit of 70 pitches, he had to leave

Horror at Home

For many players, heading home after the long and grinding journey of a baseball season is a welcome time—an opportunity to recharge their batteries while also getting a chance to be with friends and family. That includes the large international base who make up a significant share of the MLB player pool and sometimes play more baseball in leagues that aren't as competitive as the majors, but ones that still present a good training ground in which to hone and improve certain skills.

Wilson Ramos was one of those players who enjoyed returning to his native Venezuela. A talented young catcher, Ramos was signed as a free agent by the Minnesota Twins in 2004 and worked his way up the ranks of the Twins system, eventually being named the team's No. 3 prospect by *Baseball America* heading into the 2009 season.

The Twins, however, had Joe Mauer behind the plate, and he wasn't going anywhere. So, on July 29, 2010, Minnesota traded Ramos to the Nationals for closer Matt Capps. Ramos had a breakout 2011 campaign, finishing fourth in the National League Rookie of the Year voting after hitting .267 with 15 home runs and 52 RBIs. The future looked promising for Ramos as he traveled home for the offseason to play for the Tigres de Aragua, his hometown team in the Venezuelan Professional Baseball League.

Kidnapping is a lucrative business in Venezuela, with more than 600 reported cases in 2009, according to police. One did not have to be a professional baseball player to become a target, but there were several examples of MLB players and their families going through the harrowing experience.

In November 2009 former New York Mets pitcher Victor Zambrano's mother was kidnapped and rescued after three days in captivity. In June of that same year, veteran catcher Yorvit Torrealba's brother-in-law and his son were kidnapped before getting released a day later. And in 2005 the mother of former Montreal Expos reliever Ugueth Urbina was taken and held for more than five months until her rescue. "It can happen to anybody," said Nationals catcher and native Venezuelan Jesus Flores. "But at the same time, all of our families are over there. And after being in a long season over here, you want to spend time with them and be at home, eating your food, everything you miss when you are here."

Ramos knew about those cases, as did most Venezuelans. But he had never encountered any sort of troublesome behavior during his previous trips home, so he had no reason to think he was next. On November 9, 2011, the 24-year-old was taken by armed gunmen outside of his father's house and transported to a remote location in the mountains outside Caracas.

For the next 48 hours or so while Ramos was being held prisoner inside of a shack, his captors made light of the situation. "What they did was laugh, joke about my pain," Ramos told a Venezuelan TV station.

As Nationals fans set up a makeshift shrine outside the stadium, lighting candles and crafting homemade signs in support of Ramos, the wheels were in motion for a daring rescue. With the spotlight on Venezuela, controversial president Hugo Chavez ordered an airborne mission to rescue the catcher, and government agents used a hail of bullets to successfully complete the mission—just two days after Ramos was abducted. "The truth is I'm still very nervous," he said, "but thanks to God everything turned out well."

It wasn't, however, that simple. Rumors swirled about the actual rescue and the reason for Ramos' kidnapping. As the catcher remained relatively silent in the aftermath, the state-sanctioned facts surrounding the mission—which was the product of more than 200 investigating officers, a tactical helicopter strike, ground maneuvering through rugged terrain, and a gun battle that left Ramos hiding under the bed—grew cloudier.

In the end, nine people were arrested for Ramos' kidnapping, including a cousin who allegedly provided critical information that helped make the abduction easier. Ramos would wind up playing winter ball for the Tigres before returning back to the States, where he did his best to put the incident behind him. "I feel like I'm living again," he said. "I've got a new life."

early. "I'm going to go out until they tell me I'm done," Strasburg said. "That's the bottom line."

The righty took his first loss of the season on September 23 against the Atlanta Braves before bouncing back in his final start of the year on September 28, beating the Marlins with six innings of one-hit ball and registering 10 strikeouts. Five starts may have been a small sample size, but it was enough for the Nationals to know that their future was in good hands. "You have a guy that spends a summer by himself in Florida rehabbing the surgery—all those lonely days you spend by yourself working hard," Nationals broadcaster F.P. Santangelo said. "It was amazing. If you've had a serious injury, you have to have some goals, and getting back was his goal."

Strasburg finished the 2011 season 1–1, but wins and losses hardly mattered in this instance. Fighting through the pain, the doldrums, and the doubts, Strasburg showed more in the 12 months off the field than he did during his time on it. He proved to himself and to everyone else that he was a competitor of the highest degree, forging ahead to become a better pitcher despite the odds. "I'm a lot stronger," he said. "Mechanically, I'm still not quite where I was. But I still know there's room for improvement."

The Nationals knew that as well. And that was why everyone involved with the franchise was looking toward the 2012 season.

12

SPRINGING FORWARD

LONGTIME BASEBALL SCRIBES DESCRIBE THE MARCH TRIPS TO Florida or Arizona with a lyrical significance befitting poetry rather than baseball. Each spring training heralds a rebirth for teams, who feel as if this will be their year—the season when everything breaks their way, when the balls bounce correctly, when the pitching staff throws pure heat, and when the lineup turns into a Murderer's Row. It's a feeling of purity and optimism rarely matched over the course of the long and winding season. It's the first opportunity to put on the uniform, to run sprints in the cool breeze, to see youth and experience come together in a seamless mix. It's a special time shared equally by every team in the bigs.

As the Washington Nationals decamped to Viera, Florida at the start of 2012, promise and potential spilled over from the team as if it were a glass filled with Florida's finest orange juice. "We believed in ourselves from the beginning," shortstop Ian Desmond said. Not only did the Nats finish 2011 on a high note, garnering the franchise's best record since its initial year in the nation's capital, they also were returning nearly all the critical pieces from that year's team, plus adding several key players into the mix.

On December 23, Nationals general manager Mike Rizzo pulled off a stunning trade, sending promising pitchers Tommy Milone, Brad Peacock, and A.J. Cole, along with catcher Derek Norris, to the Oakland A's for lefty starter Gio Gonzalez, an All-Star pitcher who won 16 games for the A's in 2011. After missing out on acquiring mercurial Brewers pitcher Zack Grienke, Rizzo picked up the affable Gonzalez, who gave the team three front-line starters in Stephen Strasburg, Jordan Zimmermann, and now Gonzalez. "He brings a presence in our rotation. He's had success. He's been a workhorse. He's very, very young," Rizzo said. "[It] gives us a young core of starting pitchers at the major league level that really is in the realm of something we've never had here before."

Just a few weeks later, Gonzalez would sign a five-year extension worth $42 million through 2016, which covered his arbitration eligible years, giving the team a trio of pitchers under control for the foreseeable future. Rizzo continued his quest to revamp the Nats' rotation when, just before spring training commenced, he signed hard-throwing right-hander Edwin Jackson to a one-year deal worth $11 million on February 2. Jackson, who had just won a World Series with the St. Louis Cardinals, was the kind of pitcher who fit right into the Nationals' rotation and provided little risk. He was a workhorse who had thrown a no-hitter, been an All-Star, and pitched in the postseason. "We saw an opportunity to acquire a young, hard-throwing, power-pitching, eating-innings type of starting pitcher," Rizzo said. "We thought it was a good value and a good term. You can never have enough good quality starting pitching. We felt it was a good enough value to make him a National."

The successful pitching acquisitions helped take the sting off missing out on slugger Prince Fielder, who toyed with the idea of joining the Nationals but in reality never considered the team before signing a huge deal with the Detroit Tigers, the team for which Fielder's estranged father, Cecil, played. Washington, though, figured to receive an offensive boost from one of its returning players. The Nats believed that Adam LaRoche would be able to overcome the torn labrum in his right shoulder that caused him to undergo season-ending surgery in May and give them power and run production from first base. "This was the goal in spring training," LaRoche said. "This was the goal last year, when they started to put this team together."

So, when the team met in Viera to kick off spring training, there were several exciting new additions, a solid rotation, and a burgeoning offense in place. But in reality, all eyes were on two individuals—Stephen Strasburg and Bryce Harper.

After his promising return from Tommy John surgery in 2011, Strasburg returned to spring training as the anchor of what appeared to be a strong rotation, featuring himself, Zimmermann, Gonzalez, Jackson, and some combination of John Lannan, Ross Detwiler, and the injured Chien-Ming Wang. Strasburg, however, wasn't ready to anoint himself as the leader of the Nats' rotation. In fact he wasn't even ready to label himself as one of the key contributors. "I'm not sitting here, saying I need to do this or that," he said. "You have to lead by example. I'm 23 years old and I haven't even pitched a full year in the big leagues. I know my place and I know that I have to learn."

Despite Strasburg's modesty the team was counting on him to be a dominant force in the rotation, and spring training would be an opportunity to ensure that he was fully back from the surgery that sidelined him. The Nationals were aiming for a 160-inning limit on their ace, which at the time seemed like a fair number, but one that would come into play later in the season. "I went into this season not really having too high expectations. I still have a lot to learn, and it's still a process for me to figure out what it takes to get through a full season and be successful," Strasburg said. "It's great having guys like Gio and Jordan Zimmermann in the rotation to lean on and talk about stuff with."

One positive for Strasburg was that he was no longer the flavor of the month. The media's attention was largely focused elsewhere, and the influx of new players (along with Harper) made him less and less of a story. "The one thing I really benefited from in college was, they treated me just like I was another donkey," he said. "That's what they told me: 'You're just another donkey.' That's how I want to be here. I don't want the special treatment. I want to go out there, and when they tell me to pitch, I'm going to give it everything I have. When they say I'm done, I'm going to be done."

On the other side of the spectrum was Harper. After holding his own during his minor league season in 2011 and excelling during the Arizona Fall League, there was a groundswell that Harper should make the team out of spring training. But the brash Harper came to camp humbled and ready to work as hard as he could, knowing that the majors were a long shot. "The second time around, totally different," NatsInsider.com writer Mark Zuckerman said. "He comes in quiet, respectful, knew his place, said all the right things. And I think that proved that year in the minors really was necessary and what a mistake it would have been to try and move him too quickly."

Harper never wavered from his ultimate goal of getting to the majors as fast as possible but also understood that his patience would eventually be rewarded. "I was just trying to go in there and play the game I know how to play," he said. "I wanted to work hard, respect everyone around me, and not worry about anything else. Coming into this year, [I] wanted to get my at-bats in the minors and do things I could do to help us win." Harper even deleted his popular Twitter account during spring training, showing his desire to narrow the focus around him strictly on baseball and not on side issues such as his favorite basketball team. (For the record it's the Los Angeles Lakers.) Still, Rizzo's philosophy of making sure his prospects received some experience at all levels of the organization seemed to signal that Harper would start 2012 with Triple A Syracuse, New York, with a call-up to the Nats imminent later in the season.

As the Nationals entered camp, Ryan Zimmerman's contract situation was the other pressing issue. The third baseman was Mr. Nat, standing in as the face of the feckless franchise for years. Now that the team was on the cusp of respectability, it only seemed fair to reward Zimmerman for his efforts on and off the field for Washington. "The odds were in my favor that I was going to win here at some point. I love this town," he said. "They gave me a chance, took a chance on me at a young age, and put me right in the middle of it. For the team to take a chance on me like that, I felt obligated. I thought I should stay here and give them what they gave me, which is my career."

After a year of negotiations, Zimmerman and the team reached agreement on a six-year extension worth $100 million, locking up the University of Virginia graduate through the 2019 season. "I've always been comfortable here," he said. "Going to a new place would be weird for me. I know the person who lets me into the parking lot. I know the people who watch the family room, the cooks, everyone. It's not just about baseball. It's about everyone that I've met here, everyone that's helped me to get to where I am today."

As spring training started up, it didn't take long to see that this team was coming together unlike any other in franchise history. "What you saw was the talent around [Strasburg and Harper] and sensing this was going to be a good team," Zuckerman said.

Harper did all he could to make the team and impressed everyone, from hitting coach Rick Eckstein ("He's awesome.") to manager Davey Johnson, who was convinced he could play in the majors in 2012 ("I didn't see anything that told me he couldn't."), but from both a financial and baseball rationale, making the major league roster out of the spring training wasn't going to happen.

"Most people who were around understood he wasn't going to make the Opening Day roster," Zuckerman said. "There were a couple of reasons. One, Rizzo was adamant all along about making sure you take some time at each level. And two, there was just the financial component to it. Even if they only waited 21 days to call him up, they would guarantee another year of control. No matter how good they thought they might be this year, everything they've done to this point has been about building long-term, and so why would you sacrifice a year down the road in his prime just for three weeks of him at age 19?"

And so, after going 8–for–28 during nine spring training appearances, the Nationals optioned Harper to Triple A Syracuse, sending the phenom back to the minors for more seasoning. Of course, this did not sit well with the ultra-competitive Harper. "It sucks," he said. "But I've got to go down there [to Syracuse] and work hard and try to get up here as quick as I can...I just want to go down there and...get on a streak and be called up and hopefully be a game changer for the Nationals."

With Harper back plying his trade in minor league camp, the Nationals and Strasburg forged ahead, and the presumptive ace prepared for an Opening Day start against the Chicago Cubs. Strasburg went 1–4 in spring training with a 4.18 ERA, but the numbers were of no concern to anyone. What was important was that Strasburg's arm looked strong and ready to handle the rigors of a full season. "We've got a lot of talent and we've got a lot of room to grow and get better. [Rizzo] has done an awesome job, and so has [manager] Davey [Johnson], and [pitching coach Steve] McCatty," Strasburg said. "They've really helped us understand what we're capable of and what we can do, if we play the game the right way. It's fun to be a National right now. I just need to keep working on what I do out there to be successful. When I got drafted, everyone told me, 'Don't change anything,' and I try to stick to that."

As spring training wrapped up, the Nationals looked improved, but in a very competitive National League East, only the most optimistic of predictors would have placed them above the playoff-tested Philadelphia Phillies, talented Atlanta Braves, or Miami Marlins, who brought in a boatload of talent during the offseason. If anything, it seemed as if the

Nationals were perhaps a year away from seriously contending for the playoffs, and that 2012 would be a year in which the young talent would continue to marinate and gain valuable experience before making a real push in 2013.

The spring training prognostications show that the Nationals were beginning to earn some respect, but not enough to be considered a serious contender.

ESPN'S TIM KURKJIAN: (Fourth-place prediction) "The Nationals contend on the strength of an underrated rotation led by Strasburg, who dominates in his team-imposed limit of 160 innings. Bryce Harper shows he's ready for the bigs at age 19, and Michael Morse proves that last season was no fluke."

Sports Illustrated's Tom Verducci: (84-78 prediction) "The Nationals are one of these sleeper teams…This is a team that is maybe one or two players away from really being an upper-80s, 90-win team. The pitching staff is really solid."

The Sporting News' Stan McNeal: (Fourth place) "The Nationals have plenty of talent up and down the roster led by Stephen Strasburg and Ryan Zimmerman. What they don't have is much experience of playing in a pennant race. This year will be about maturing. Their time will come next year."

"I was among those this spring who thought they were a year away," CBSSports.com baseball columnist Scott Miller said. "I thought they had something special, but it was more like just that young tree that had been planted with a stick coming up through the ground instead of a big, beautiful tree. I thought they were a year away despite the young talent."

The Nationals had something else in mind. A television reporter asked Johnson during spring training if his team would make the playoffs. "No question in my mind," Johnson said. "You know, and they can fire me…I mean, we should make the playoffs. There's no doubt in my mind."

At the time Johnson's words seemed overly optimistic, but they would prove to be prophetic.

13

HOLLYWOOD BEGINNING

WASHINGTON'S MAGICAL 2012 CAMPAIGN BEGAN AT VENERABLE Wrigley Field in Chicago, where the ivy had not yet covered the walls and the surprising dominance of the Nationals had yet to be discovered.

Stephen Strasburg, recovered in full from Tommy John surgery and with his arm and mind back in battle mode, strode to the hill for the Nationals on April 5 as the Opening Day starter and immediately established himself as the team's ace, plowing through the Cubs hitters with ease. It took just 14 pitches for Strasburg to get through the first two innings of the Chicago lineup, and later in the game he would retire nine of the final 10 hitters he would face. But in a tight game, Strasburg wouldn't factor in the decision, as two unlikely heroes would step up for the Nationals, a theme that would carry the team early on.

Veteran infielder Chad Tracy, who only made the team due to an injury to Rick Ankiel, delivered a two-out double in the ninth inning of a tie game, and shortstop Ian Desmond followed with an RBI single to give the Nationals a 2–1 edge. With closer Drew Storen on the disabled list with a bone chip in his right elbow, the rejiggered Nationals bullpen stepped up as Tyler Clippard earned the win, and veteran Brad Lidge picked up the save to start the season in dramatic fashion. "If you didn't like that ballgame, you don't like baseball," manager Davey Johnson said. "Every pitch meant something."

Washington opened the season by taking two of three from the Cubs, two of three from the New York Mets, three of four from the Cincinnati Reds and Houston Astros, two straight from the Miami Marlins, and two of three from the San Diego Padres, putting them at an astonishing 14–5 with a two-game lead in the National League East through the first three weeks of the season.

During that stretch the Nationals played an array of taut affairs, thanks to the absence of slugger Michael Morse from the lineup with a back muscle injury and the struggles of Ryan Zimmerman, who was dealing with a shoulder inflammation of the AC joint.

It was Zimmerman's injury that led to the second most anticipated roster move in Nationals history on April 28. Bryce Harper was headed to the majors.

"We still have a very good and committed developmental plan for Bryce in place," general manager Mike Rizzo said. "I still believe very passionately in the plan and I'm going to be very committed to it. But this was expedited by the circumstances and by two of our middle of the lineup guys going down in Morse and Ryan Zimmerman. We felt we needed to bring in an impactful, left-handed bat that can play the corner outfield."

There had been a lot of speculation regarding whether the Nationals would even consider calling up Harper this early in the season, when it meant that doing so likely would qualify him for a Super Two contract, meaning he would get an extra year of arbitration eligibility. Although Harper remains under contract to the Nationals through 2018 (thanks to the 21 games he played at Triple A Syracuse, New York) if he is one of the top 22 percent of players between two and three years of experience, he will enter the arbitration process one year earlier and be in line for a hefty bump in salary. Washington has not shied away from making players Super Two eligible, with the most recent example being Storen, who earned Super Two status after the 2012 season.

Harper hadn't lit up the minors during his time with the Syracuse Chiefs, batting just .243 with one homer in 21 games, but calling him up would help fill the void that Morse and Zimmerman left in the Nationals lineup. "If you develop properly, a by-product of developing properly is winning," Johnson said. "Harper has had great springs in spring training. He is a formidable talent and he has been swinging the bat good down there. We had a need here for a left-handed bat. We're trying to get more of a left-handed presence in our lineup, and he is the guy who fit that role."

Harper's dream of making it to the majors was coming true—quickly. "I had to get on a plane within an hour," he said. "I had to go to my house, pack up really quick, and bam!"

In a scenario that even a screenwriter might reject for being too cliché, Harper would be making his MLB debut at storied Dodger Stadium, and the other Nationals building block, Strasburg, would be the starting pitcher.

Harper's call-up was the talk of the majors, and a media horde descended upon Los Angeles to see the 19-year-old's first game. As is his nature, Harper handled the pregame media scrum, which threatened to spill out of the Dodger Stadium dugout and onto the field, with ease, showing a maturity well beyond his years and a playfulness that would suit him well in the high-stress situation.

As Harper was announced for his first Major League Baseball at-bat and with his parents sitting in the stands, a surprising cascade of boos rained down from the Dodger Stadium faithful, likely a result of Harper's perceived attitude rather than anything he'd ever done on the field. Harper's first two at-bats—a comebacker to the mound and a routine fly to left—were uneventful. But in his third at-bat, Harper flashed some of his tantalizing power, ripping a ball off the wall in dead center for his first major league hit.

Harper also showed off his arm, throwing a perfect strike to home that should have nailed the Dodgers' Jerry Hairston Jr., but catcher Wilson Ramos dropped the ball to allow L.A. to tie the score at 1–1. Harper, though, did his best to become the hero again, delivering a sacrifice fly in the ninth inning to give the Nationals a 2–1 advantage. The fact that Washington would go on to lose 4–3 in the 10th inning did little to dampen the luster of seeing Harper and Strasburg play and pay dividends for a first-place team.

Just 19 years, 195 days old during his debut, Harper resembled a composed veteran against the Dodgers. "I really didn't have butterflies at all. I think that's one of the first times I've never gotten butterflies," Harper said. "I was sitting in the dugout before the game and I was thinking to myself, *Wow, I'm in the big leagues.* But I was talking to Adam LaRoche before the game and I told him: 'Hey, I'm really calm right now.' I was just trying to look for my pitch and got into some good counts. I think, in the next week or so, it'll really sink in."

In just one series in Los Angeles, Harper began to turn the tide of public opinion in his favor and give the Nationals a much-needed jolt. "I admit I was basically a grumpy old man, old school, show-me-something-before-I-join-the-chorus-of-hype kind of guy, but I covered Harper's debut at Dodger Stadium, and within the first couple of games, he sold me," said CBSSports.com baseball columnist Scott Miller. "It was very easy to see—not just the talent—but the grit and enthusiasm and joy with which he played the game."

The whirlwind start to Harper's major league career took another turn when he made his debut in D.C. before adoring Nats fans on May 1. Whether it was from his rocket arm to hold runners at bay, his willingness to sacrifice his body, his aggressiveness to take the extra base, or his savvy to work the count in his favor, fans could not ignore the ebullience Harper brought to the field, which showed none of the hesitation one might (rightly) expect from a teenager. "I'm just excited to be here and play in the big leagues. It's a winning ballclub, and that made it better and easier for me," he said. "I'm busting my butt every day."

THE NATIONAL PASTIME IS AN OLD, TRADITIONAL, and sometimes funny game replete with unwritten codes and tacit rules to match. May 6, 2012 was one example of that. When the Nationals hosted an ESPN Sunday Night game against the Phillies, Philadelphia starter Cole Hamels drilled a first-inning fastball into Harper's back, a pitch that clearly was destined to end up between the teenager's numbers.

Instead of reacting to the plunking in an emotional way, Harper would get revenge on Hamels through his hustle and guile. He took an extra base on Jayson Werth's single and stole home, becoming the first teenager in nearly 50 years to pull off that rare theft.

After the game, a Phillies victory, Hamels admitted he'd hit Harper on purpose. "That's something I grew up watching. That's kind of what happened. So, I'm just trying to continue the old baseball because I think some people are kind of getting away from it," Hamels said. "I remember when I was a rookie. The strike zone was really, really small, and you didn't say anything, because that's the way baseball is. But I think unfortunately the league's protecting certain players and making it not that old-school, prestigious way of baseball."

"It's just, 'Welcome to the big leagues.'"

Harper responded by keeping his cool and saying all the right things. "Hamels threw a great game tonight," he said. But, if Harper was blasé about the whole scenario, his GM wasn't. When reached by *The Washington Post* the next day, Rizzo attacked Hamels and defended his player. "[Hamels] thinks he's sending a message to us of being a tough guy. He's sending the polar opposite message," Rizzo said. "He says he's being honest; well, I'm being honest. It was a gutless chicken [bleep] [bleeping] act. That was a fake, tough act. No one has ever accused Cole Hamels of being old school. This goes beyond rivalry and all that stuff. This points to—you take the youngest guy in baseball. He's never done a thing, and then Hamels patted himself on the back. Harper's old school. Hitting him on the back—that ain't old school. That's [bleeping] chicken [bleep]."

But wasn't Harper supposed to be a hothead who would blow up at the slightest provocation? The Hamels incident certainly proved otherwise, and nearly everyone who has encountered Harper over the course of the year said that is a more accurate depiction. "The media is incredibly irresponsible in judging and labeling people they've never met," Nationals broadcaster F.P. Santangelo said. "In today's world you have so many talking heads forming opinions about people they've never researched or met. You can say whatever you want without prep work to justify it. My favorite trait isn't [Harper's] arm, speed, power, or hitting ability. He's fearless in whatever he does on the baseball field. Baseball is the one sport, where for some reason, you really stick out when you're scared. But from Day One, he's been fearless."

(In the end, Hamels would tell reporters that he voted for Harper in the All-Star Game, signifying that perhaps the Washington rookie had earned his respect.) The rookie certainly earned respect from the rest of the baseball world. "In watching how that whole thing played out, Harper handled things beautifully and he answered [Hamels] in the perfect way," Miller said. "He took his base and then went to work on the bases. After the game, he came out looking better than anybody by saying 'Cole's a great pitcher.' Here was this 19-year-old kid, and he, in that moment, was more mature and handled things so much better than anyone that evening. It was a telling thing about him."

Harper's philosophy was to go all out on the field while trying to earn the worth of his peers. He played hard on the field and listened carefully to his elders in the clubhouse. "There are people who want to see you succeed, and people who want to see you fail. You just try to take it in every single day and play the game the right way," he said. "You gotta control what you can control—playing the game hard, running the bases the right way, and respecting everybody around you. Once you have respect from your peers, that's the highest thing you can get. I'm going to play it hard, and if at the end of the day I played terrible, then I played terrible. Nobody can get as mad at myself as I can."

That anger came out in early May during the middle of the worst game of his young career. After grounding out against the Cincinnati Reds, Harper went into the tunnel and smashed his bat against the wall. But the bat fought back, breaking off and sending a shard into Harper's face—right below his eye. "I just got caught up in the moment," Harper said. "I want to do so well. It just got me." A few inches different, and the phenom could have done serious damage, perhaps jeopardizing his vision and career. Still, the wound bled furiously, and Harper stood in for his last at-bat with blood pouring down his face.

On May 14, Harper tallied another first, crushing a pitch from San Diego Padres starter Tim Stauffer to straightaway center at Nationals Park, where it landed on the grassy berm for his first home run. Harper sprinted around the bases as if he were running the 100 meters in the Olympics but had to be coaxed out of the dugout for a curtain call. "I've got no words for it," Harper said. "Hopefully it's one of many."

Each day seemed to create a new milestone for the teenager, as his comfort level seemed to grow with each pitch he saw and each at-bat he received. "His swing, at times, is as technically sound a swing, as I've ever seen," said Santangelo, who also worked as a minor league hitting coach. "From a technical aspect, his knowledge of the strike zone at age 19 is ridiculous. For a 19-year-old to have that grasp is unreal."

By the time Harper delivered his first game-winning hit—a two-out single to give the Nationals a 7–6 win against the New York Mets on June 5—his teammates were running out of words to describe what they were seeing. "[Harper]'s a man-child," Morse said. "This guy's unbelievable. He's really learning this game. Every day, I think he's taking something in…When he plays like he plays, it's fun to watch and it's good to have him on our side."

Based solely on some murky YouTube videos and the notion that a confident kid playing in the bigs must be a jerk, Harper came into most towns as the villain, but by the time the Nats left each city, he had just about won them over. "I do think some people were too hard on him," Mid-Atlantic Sports Network (MASN) play-by-play man Bob Carpenter said. "He's not one of those guys who came up, saying outrageous things and making stupid tweets. Most of the stuff he got criticized for was for hustling and projecting himself on the field. That's him being him. We would go to ballparks, and fans that had never seen him before would boo him. But then he did something, and you didn't hear boos the second and third times he came up, because it was like, 'Oooh, here's something different.'"

"He's come a long way. I was in spring training with him last year, and to see the changes he's made—both physically and the mental side of it—he's grown up a ton. He's now got the respect of all his teammates, and we all back him 100 percent," LaRoche said. "A lot of people on the outside, if they're watching a guy like Bryce and only see him once a month, it might be like, 'Man, that's kind of tired. He's going 1,000 miles an hour on a ball hit back to the pitcher?' But when you see it every day, that's the only way he knows how to play the game. If we're down three or four runs, and Bryce turns a routine single into a double, it can fire some guys up. It's motivating. He's been a spark plug since the day he got up here, and I don't think that'll ever change."

Harper and the Nationals took off during a stretch that encompassed interleague play, sweeping the Boston Red Sox at Fenway Park before moving on to Toronto, where a series against the Blue Jays would once again put the teenage superstar into the limelight.

Harper connected for a titanic homer on June 12 to lift the Nationals to a 4–2 victory against the Blue Jays. In the postgame press conference, a reporter for Toronto radio station The Score asked Harper what kind of Canadian beer Harper would celebrate with after his big day. Even though the drinking age in Canada is 19, Harper is a Mormon and does not drink alcohol. After a Nationals public relations staffer tried to brush off the inquiry, Harper responded with a retort that would live in infamy. "I'm not answering that," he said. "That's a clown question, bro."

The simple put-down spread like wildfire, going viral on Twitter thanks to Harper's turn of phrase. Before long, U.S. Senate Majority

Leader Harry Reid—from Nevada like Harper—used "clown question" during a debate on…immigration reform, specifically. the Development, Relief, and Education for Alien Minors (DREAM Act), a bill designed to provide residency to foreign residents who arrived in the United States as minors.

In the hopes of getting Republicans on the record about this immigration issue, a reporter from CQ Roll Call asked Reid about his plans to bring the DREAM Act to the Senate floor. "I don't want to answer that question," Reid said after pausing. "That's a clown question, bro." The response drew peals of laughter from the assembled reporters. Later, Reid, a Nats season-ticketholder who met Harper before a May game and received an autographed jersey from him, tweeted, "I quoted a great Nevadan in a press conference today," with a link to the video of his response.

And soon after, the shirts started appearing, some more official than others, considering Harper trademarked the phrase shortly after saying it. A Denver brewery, the Denver Beer Co., announced they would create a Canadian lager in Harper's honor called "Clown Question, Bro." that would be available in time for the Nationals' trip to play the Rockies. "Maybe he'll come here, although he can't drink it here," said brewery co-owner Charlie Berger. "It is definitely his favorite beer, and maybe we'll serve it with a big red clown nose."

Harper, again thinking beyond his years, turned the a light situation into something better by suggesting to Berger that a portion of the proceeds for the beer go toward the memorial fund of Celina Hollis, a veteran Denver policewoman who had been killed in the line of duty. "It's exciting to hear from Bryce," Berger said. "We were making this beer just for fun. We never thought it would pick up to this extent. First of all we're definitely flattered. More important, the fact that he was making a lot of good come from it, it's valiant. It says something about Bryce."

As well as his benevolence, Harper would reveal a sense of humor regarding the whole situation. After his rookie season had finished, he dressed as a clown for Halloween and posted a picture of the costume on Twitter. Accompanying the photo, he wrote, "Come on kids! Get some candy! #Halloween."

Harper's rookie season wasn't all fun and games. Like any rookie, he experienced adversity, and his came during a critical series. Harper and the

Nationals' stunning June had opened eyes around baseball, but a showdown with the first place New York Yankees at Nationals Park would provide a measuring stick against the famed Bronx Bombers. The stadium was filled with Yankees fans who snapped up tickets long before Washington got off to a hot start. Adding intrigue was the fact that Harper had proclaimed himself to be a lifelong Yankees fan before his allegiance switched to the Nationals.

The middle game of what would turn out to be a dispiriting three-game sweep by the Bronx Bombers would be one of the worst of Harper's golden start to his MLB career. Veteran left-hander Andy Pettitte flummoxed the rookie, making him look foolish against an array of off-speed pitches. Pettitte took Harper's aggressiveness at the plate and turned it against him. When the 14-inning marathon was all said and done, Harper had an 0–for–7 day in the books with five strikeouts. He would see 22 pitches on the day and only make contact with two of them. "This is probably his first really tough game where he was overanxious," Nationals manager Davey Johnson said. "That's showing some of his inexperience. He was really amped up against Pettitte. I've never seen him swing at balls out of the zone, and he was chasing balls. You get in that mode where you try to make something happen, and that's part of youth."

But that youth was what made Harper so exciting, and a player that everyone wanted to see. The talk around baseball regarded Harper's numbers and whether or not the 19-year-old deserved a trip to Kansas City, Missouri, for the All-Star Game. Midway through June, Harper was hitting over .300 and had displayed power, speed, and savvy for a first-place team—traits that certainly warranted All-Star consideration. "This is a guy you just can't take your eyes off," Miller said, "when he's in the field."

By the time the lineups were announced, Harper had been in a mini-funk that eliminated him from being a lock to make the team, but he was nominated as one of the five players on the final vote ballot. Showing his appreciation and respect for baseball history, Harper immediately announced that retiring Braves third baseman Chipper Jones should win the contest, and that was who he was voting for. "I texted him last night and said, 'That's a very classy thing for a 19-year-old kid to say,'" Jones said. "He's going to be in his fair share of All-Star Games throughout the years. He's an unbelievable talent. I just let him know I appreciated what he said. It was classy."

If Nationals manager Davey Johnson had his druthers, his teenage prodigy would get a few days rest instead of heading to Kansas City, and it seemed like he would get his wish when Harper came in third in the final vote to St. Louis Cardinals third baseman David Freese and Atlanta Braves outfielder Michael Bourn. But when Marlins outfielder Giancarlo Stanton was forced to go on the disabled list with a knee injury, Harper was given the nod by National League manager Tony La Russa, making him the youngest position player ever selected to an All-Star roster. He was the third youngest All-Star in history after a pair of 19-year-old pitchers: Dwight Gooden of the New York Mets in 1984 and Hall of Famer Bob Feller of the Cleveland Indians in 1938. "It would be nice to put the National League phenom against the American League phenom," La Russa said. "And it's been good to see [Mike] Trout and Harper come into the game."

Harper joined Strasburg, Gio Gonzalez, and Ian Desmond as Washington's representatives, though Desmond would miss the game with an oblique injury. "It's going to be fun to go down there and take it all in," Harper said after he was selected. "I'm excited, but I'm not going to be jumping up and down and yelling and screaming."

In 63 games, Harper had energized a fan base, proven the naysayers wrong, played an integral role on a first-place team, uttered the quote of the year, garnered the respect of teammates and foes alike, and earned a spot on the All-Star team. And the ride was just beginning.

14

DYNAMIC DUO

IT'S HARD TO IMAGINE TWO PLAYERS MORE WILDLY DIFFERENT from a personality standpoint than Stephen Strasburg and Bryce Harper. They may have a shared experience as can't-miss, No. 1 picks, but otherwise the two men were as different as night and day. "Early on they were both asked a lot about each other and they didn't really have a lot to say," Nationals reporter Mark Zuckerman said. "They don't hang out. They don't speak. It's not like they don't like each other. It's just that they have different personalities, different backgrounds."

Strasburg is the prototypical introspective pitcher who'd rather spend his time away from the ballpark at home with his wife. During games he will sit quietly at his locker in the clubhouse. His demeanor is not much different from his early days. "He didn't talk that much," said Strasburg's high school coach, Scott Hopgood.

Like most pitchers, Strasburg can dissect his starts with clinical precision, but getting answers from the ace can require some heavy lifting. Having to bear the burden of being the No. 1 pick sometimes weighed on Strasburg during his rookie season, resulting in the perception that the young pitcher was a dour sort when in fact he was merely laconic. "He tends to be a quiet, soft-spoken guy," Nats play-by-play man Bob Carpenter said.

The majority of pitchers don't want to be disturbed on gameday, and when Strasburg slips on his game face prior to a start, everyone is keenly aware that his area is no-man's land. "He's focused, intense, and into baseball. [He] eats, drinks, and sleeps it," Nats broadcaster F.P. Santangelo said. "He wants to be the best, wants to be the greatest. There's nothing wrong with that."

With his impassive facial features and controlled mannerisms, one might assume that Strasburg is going through the motions, but he assures you that is not the case. "I try to show no emotion out there. I'm having fun, even if it doesn't look like it," he said. "I don't think I'll ever be able to go out there and just laugh and tell the opposing batter, 'Hey, nice hit,' like Gio [Gonzalez] does."

Teammates past and present are impressed by Strasburg's demeanor and his dogged approach to the game. "Obviously, on the mound, he is what he is," former teammate Adam Dunn said. "Off the field, how he handles stuff is really impressive. He's just a quiet kid. I don't think he's shy. I don't think he's arrogant. He's just…he's not like me. I'm loud. I can't help it. I try to be quiet, and it doesn't work. But he's just awesome. I really enjoyed my time with him. He's a great dude. He's got it going on upstairs, for sure."

Harper said, however, that Strasburg has a side that very few outsiders get to see. "You guys don't know Strasburg very well. He's very funny," Harper said. "In our clubhouse he's funny. He's hilarious. Some of the things he'll pop off with are pretty good. On gamedays he's totally different. But on other days, he's just another guy."

Strasburg, perhaps, is the clown behind the scenes, while Harper is the one openly responding to clown questions. But the two phenoms, who forever will be linked, are more similar than one would initially think. "Harp's a good guy, and in a lot of ways, we're a lot alike," Strasburg said. "He's the type of player that wants to go out there and not just beat people, but kick the crap out of them. So do I, absolutely."

Harper's reputation was that of self-absorbed showman. Although the teenager proved that he was far more mature than given credit for, Harper is no wallflower. Going back to his high school and college days when he slathered eye black all over his face and went through his elaborate hitting routine, Harper welcomed the attention of being a phenom. From magazine covers to TV interviews, Harper was a household name well-versed in handling the media and fans. Now, as a pro, he says all the right things, but as the "clown question, bro" situation proved, he's got a way with words.

Harper's teammates enjoy razzing their teenage counterpart, but it's all in good fun. "You've got a bunch of players around him who love him as a teammate and protect him and don't let anybody mess with him, except for them," general manager Mike Rizzo said. "It's like your brother. You can mess with your brother as much as you want. Don't let somebody from the outside mess with him."

Despite his burgeoning fame, Harper never overstepped his boundaries within what can be a rigid clubhouse culture. "When we're on the plane and going on a trip, he's sitting up front behind the media where the rookies sit, not with the veterans," Carpenter said. "He's pretty good at accepting his role. A baseball team is like an office or a family. Some of [the players] are going to want to test the kid, bust his chops, and some are willing to let him do his own thing. There's a mix of it, and I don't see anything that tells me that he hasn't fit into this team really well."

Curious reporters and announcers from around the country wanted the scoop on Harper, and Santangelo was more than happy to give it to them. "I'm the president of the [Harper] fan club," he said. "I'm always pumping him up. I would pump him up, even if I was the broadcaster for the Phillies. He's one of the better kids you'll ever meet. His parents did a great job. I pump him up not because I have to, but because I want to."

Before deleting his Twitter account in February, Harper fielded questions from fans, opined on various topics, and maintained a running dialogue through the social media channel. (Harper re-started his Twitter feed in September.) On the other hand, Strasburg's Twitter account is filled with simple retweets and bland offerings.

Harper has a dog named Swag and a white Mercedes with a customized bat rack in the trunk. He hangs out with rappers and country artists. Strasburg catches fish and makes Toyota truck commercials but doesn't watch sports shows. "I don't watch MLB Network or anything," he said. "That's baseball overload."

So the two teammates aren't mirror images. The fact that they play different positions also limits their interactions with each other. In the Nationals' oval-shaped and cavernous clubhouse, their lockers are on opposite sides of the wide portion of the oval and separated by a TV and couches. They, however, do share a love for the game and a joint history as No. 1 picks. "He's a big part of our team," Strasburg said of Harper. "Once we called him up, he really sparked our offense a little bit. He's exciting. There's nothing wrong with that."

At the All-Star Game in Kansas City, Strasburg and Harper, along with Gonzalez, had the chance to showcase their personalities for a national audience. "I have that love and passion for the game and I hope I can keep it going," Harper said. "Hopefully, I will play for the Nationals for a long time. Any time I can be that guy who is a face of baseball, that would be great. I think that would be a lot of fun...If they want that, I'm all in."

The All-Star festivities also provided a showcase for the Nationals, who, given their previous history, had not made much of a dent outside the D.C. area. Having two of the game's most recognizable names on the roster was a boon to the Nationals brand. "Nobody expected us to be where we're at," Strasburg said. "It's great to bring national recognition to the Nationals. A lot of people didn't even know that there was a team in D.C. until the last couple of years."

At All-Star media day, both players got their turn to field a wide array of questions—both insipid and inspired—from the huge gathering of reporters, and the Nats pair held their own in the onslaught.

Strasburg on...

Fellow players: "I think I'd like to see everybody. It would be cool to see [Clayton] Kershaw pitch...just to see their routines and how they go about throwing their pitches in the bullpen. Obviously, it will be great to see [Justin] Verlander again. [R.A.] Dickey's knuckleball. [Craig] Kimbrel."

The Nats' All-Star future: "It might not be the same faces every year, but if we're playing well, we're going to have some guys in there. With the direction of how our team is going, it could be any guy."

His popularity in Latin America: "It's awesome. I never expected it. Hopefully Gio [Gonzalez] has given me some good exposure down there. To think that I have more fans worldwide than in the U.S. feels great. People just appreciate good baseball."

Texas Rangers pitcher Yu Darvish: "Who? Who is that? I know who it is. He pitched against us in Beijing. He pitched against us in 2008. I've seen him on TV, but we play every day, too. He's a good power pitcher."

Harper on…

All-Star festivities: "I just want to hang out and joke with the guys and get all the free stuff I can."

Fellow phenom and former Scottsdale Scorpions teammate Mike Trout: "He is an unbelievable talent. He's been very impressive. He's a game changer."

His musical choices: "It depends. Gametime, I listen to Motown stuff. Hanging out, I like to listen to country, rock. It all depends."

People referencing "clown question": "I don't know why. It's not that big of a deal. It's just something I said. It's something I grew up saying."

However Harper is characterized, he certainly has an appreciation and respect for baseball history. During All-Star week, he met Kansas City Royals legend George Brett, a Hall of Fame player known for his gritty style, whom Harper idolized. "ESPN Classic was always on, when I was growing up—whole games, even back to Mickey Mantle and Yogi Berra. My dad would say, 'Here are the guys.' Cal Ripken, Pete Rose, and Brett…were the ones I wanted to be like," Harper said. "They gave it everything, made their town and their fans proud. I was more a student [of them] than a fan." So when Harper got to chat with Brett during batting practice, it was a special moment for the precocious teenager because it was an opportunity for Harper to do one of his favorite things—talk purely about baseball with one of the greatest hitters of a generation, a player who earned batting titles in three different decades.

After all the festivities, there was an actual game to play, and in Kansas City, the Nationals contingent made an impact on both the good and bad sides of the ledger. Gonzalez entered in the third inning, replacing starter Matt Cain and blew through the American League hitters in just 11 pitches. He showcased his fastball and looping curve in striking out Mike Napoli (then with the Rangers) and then had no problem with a pair of New York Yankees, getting Curtis Granderson on a routine fly ball to left and a ground-out to second by Derek Jeter.

Strasburg pitched the fourth and navigated his way through Robinson Cano, Jose Bautista, Josh Hamilton, and Prince Fielder—a group of sluggers who would later lead Strasburg to tweet, "Insane!" He allowed a leadoff single to Cano, who served Strasburg's fastball right up the middle. Hamilton followed with another shot headed for center, but with the shift on, Rafael Furcal was able to snag the ball to start a double play. Strasburg walked Bautista, bringing up Fielder, who ripped a shot to left that Ryan Braun had to chase down to end the inning and preserve the National League's huge lead. "I love the challenge," Strasburg said. "It was great. Gio finished up a good inning, and I knew I was going to be going in there, facing the middle of the lineup guys. It was great to get the opportunity to face them. Me being in the National League, I don't know when I'll be able to face them again."

Harper spent the early part of the game sitting next to Chipper Jones, who called out Harper in his stirring pregame speech to the National League veterans. "You belong here," Jones said. "It doesn't matter if you're 19 [points to Harper] or 40 like me. We are all equals here." The 19-year-old entered in the fifth (wearing gold spikes) and drew a walk off Los Angeles Angels ace Jered Weaver and then showed off his signature hustle by tagging to second on a fly ball hit by Giants catcher Buster Posey.

New York Mets third baseman David Wright then hit a chopper up the middle that looked like a hit. Weaver, however, snagged the ball and caught Harper in a rundown off second base—an example of where Harper's eagerness cost him.

The ball continued to find the Nationals rookie in the next inning. Napoli lofted a fly ball to left into the lights of Kaufman Stadium. Harper took a few steps in, looked up, and threw his arms out as the ball plunked in behind him. The scoreboard operator quickly cued up the scene from the movie *The Sandlot*, where a kid gets bonked by a fly ball, drawing laughs from the crowd. "It didn't hit me in the head," Harper said. "So, I think I'm doing okay."

In his final at-bat of the night, Harper was struck out looking by Ryan Cook of the Oakland A's, ending his first All-Star appearance at 0–for–1, one walk, one baserunning blunder, and one wild ride in the outfield.

Harper had warned everyone that he was terrible in All-Star Games. (He went 0–for–4 with two strikeouts at the 2011 MLB Futures Game, drawing boos from the crowd at Phoenix's Chase Field.) The 2012 Midsummer Classic, however, was still an experience he'd never forget. "Being able to sit there with Chipper in the dugout for the first five innings was an unbelievable experience," Harper said. "It was so much fun just sitting there talking with him and shooting the bull. It was pretty amazing. He's just an unbelievable player, and it was pretty special getting to meet him."

In the end the trio of Nats contributed to the National League's 8–0 victory, ensuring the NL home-field advantage for the World Series. In previous All-Star games, this would have meant nothing to the sole Nat representing the floundering franchise. Now, there was a possibility that this win would give Washington a chance to host Game 7 of the World Series. But there was still more work to be done. "It will be a tough second half for us," Strasburg said.

15

THE FUTURE IS NOW

THE NATIONALS CAME OUT OF THE ALL-STAR BREAK WITH A 49–34 record and a four-game lead in the National League East. This was heady territory for a franchise that had never sniffed this kind of rarified air. Washington was supposed to be a year away from seriously contending, but the Nationals threw that plan out the window, stunning the baseball world with just how good they were. "The more and more we win, the more of a target there is on our backs," Stephen Strasburg said. "We've just got to keep focused and can't try to do too much out there. Just go out there, have fun, play hard, and limit the mental lapses out there. I know what we have in our lineup and in our rotation and bullpen. Everybody thinks it's a surprise because of the teams we have in our division."

And keeping the Atlanta Braves, Miami Marlins, New York Mets, and Philadelphia Phillies at bay was a balanced effort, seemingly featuring a new hero each day. Unheralded veterans, callow rookies, and emergency fill-ins played as big a role as the everyday starters and the marquee names of Bryce Harper and Strasburg. "There are 23 other guys who have played their ass off," Nats broadcaster F.P. Santangelo said.

The Nationals were hit hard by the injury bug, with Michael Morse, Ryan Zimmerman, and Jayson Werth all missing extended time in the first half of the season, but that hardly seemed to slow them down. "The character of this team really came out early in the first half with a lot of the injuries," Washington manager Davey Johnson said. "The first two months with the offense, because the middle of the lineup was struggling, we were in a lot of dogfights. And the pitching staff, by and large, kept it close. We won a lot of series by maybe one or two runs. That builds character. The hotter the fire, the harder the metal."

After laboring through the 2011 campaign, the Nationals were counting on Werth to regain his form and anchor the lineup. He had gotten off to a solid start when—in the same May 6 game that Phillies pitcher Cole Hamels plunked Harper—Werth, a former Phillie, broke his wrist while attempting a sliding catch on a tailing fly ball. "When Werth broke his wrist, I thought, *Okay, it was a nice little start, but it's about time for them to be dropping back to earth*," CBSSports.com columnist Scott Miller said. "But they never did. Once they got beyond a month past [the injury] and didn't miss a beat, that's when they made a serious statement."

Ian Desmond was one of several young Nationals who blossomed in 2012. The shortstop had overcome an erratic rookie season, in which he made 34 errors, to become a solid defensive player, and now his bat was coming around, giving the team a power-hitting middle infielder who was just fully realizing his gifts. "He's just playing up to his potential," Johnson said. "I told him three years ago, 'You're going to be awful good.' Then, I compared him to [Cincinnati Reds Hall of Famer Barry Larkin], and in my conversations with him, I said, 'When you find out who you are, like I understand who you are, you're going to be a heck of a player.' And he's still learning. He's real comfortable in his own skin right now. Our job as baseball coaches is to help [players] know who they are. I think he's comfortable there."

Adam LaRoche rebounded from a miserable 2011 to provide a huge boost to the Nationals' offense while some of the team's big guns were sidelined, jumping out to a fast start before cooling down prior to the All-Star break. LaRoche's steady presence and run-producing abilities, however, were crucial to keeping the team afloat. "At some point during the year, I don't know when it was," LaRoche said. "I started to think we were really good."

Rookies Tyler Moore and Steve Lombardozzi stepped in and delivered quality at-bats and versatile efforts at several positions in the field, while Chad Tracy and Roger Bernadina proved to be invaluable additions off the bench. Tracy, in particular, didn't even create a blip on most fans' radar screens when he was signed and made the team, but he is the type of player successful teams always have on their rosters.

He got his start with the Arizona Diamondbacks (and was drafted by Nationals general manager Mike Rizzo) as a power-hitting third baseman.

In 2005 Tracy hit .308 with 27 homers and 72 RBIs for the D-Backs and seemed well on his way to a solid career. But over the next four years, he struggled with the bat and the glove largely due to the microfracture knee surgery he underwent in 2007, and fell out of favor in Arizona. He signed with the Chicago Cubs in 2010 but was released during midseason. Stints with the New York Yankees and Florida Marlins during that season were also short-lived. By 2011 Tracy had run out of options. He signed with the Hiroshima Carp of the Japanese League in an attempt to jump-start his career. "I didn't hesitate [with this decision]. I thought Hiroshima's offer was my best chance," Tracy told Nikkan Sports. "If I stayed in the U.S., I probably would have had to start in the minors and work my way back up to the majors. Coming to Japan means I'll get a chance to play. Right now is probably the best time for me to be here."

But Tracy's stint overseas would be brief. After just 40 games with the Carp, he had to return to the U.S. because of a lingering hip and groin injury. He hit just .235 with one homer for them in 149 at-bats. The Nationals signed Tracy to a minor league contract before spring training started, and he seemed like a long shot to make the club. But the veteran kept grinding and was one of the final players to make the roster. He immediately made his presence felt by coming up with a clutch hit in the first game of the season and continued to provide a valuable bat off the bench and an emergency infielder as the team dealt with its various injuries.

More important, however, was Tracy's clubhouse role. He was not a player who was embittered by his reduced playing time. He embraced it, becoming a sounding board for the Nationals' young players and a leader for the guys who weren't everyday starters. Tracy helped create the "Goon Squad," a nickname for the Nationals' bench players and a moniker that ended up on T-shirts. "During spring training we all kind of figured out the mix that was going to be on the bench," Tracy told Mid-Atlantic Sports Network. "I don't know where I heard it, or if I came up with it, but it sounded right. I was looking around and I said, 'We're the Goon Squad over here.' It fit and it's kind of caught fire a little bit."

Mark DeRosa was another veteran leader, even suggesting to Bernadina that he use a lighter bat instead of the heavy lumber he was swinging. That bit of wisdom helped result in the best year of the outfielder's career, as Bernadina hit .291 with a .372 on-base percentage and a .777 on-base plus slugging percentage. Tracy would finish 2012 with a line of .269/.343/.784—the best numbers he'd put up since 2007—and the Nationals pinch-hitters would end up hitting a league-best .288 with seven game-winning pinch-hits.

Although the bench provided a huge lift, you cannot discount the energy that Harper brought to the team after his call-up. The team fed off his boundless enthusiasm, and Johnson could see his teenage star maturing before his eyes. "Every game Harper plays," the skipper said, "the more comfortable he gets."

But if the Nationals had an MVP in the first half of 2012, the honor would have had to be shared by the entire pitching staff, which was so dominant that it allowed the team to overlook some of its offensive woes. Starters Strasburg, Jordan Zimmermann, and Gio Gonzalez were simply masterful, with Strasburg and Gonzalez earning All-Star nods for their efforts, and only a lack of run support keeping Zimmermann from the 10-win plateau at that point of the season. Edwin Jackson proved to be an effective workhorse, and Ross Detwiler, who earned the No. 5 slot over veteran John Lannan, showed that the Nats' decision was correct with a string of steady efforts. Strasburg showed his skills at the plate at well, developing into a difficult out. He would finish the season with a .277 average, a stunning number for a pitcher of his caliber. And against the rival Baltimore Orioles on May 20, Strasburg smacked a home run into the visiting bullpen, shocking the crowd and delighting his teammates as he loped around the bases. "Look at the pride he takes in his hitting," Nats broadcaster F.P. Santangelo said. "Throw the pitching aside. The pride in his hitting tells you everything. Pedro Martinez would go up, strike out, and come back smiling. This guy would grind out every at-bat."

In the bullpen Tyler Clippard stepped into the closer role for the injured Drew Storen after Brad Lidge and Henry Rodriguez failed to hold on to the position and make it their own, helping to nail down close wins throughout the first half of the season. Set-up man Sean Burnett, long reliever Tom Gorzelanny, and specialists Michael Gonzalez and Craig Stammen all carried their weight in the bullpen, which Johnson turned to time and again in the first half of the season.

But for all the successes the Nationals achieved in the first half, there were plenty of doubters waiting for the other shoe to drop, as the pressure of playoff baseball and the dog days of August loomed for a franchise whose biggest second-half goals to date were to get above .500. "The real push comes in the second half," Johnson said. "There's nothing that beats a pennant race, and we're right in the thick of it. We've got a big game every day for the next three months. I don't believe in getting too high and I don't believe in getting too low. I try to keep them all at the same level. This team is very well-founded. There's a lot of good character."

The second half started with a dose of controversy from an always controversial manager. The Nationals' trip to Miami on July 15 made national news when Marlins manager Ozzie Guillen grew upset about the amount of pine tar that Harper was using on his bat. After Guillen complained to the umpires that his bat had too much of the sticky substance, Harper pointed his new bat at Guillen before his next plate appearance, which resulted in a stream of invective from the dugout by the fiery manager, who labeled the teenager "unprofessional." "Ozzie complained that the pine tar was too high up on Harper's bat," Johnson said. "So, we changed it. Then he was still chirping about it. It got on the umpire's nerves. It got on my nerves. He was trying to intimidate my player, I guess. He was hung up on our player. He does what he has to do. One of my pitchers complained one time, and it was the first time I saw him do it all year. Some strange things go on out there."

Asked about his verbal fusillade from the dugout, the outspoken Guillen said, "I was just telling him how cute he was. Something happened the inning before, and I don't like it. I was talking with the umpire about it. But for the first time, it's going to stay between us. I could say a lot of [stuff] about this kid. I've been praising this kid. The last three times [the media] asked me about him, I said he is a great player. What he did today was unprofessional. I'm not going to tell you guys what he did. I'm not going to be talking about this guy on ESPN or *Baseball Tonight* or everywhere. I'm going to talk to his manager in a little while."

Guillen later attempted to talk to Johnson about Harper and the pine tar, but the Nationals manager rebuffed him. "I told [Guillen] it was not a big deal. Enough said about it," Johnson said. "That's Oz...I don't like any time an opposing manager talks to my players at the plate, has any conversation with my hitter, whether my hitter instigated it, or he instigated it. It's nothing I like to see happen in a ballgame."

That got Guillen's juices flowing, and the manager responded with one of his classic tirades. "I don't know if I did it the right way, the wrong way. I just did it my way," Guillen said. "If that happened two years ago, whew, it would be fun. They'd be talking about this the next two months. I think this kid don't respect myself doing that and I don't think that was appropriate to do because I didn't try to make it a scene or a big deal. He reacted the wrong way. I tried to call [Johnson]. He told me to [expletive] away from here.

"If [Harper] had showed me the bat a couple of years ago, I might shove his [expletive] on the grass. Right now, I'm too old to be fighting... This kid's [6-5, 200-pounds of solid muscles]. I'm 48. I can't intimidate my own wife. I might intimidate Davey but not that kid. He's going to kick my butt. When you try to intimidate people, you don't say anything. I drill his [expletive]...If this kid continues to do that [expletive], he might not make it because he's going to fool around with the wrong guy, and that one guy will kick his [expletive]. And I love this kid. He plays the game right. He's only 19 years old, too. He's a baby. That's why I respect him, because he didn't know what he was doing. If he did that to Tony La Russa or somebody else, he's going to get in trouble. To me, I just laugh...Thank God I was a manager. If I was a player, that's a different scenario. As a player I could fight with him, as a manager I'd look like an [expletive] fighting with a kid."

Harper once again showed maturity beyond his years and turned the other cheek. "[Guillen]'s a great manager to play for," Harper said. "He's going to battle for you, no matter what. That's a manager you want to play for."

That was the second strange pine tar incident to involve the Nationals during the 2012 season. During a game against the Tampa Bay Rays in June, Johnson brought to the umpires' attention that reliever Joel Peralta had a foreign substance on his glove, which turned out to be pine tar. Peralta was ejected from the game. There were rumblings that the Nationals had been tipped off about the use of pine tar by Peralta, who played for Washington in 2010, from someone on the Nats, and that sparked a war of words between Johnson and Rays manager Joe Maddon.

"To single out Joel Peralta and make him look like a bad guy or a villain, that's what upsets me," Maddon said. "Before you start throwing rocks, understand where you live...It's insider trading, man. It's bush, it's bogus, it's way too easy."

After hearing Maddon's comments, Johnson had an amusing response when asked the next day if he would meet with the Rays manager. "No, I don't know him that well," Johnson said. "But I thought he was a weird wuss anyway, so, no." Johnson also took a shot at the media-savvy Maddon's use of Twitter. "I don't want to get into a shouting match with Joe. I looked him up on the Internet and found out he is a tweeter, so he can get to more people than me," he said. "But it was interesting reading. But you can tell him I have a doctorate of letters, too. Mine's from Loyola in Humanities, and I'm proud of that, too."

Maddon responded, suggesting that free agents should look elsewhere when searching for a new job. "If I'm a major league player who might want to come play for the Nationals in the near future, I might think twice about it," he said. "This is one of their former children who performed well, and all of a sudden he's going to come back to this town, and they pull that on him based on some inside information." The dust eventually settled, but don't expect the two men to exchange Christmas cards—or retweet each other's comments—in the future.

The next major hurdle for the Nationals came later that month during a four-game series at Atlanta. Entering the series, Washington held a three-and-a-half game lead over the Braves, turning the set into a critical swing for both teams. The series could not have gotten off to a worse start for the Nationals, who blew a 9–0 lead in the first game to lose 11–10 in 11 innings. "Arguably the worst game I've ever managed in my life," Johnson said. "I've never lost a nine-run lead when it was my part of the game to handle the pitching, and it'll be hard for me to sleep. I had a worse night than the guys did."

That crushing loss put the Nationals on edge as they approached a doubleheader with Atlanta. A desultory effort in the opener resulted in a 4–0 loss and moved the Braves to within one-and-a-half games of the Nationals, the closest anyone had been to Washington since June 9.

Instead of folding, however, the Nationals responded in the nightcap of the doubleheader, besting the Braves 5–2 to begin a run in which they won six straight and eight of nine to open up some breathing room against their closest pursuers. The Nats ran off another eight-game streak in August, proving once and for all that 2012 was a new day for this franchise. All the embarrassing, awkward, hopeless moments for the Nationals were no more. This was a team built to last.

And Washington was doing it without much help from Harper, who had gone into the first prolonged funk of his major league career. Whether the league had figured him out or it was fatigue from playing in more games than he ever had, Harper was out of sync after the All-Star break. Harper hit .222 with 22 strikeouts in July and .243 with 25 strikeouts during August. More often than not, pitchers attacked him with sweeping breaking balls out of the zone, and Harper chased them. Being such a competitor, this rare bout of failure frustrated him to no end. "I'm trying to find some mellowness at the plate and in the box," he told *The Washington Post*. "Just trying to work at it every day and try to take something good from every at-bat and take something good from every game."

But there were some flare-ups. After striking out against Miami's Ricky Nolasco on August 5, Harper slammed his bat on home plate, shattering it in front of stunned Marlins catcher John Buck. Before his next plate appearance, Harper apologized to the catcher. "I told him, 'Don't worry about it,'" Buck said. "'I did the same thing when I was your age. It was a metal bat, and I was in high school.'"

Later in the month, Johnson removed Harper from an eventual 4–1 loss to the Phillies as part of a double switch, and the outfielder threw a tantrum, smashing helmets in the hallway between the dugout and clubhouse. And then, in an odd turn of events, after hitting two home runs against Miami—the first sign that Harper was coming out of his slump—he was ejected by first base umpire C.B. Bucknor for slamming his helmet to the ground following a close play at the bag. It was the first ejection of Harper's young career. "He's just a 100 percenter," Johnson said. "And he expects great things out of himself. He breaks bats, throws his helmet. He's just got to stop it. [We] can't afford to be losing him in a ballgame with that. He'll learn. He's young."

Harper, for his part, was contrite about the situation and admitted needing to get his temper in check. "I just need to stop getting [angry] and just live with it, and there's nothing you can change," he said. "I just need to grow up in that mentality a little bit. Try not to bash stuff in, and things like that I've always done my whole life, and those need to change."

Harper was learning, the Nats were winning, and the team could smell the finish line. "Great ballclubs are built from within, and that's what we're seeing happen here," Nationals play-by-play man Bob Carpenter said. "Zimmerman, Strasburg, Harper, [Danny] Espinosa, Desmond—they're all organizational guys. Zimmermann, Storen—that's the foundation. And then you sprinkle in guys here and there and you've got a solid organization. Did we think we're going to be in first place with best record in baseball? I don't think anyone envisioned that."

But there was one issue looming over the feel-good vibes the Nationals had created for themselves, one that threatened to wreck the chemistry in the clubhouse and make the team's path to the postseason more difficult. Strasburg's innings limit was rapidly approaching, and with it, the eyes of the baseball world once again focus squarely on D.C.

16

THE DEBATE

"I expected a lot more people to ask me about the innings limit. I contemplated making a recording and pressing play. Everybody expects me to have all the info, and I really don't."
—Stephen Strasburg at the 2012 All-Star Game

FROM THE TIME STEPHEN STRASBURG MADE HIS TRIUMPHANT return back from Tommy John surgery in 2011, it was clear the Nationals were taking a rightfully cautious approach with the young ace. He was on strict pitch limits during the five starts he made at the end of 2011, and it was clear from spring training that Strasburg would not pitch a full season in 2012, though no specific innings limit was set.

It was the same strategy the team employed in 2011 with Jordan Zimmermann, another young starter who had the same surgery. The team capped Zimmermann's innings at 160, and the pitcher was shut down in September after having thrown 161⅓ innings. Of course, the Nationals weren't in the middle of a playoff chase, so the decision was seen as good for the interest of keeping a talented young pitcher healthy. "I'm definitely happy," Zimmermann said. "We were out of it, so it was probably the best thing to get shut down. But if we were in the hunt, I'm sure I would have said a little something."

From the beginning of the 2012 season, general manager Mike Rizzo intimated that the Nationals would shut down Strasburg per the team's long-standing policy of not letting young pitchers exceed their previous season's work totals by more than 30 percent. The pending shutdown simmered under the surface for most of the season, with scribes keeping track of the innings and pitch totals, but most insiders believed the

Nationals would budge on their stance as the team continued to contend for a postseason berth.

Strasburg looked as dominant as he had ever been, despite his claims that he wasn't fully recovered from the surgery and rehab. "I'm not necessarily where I was or where I was headed before I got hurt. So, I know it's going to be a process," he said. "It's been going well so far this year, and I have to roll with the good or bad."

At the All-Star break, Strasburg was cruising along with a 9–4 record, 2.82 ERA, and 128 strikeouts in 99 innings. He looked sharp and ready to carry the load for the Nationals as they made a second-half playoff push. "Every outing is a learning experience for him," Nats broadcaster F.P. Santangelo said. "He's gone from a guy who was a max effort thrower to a pitcher. He'll throw 2–0 curves, 3–1 change-ups. He's really thinking along with the catcher. It's a pleasure and honor to see him develop from a young guy, just throwing, to a Major League Baseball pitcher."

Strasburg, ever the competitor, stubbornly ignored the talk about the limits, focusing his efforts on pitching every five days. "I'm in the dark. I just go out there and pitch," he said. "Every time I go out there, I'm going to pitch hard until they take the ball out of my hand."

But when would that be? The rumblings about the shutdown began in the second half, as Strasburg suffered through several tough starts and started pressing. "He's a perfectionist," Santangelo said. "He gets in a little bit of trouble with that sometimes. When he realizes he doesn't have to be perfect all the time, he'll be even better."

After an August 10 victory against the Arizona Diamondbacks improved his record to 13–5, Strasburg stood at 133⅓ innings, which appeared to be on the cusp of the team's plateau. But with the Nationals leading the National League and set up to play deep into the postseason, would Rizzo still stick to his guns?

The answer was a resounding yes. "It's not on Davey Johnson or [owner Ted] Lerner. It's on me," Rizzo told *The Washington Post*. "I know it may stain my reputation or my career. There's no way it can ever be proved, if I was right. The easy thing for me is just to do nothing. But I'm hardheaded. The decision was made five months ago because it was the best decision for Stephen and the Nationals. And nothing is going to change it."

The debate raged across baseball and even within the Nationals dugout, where several of Strasburg's teammates questioned the validity of the shutdown. "You take the best pitchers off any team that has a chance to make it to the postseason, and it's devastating," utility player Mark DeRosa said in mid-August. "At the same time, we knew it going in. You kind of hoped the better we played, the more the decision changed to the opposite."

Former Atlanta Braves pitching coach Leo Mazzone threw his hat into the ring during an appearance on ESPN's *Mike & Mike* radio show, castigating the Nationals for their stance. "I think it's absolutely pathetic, to be honest with you," Mazzone said. "If I'm Strasburg, here's what I'm saying. I'm saying, 'You take the ball away from me, and I'll save my arm for some other team to pitch for.' I think it's absolutely ridiculous. I think that it's been 79 years since Washington's gone to a postseason. And you know what, you think of the Adam LaRoches of the world. These guys have a shot. They have a *legitimate* shot—with the best rotation in baseball with Strasburg in it—to go to the World Series. And to shut this down like this is absolutely ridiculous."

Across the country, voices of all sorts chimed in on the Strasburg debate, including those close to Strasburg. "The Nationals, you can't fault anything they've done, but I hope they don't shut him down," Strasburg's high school coach Scott Hopgood said. "I cringe at that. Just make him the closer."

Chicago White Sox hurler Jake Peavy, who has endured his own slew of injuries, though not Tommy John surgery, weighed in. "It would just blow my mind, thinking that the Nationals are going to the playoffs and Stephen Strasburg not being part of it." Peavy said. "He's arguably the best pitcher in the game. Don't you want to seize the moment?"

Chipper Jones, who played for the NL East rival Atlanta Braves, agreed. "Everybody knows he wants to pitch. He's a competitor," Jones said. "He's not in it in a 162-game regular season for nothing. He wants that pot of gold at the end of the rainbow just like everybody else. I see both sides. I get it, but as baseball players, we want to hunt it down and kill it right now. And they have a chance to slay the dragon, and I'm sure 24 other guys over there feel much the same way."

Former Nationals catcher Ivan Rodriguez, who was Strasburg's battery mate during the 2010 season, was dubious. "I think that all depends [on] where the team [is] going to be at the end of the year," he said. "My opinion [is] they're not going to shut him down, if the team is in the race at the end of the year. I think this all depends on him. I know him. He's a very competitive kid and player, and I think if you see the team in the pennant race at the end of the year, he's going to ask the team to continue to let him pitch. I think he works hard. I've seen him, the way he works. He's a workaholic, so I think he's going to be fine. Let's see what's going to happen with the team in the second half. I think the team [is] going to have a great second half, too with the pitching staff that they have, with the relief pitchers that they have, and now the offensive team that they have. So, I think good things are going to happen, but we have to wait until the end of the season, like in September, late September, so I think if the team is in the race, they're not going to let him shut it down. They're going to let him keep pitching."

The Strasburg shutdown made for a juicy story—a talented player, a first-place team, a controversial decision, intra-team turmoil, a stubborn leader, and historical precedent. So it's no surprise that this was provocative baseball issue with a cacophony of voices who wanted to chime in. Here's a sampling:

Jon Heyman, CBS Sports: "The dissent isn't a shock, of course, since the call is so unusual for an old-time baseball person like Rizzo, who was around seemingly forever before getting his first GM shot in Washington a couple years back. But in some ways, to stand up and shout about the Strasburg call might fit somewhere between rude and selfish. The other obvious reason to accept the plan is this: Rizzo is doing it for the right reasons. He is doing it to save the kid's career. Some have said that Rizzo is only sparing Strasburg for his expected future as a rich Yankee or a richer Dodger. But Rizzo can't worry about that now. Strasburg, 24, has a long and terrific future, and at least three more of those years will be with the Nats."

Jayson Stark, ESPN.com: "We're never going to know whether this was the right move or the wrong move. Never. Doesn't matter if the guy goes on to make his next 486 consecutive starts. Doesn't matter if he breaks down in 2013 or 2018 or 2028. We'll never know. Never. Can't possibly know because we don't live in a what-if world. It would be awesome, if real life were scripted by, say the creators of *Lost* or the screenwriters from *Sliding Doors*. Then, we would know what might have been, if the Nationals were to decide, 'Aw, what the heck. Let's let this guy keep pitching.' But in the absence of parallel universes, we're stuck with this universe. So, as Shutdown Day draws ever closer, the Nationals understand they have no choice but to live with whatever happens. And we give them credit. They're prepared to do that. Or that's what they tell us now, at least."

Jake Simpson, *The Atlantic*: "Strasburg has the makings of an all-time great pitcher—Nolan Ryan with a breaking ball and better command. More to the point, he's a human being, not a cog in a championship-winning baseball machine. Strasburg's absence could very well prevent Washington from finally bringing a World Series title back to the nation's capital. But an organization cannot in good conscience start a player when its own doctors—bound by the Hippocratic oath to 'never do harm to anyone'—recommend that the player be sat to preserve his long-term health."

Tom Verducci, *Sports Illustrated*: "It all sounds so easy, until you understand the study Rizzo has put into this, and that we really are talking about a human with a $200 million career in front of him, not the simple mathematics of innings. The fact is that Strasburg, like most starting pitchers, is a routine-oriented, highly trained athlete. He also employs mechanics and high-velocity stuff that put him in a high-risk group to begin with. (His late load, in which the baseball is not well above his shoulder at front foot strike, is reminiscent of how [Mark] Prior threw.) He's not the kind of pitcher or asset to subject to an off-the-cuff plan, now that the Nationals are winning. Recent development failures of Joba Chamberlain, Phil Hughes, Daniel Bard, and Neftali Feliz speak to the difficulty of changing roles for young pitchers."

David Lariviere, *Forbes*: "If they chose to, they could even limit him to one start in each round of the playoffs, if they got to the World Series, which a Washington team has not won since 1924, its only victory in the Fall Classic 88 years ago. That would mean the most innings he could reach is about 190 innings, hardly a blow-up of the original plan. The bottom line is the team cannot, in fairness to the rest of the players on the team and the fans who have supported them all season, shut Strasburg down, despite what the preseason plan was. Plans are made to be changed, and the opportunity to win a World Series doesn't present itself every year, especially if you play in Washington."

Tim Cowlishaw, *The Dallas Morning News*: "The noise level surrounding the Nats' decision to pull the plug on Strasburg, when he reached 160 innings, has been rising for weeks. As far as the team is concerned, there is evidence to suggest the cautious approach makes at least some sense. But the failure to limit his innings earlier in the summer, when it became clear this team was playoff-bound, was a terrible one for Nats fans and for Strasburg himself. As far as baseball and sports in general are concerned, it's an alarming decision and a terrible precedent we can only hope others won't follow."

Richard Justice, MLB.com: "Most of the noise about the decision comes down to the Nationals having a chance to win the World Series. With Strasburg at the front of their rotation, they might be the best team in baseball. Most franchises aren't in this position very often, so why not go for it? And if the kid gets hurt, well, he gets hurt. Rizzo just can't bring himself to go down this road. His good reputation in baseball begins with his gift of being able to identify and develop talent. The first-place Nats, with all that young talent, are a tribute to his work. He can't bring himself to risk injuring Strasburg for the sake of winning a championship. Washington drafted Strasburg with the idea of building a franchise around him way beyond 2012, and that's still the plan. Rizzo's decision will be as tough and as controversial as just about any decision any general manager has ever made. But he's a baseball guy, a player development guy. He knows the right thing to do for both the player and the organization. He'd have trouble living with himself if he did anything else."

Ken Rosenthal, Fox Sports: "Instead of backing himself into a corner last spring, all Rizzo needed to say was this: 'We're going to monitor Stephen closely. Our eyes and our doctors will tell us when he needs to be shut down, if at all.' With that, there would have been no story, nothing to distract from the Nationals' brilliant season—a season that, by the way, is testament to Rizzo's masterful work in putting the Nats together, work that should make him a leading candidate for Executive of the Year. The Nats still might have shut down Strasburg, if he became fatigued, lost his command, lost velocity, whatever. But they would have made their determination for a specific reason, rather than some vague notion of what is best for the pitcher. The truth is no one knows for certain what is best, not even the doctors."

It was clear that there was no right answer for how Rizzo and Johnson should handle their pitcher, but the debate roiled on. Another wrinkle in the Strasburg shutdown discussion emerged when agent Scott Boras gave an incendiary interview to columnist Mike Wise of *The Washington Post*, suggesting that he played a role in helping build the Nationals and that he and Rizzo discussed how to handle the young pitcher's workload. "Look, you want to draft these players? Great, but you know what, I'm not on board," Boras allegedly told Rizzo. "We won't sign, and I'll send them back to college. I want to make sure we have an organization that will put the health of these players first. How about everyone was given notice by Rizzo that this was going to be what the format was, that he is going to, hopefully, pitch the Nationals into [pennant-winning] position. Rizzo and I put this team together. I got eight or nine guys on the team.

"I told Rizzo, 'I'll be honest with you. You got a guy who is a No. 1 pitcher. There are only a few of them in the game. He's worth $30 million dollars a year.' You have four years that cost you $120 million dollars. Because of the reserve system, you only have to pay $40 million dollars. So, you have an $80 million dollar decision of profit in an asset that you have under your control. You better look at it that way. You know what else you better look at. With your insurance coverage, if you go against medical recommendations, are you liable for negligence as an organization?"

Boras quickly backtracked on his statements, telling the *Post,* "I don't make the decisions. I don't even know, when they're shutting down

Strasburg, and I don't need to. They're following expert medical opinion, and that's all I care about."

The entire Boras episode was bizarre and left Rizzo in a no-win situation. "Did Rizzo overreact initially, trying to eliminate any notion that Boras was behind the decision?" Rosenthal said. "Or did Rizzo truly act on his beliefs, trying to demonstrate leadership and shield the rest of the organization from criticism? Either way, he's now stuck."

Dr. Lewis Yocum, the surgeon who performed Strasburg's Tommy John surgery, told the *Los Angeles Times* that he had not been consulted by the Nationals regarding the pitcher's health, saying that he had not spoken to Rizzo since last year and Strasburg since spring training. "I wasn't asked," he told the *Times*.

Then like Boras, Yocum quickly backtracked, responding to the article by saying that he had spoken with the team while leaving the exact decision up to Rizzo. "I would like to correct the misimpression generated from today's *L.A. Times* article that I have not been a participant in discussions with the Washington Nationals regarding the recovery strategy for pitcher Stephen Strasburg," Yocum wrote in a statement. "In fact, I have been contacted repeatedly and have had numerous discussions with the Nationals GM Mike Rizzo and the team's medical personnel, as recently as mid-August. While the final decision was up to the team, as is standard practice, I was supportive of their decision and am comfortable that my medical advice was responsibly considered."

The question about Strasburg's limit even moved into the political realm, where Washington, D.C. mayor Vincent Gray told reporters that the shutdown was "very wise." Former New York mayor Rudy Giuliani joined the chorus of voices as well, saying on NBC's *Meet the Press*, "The guy's a big strong guy. The operation seems to have worked. A lot of guys for 100 years have been pitching until the end of the season."

Even Tommy John, the former pitcher and patient for whom the surgery is named, chimed in, saying that Strasburg should be allowed to pitch because he threw more than 200 innings after his the elbow operation, which brought on this tart-tongued response from Boras: "Should we follow the expert medical opinion of a licensed surgeon, who performed Tommy John surgery—or of the patient who was asleep?"

By this time, everyone involved with the Nationals was irritated with the entire situation, perhaps no one more than Strasburg himself. The laconic pitcher dreaded having the spotlight turned on him, but after Strasburg's start on September 2 against St. Louis, Johnson said his ace would start two more times in 2012, putting a firm deadline on the rampant speculation that had overtaken the team in the midst of its playoff run. "I'm just focused on the next start," Strasburg said. "We're going to have a sit down and talk here soon."

Rizzo reiterated that the team had Strasburg's best interests in mind with the decision. "When we feel that he's had enough in and around that area of innings, and we take into account all the things," he said, "stressful innings, pitches, and that type of thing, then we'll make that decision and shut him down. I don't think he's going to fight me on it. I think he's going to be unhappy about it. I know he'll be unhappy about it. He is an ultimate competitor, but we've taken that out of his hands. We've made [a decision] five months ago and we're going to stick to it. Stephen Strasburg is one of the most popular players in baseball, and it is a good conversational piece. It is a debatable subject, but most of the people who have weighed in on this know about 10 percent of the information that we know."

The Nationals used exhaustive research in coming up with their strategy, carefully studying pitchers who had undergone Tommy John surgery and what happened the next season with an increased workload. While John was a medical marvel who never missed another start, there were hundreds of cautionary tales—both past and present—that helped make the Nationals' decision.

Cardinals pitcher Jamie Garcia was shut down in 2010 after 163⅓ innings following his surgery. The next season, when St. Louis won the World Series, he was bumped up to 220⅓ innings, including the postseason. The pitcher would suffer through shoulder trouble in 2012, and his elevated ERA would show his ineffectiveness. (Garcia would later leave Game 2 of the Cardinals playoff game against the Nationals with shoulder trouble.)

Josh Johnson, traded from the Miami Marlins to the Toronto Blue Jays during the 2012 offseason, threw 209 innings in 2009 in his first full season after coming off surgery. Since then, he has suffered back and shoulder injuries and was 8–14 with a 3.81 ERA in 2012. After throwing almost 200

The Forgotten Starter

The discussion about shutting down Strasburg was so loud and divisive that the question of who would replace him in the rotation almost became an afterthought. The answer was a familiar face in an unfamiliar place. John Lannan was drafted by the Nationals in the 11th round of the 2005 Draft, making him one of the original members of the "new" franchise. He made his first start for the team in 2007 and served as the Opening Day starter for the Nats in both 2009 and 2010.

Although Lannan was never considered an upper-tier starter, he filled the void on some horrid teams and never shied away from taking the ball. Lannan went 10–13 in 2011 with a 3.70 ERA in 33 starts. In spring training, Lannan, however, lost a battle with Detwiler for the No. 5 spot in the rotation and was sent down to Triple A Syracuse, New York, but not before requesting a trade. "If the Nationals feel they don't need me or want me with the current makeup of the team, I can respect their decision," Lannan said. "However, I'm very confident that I am capable of making a meaningful contribution to a major league team."

The Nationals held on to Lannan, knowing they would need him down the stretch. To his credit Lannan acted like a pro in Triple A, using the time in the minors to refine his delivery. It was a far cry from the baseball life to which he was used, but Lannan made the best of a difficult situation. The lefty was called up twice to the big club for spot starts in doubleheaders,

innings in 2010, Francisco Liriano has struggled to regain his form and was traded by the Minnesota Twins to the Chicago White Sox and is now with the Pittsburgh Pirates.

Others suggested that the Nationals had already done enough to protect Strasburg and were actually taking unnecessary steps. "If you look at it superficially, you could argue that the way MLB has improved the way it handles young pitchers proves the Nationals' point—that reducing a starter's workload reduces his risk of injury, so shutting down Strasburg will keep him healthy," wrote Grantland's Rany Jazayerli. "But the sabermetric argument is the opposite: That precisely, because the industry has *already* reduced the risk of pitcher injuries significantly, there is less to be gained by further reducing Strasburg's workload.

and Lannan won both games—on July 21, when the Nationals were reeling after blowing a nine-run lead to the Atlanta Braves and dropping the first game on the double-dip and August 3 against Miami. "I understand the situation. Going down there and pitching was a little weird," Lannan said. "I wish I could stay up here, but I know the deal."

Lannan would get his chance when the Strasburg drama was over, taking the young ace's spot in the rotation on September 12 against the New York Mets, where he went 5⅔ innings to pick up his third win of the season. In six critical starts, Lannan compiled a 4-1 record with a 4.13 ERA—certainly not Strasburg numbers—but good enough to help the Nationals finish their playoff run.

He performed particularly well in a huge start at Citizens Bank Ballpark on September 26 against the Philadelphia Phillies, a place where he normally struggled. With the Braves making a late run, Lannan helped the Nationals keep pace. "Pretty much the whole night was an adrenaline rush," Lannan said. "I just rode with it."

Lannan won't make anyone forget Stephen Strasburg and he knows that. But after the toughest year of his career, he was simply glad to play a role. "It's night and day. The one thing I realized watching this team from afar and then coming up and seeing it every once in a while, you realize how special it was," said Lannan, who signed with the Phillies after the 2012 offseason. "You ask yourself, 'What's it all for?' and you realize this is why. It's a stepping stone for something greater."

"Strasburg, like every pitcher of his generation, has had his pitches monitored from the moment he signed a pro contract. Strasburg never threw even 100 pitches in a game as a rookie before he blew out his elbow, nor did he throw even 100 pitches after returning from Tommy John surgery last year. This year the gloves have come off a little; he threw 119 pitches in one start, 111 in another, and no more than 108 pitches in any other start. Strasburg is the product of an era, in which a pitcher's well-being already comes first. This approach has succeeded in reducing injuries significantly, but not entirely. There's only so much risk that can be squeezed out of the equation, no matter how much you protect a pitcher's arm. Some pitchers will get hurt, no matter how well you protect them. You know which pitcher illustrates this best? *Stephen Strasburg.*"

Once again, Rizzo's principled stand was met with howls of disgust from the let-him-pitch camp and nods of approval from the protect-your-pitcher folks. "When Rizzo explains it to you, and you're around it every day, it makes perfect sense," Santangelo said. "If you don't know all the details and you aren't around the club, you're formulating ridiculous opinions. I guess we're lucky that we're around it every day. He has a game plan and he's sticking to it. He's stuck to his guns and is a man of his word. There are not too many of those guys in baseball."

The Nationals began making plans for life after Strasburg, which was made easier by the fact that the rest of the rotation—featuring Gio Gonzalez, Zimmermann, hard-throwing Edwin Jackson, and emerging starter Ross Detwiler—was arguably the NL's best, even if you took Strasburg's stats out of the equation. Gonzalez finished the season third in the voting for the NL Cy Young Award.

Strasburg's next start, on September 7 against the Marlins, might have sealed his fate. The right-hander was flat from the start and lasted only three innings against a last-place club. None of his pitches had the usual snap, and Strasburg's body language suggested that he had had enough. Had the stress of the shutdown debate finally cracked Strasburg's steely resolve? His manager thought yes. "To be honest with you, I think he just is thinking too much about the decision, when we're going to shut him down," Johnson said. "And he kind of wore it. He didn't like it. But that's the way it is."

The next day, September 8, Johnson walked into the training room and told Strasburg he was done for the year, ending the long, drawn-out debate about the innings limit one start earlier than planned. "He's had a great year. I know what he's going through for the past couple weeks. The media hype on this thing has been unbelievable," Johnson said. "I feel it's hard for him, as it would be anybody, to get mentally, totally committed in a ballgame. And he's reached his innings limit that was set two years ago, so we can get past this and talk about other things for a change. I wouldn't have done anything differently. And even with all the so-called experts commenting on how to use him, how to get him through October, how to do this, how to do that, I have a little bit of experience in how to handle a pitching staff. And none of those scenarios fit. I mean, if they did, I would've pursued them."

Not surprisingly, Strasburg was not happy about the decision to end his season earlier than expected. "It was pretty shocking, and honestly, I'm not too happy about it," the 24-year-old said. "I don't know if I'm ever gonna accept it, to be honest. It's something that I'm not happy about at all. That's not why I play the game. I play the game to be a good teammate and win. You don't grow up dreaming of playing in the big leagues to get shut down when the games start to matter. It's gonna be a tough one to swallow, but like I said, all I can do is be the best teammate possible for these guys."

After undergoing ligament replacement surgery in 2010 and working his way back through a grueling rehab process, Strasburg's brilliant season came to a close with the pitcher sporting a 15–6 record and 3.16 ERA in 28 starts. He struck out 197 batters in 159⅓ innings—two-thirds of a frame short of the mystical 160 innings limit.

By all accounts it was a fantastic season, but one that will forever be judged by the decision the team made. "I respect them for going with their heart and trying to do best by the kid for his future," CBSSports.com baseball writer Scott Miller said. "The easy thing to do would be to simply hand him the ball and let him keep pitching. But I don't think anybody knows…I know nobody knows what the best way to handle a young pitcher is. While it's easy to knock the Nationals, at the same time, you have to respect the decision they made in keeping the foundation or a cornerstone of the franchise healthy."

With the playoffs looming and the chance to finally rewrite the record books, it was a hard pill for many Nationals fans and quite a few of Washington's players to swallow. Rizzo understood their pain. But his world view went beyond October. "I'm going to say to [fans] that we're going to be good for a long, long time," Rizzo said. "And Stephen Strasburg is going to be a prime reason why we're going to be good for a long, long time. This team wasn't constructed to have a short glimpse of prosperity and fade away. This team is built for the long haul. And by shutting down Stephen Strasburg and Jordan Zimmermann last year, we've proven that we care for our pitchers. We care for the long haul and we're going to do what's best for their careers and their future, because what's best for their careers and their future is best for the Washington Nationals' future."

17

PLAYOFF PUSH

WHILE THE REST OF THE BASEBALL WORLD WAS EMBROILED IN the Strasburg shutdown scenario, the Nationals were in the middle of a pennant chase, battling the ghosts of seasons past and the pesky Atlanta Braves and Cincinnati Reds for the best record in baseball. To say this was uncharted waters for the Nationals would be a huge understatement, but having been in first place since April, with each day the team was growing more comfortable with its status as front-runners. While teams scrambled to make moves around the July 31 trading deadline, the Nationals stood pat, as general manager Mike Rizzo felt good with just about every spot in the lineup. It helped that the Nationals were finally getting healthy.

Ryan Zimmerman struggled with a shoulder injury for a large portion of the first half of the season, but a cortisone shot on June 24 helped save his year. Prior to receiving the shot, Zimmerman was hitting .218 with three homers. After receiving the injection—the third he had endured in hopes of finding a solution—the veteran third baseman looked like an entirely new player, blasting 22 homers and hitting .321 over the season's final three months. "It's very satisfying to look back to where I was at the end of June," Zimmerman said, "to look at my numbers then, and to know what I was thinking then and how bad I felt for not producing, and to look at my numbers now."

After breaking his wrist in May, outfielder Jayson Werth returned to the lineup in August and provided a spark from an unlikely position in the batting lineup—leadoff. Werth, who spent most of his career as a No. 5 hitter and run-producing threat, moved to the top of the lineup and utilized his versatility to get on base and make things happen in front of both Bryce Harper and Adam LaRoche. "The guys just kept plugging along and kept playing hard every day," Werth said.

And even more than Werth's stats—a .300 batting average, .387 on-base percentage, and .440 slugging percentage—would indicate, his effort, hustle, and dogged determination to change the entire mind-set of the organization was beginning to take hold. "Anyone who's gone through a new team knows it's a process," Nats broadcaster F.P. Santangelo said. "It will take some time. He was a fish out of water [in 2011]. It's funny how last year there wasn't one sentence that didn't end with 'Seven years, $126 million.' You don't hear that now. But he is still the guy that everyone looks to. If he's okay with the team losing 2–1, because they played well, then it's okay. If he's hanging his head after a loss, then so is everyone else."

Michael Morse didn't make his debut until June after battling through a torn right lat muscle and then battled through several nagging injuries throughout the rest of the season. But just the threat of his power did wonders for a flagging offense, and Morse delivered several big blows during the stretch run, finishing with 18 home runs in 102 games. "I guess it's never too late to get going. I feel good. It has been a tough year for me, but this team has been doing so great that everybody has been picking up everybody the whole year," he said. "I guess that's what good teams do."

Morse had one of the more unique home runs in baseball history in a game against the St. Louis Cardinals on September 29, when he appeared to line a grand slam just over the wall in right at Busch Stadium. But the umpires ruled that it did not go out, and Morse was thrown out, trying to scramble back to first base. The officials then took a closer look on replay and overturned the call. They determined the ball did go over the wall before striking an advertisement and bouncing back onto the field.

So, the umpires made everyone return to their original bases and reenact the play, including Morse, who stood confused in the batter's box. He pretended to swing but did so without a bat—almost like a little kid pantomiming the action in his backyard. "I was like, 'What do you want me to do?'" Morse said. "So, I look over to the dugout, and everyone told me to swing and I was like, 'I'm not going to swing.' But then [Cardinals catcher Yadier Molina] goes 'Swing! Swing!' I was like, 'All right!' So, I swung. And it was pretty cool. It felt like spring training. It felt like a drill. I guess I didn't have to [swing again], but if they had called me out, I never would have slept again. I felt like everyone was waiting for me to swing…I

wasn't going to do it at all, but it was such a crazy moment, that I might as well have some fun with it."

The Nationals broadcasting crew had some fun with it, too. Play-by-play guy Bob Carpenter even called the action as if it was really happening. "That is the greatest thing I've *ever* seen in my life," Santangelo told the DC Sports Bog. "I mean, right when you thought you've seen everything in a Major League Baseball game, they pressed rewind on the video, and Michael Morse went phantom grand slam."

Along with ailments to Morse, Zimmerman, and Werth, the Nationals had been hurt by injuries at the catcher position, with Wilson Ramos, Jesus Flores, and Sandy Leon all missing significant chunks of time. On August 3, three days after the non-waiver trading deadline had passed, the team made a move that barely registered on the radar but would prove to be a huge acquisition down the stretch. Rizzo swung a deal for veteran Oakland A's catcher Kurt Suzuki, giving Washington depth and defensive help at a position of need.

Suzuki was hitting just .218 at the time of the deal, but his veteran presence and acumen handling pitching staffs made him a perfect fit. In addition he found his offensive stroke, finishing the regular season hitting .267 with five homers and 25 RBIs in 43 games with the Nationals. "It's been such an easy transition. There are a great group of guys in this clubhouse," Suzuki said. "They welcomed me in nicely and really allowed me to be myself."

Each day seemed to bring a new milestone for the Nationals. After an August 20, extra-inning win against the Braves, Washington improved to 76–46, 30 games over .500. A 2–1 triumph against the Chicago Cubs on September 3 gave the Nationals 82 wins, ensuring the first winning season for a D.C.-based franchise since the 1969 Washington Senators. "We've come a long way," Zimmerman said. "I guess you can't try to start an organization like we did here from the ground up and expect that to happen really quickly. We've gone through the process, and they've done things the right way. It's been a struggle sometimes and it's been frustrating, but I think now we're going to be set for not just this year, but a lot of years to come."

Individually, the Nationals continued to surge. Starter Gio Gonzalez earned his 21st victory of the season, making him the first National League left-hander to win more than 20 games since Dontrelle Willis did it with the Florida Marlins in 2005. Gonzalez would finish third in the voting for the 2012 NL Cy Young Award. "Everyone has been doing their part," he said. "I can't explain how great everyone has been playing."

Harper continued his remarkable rookie campaign, coming out of another slump to finish with a .270 batting average, 22 home runs (the most by a teenager since Tony Conigliaro), 18 steals, 26 doubles, nine triples, and 98 runs scored, which would earn him NL Rookie of the Year honors. (His friend and teammate from the Scottsdale Scorpions, Mike Trout, would receive the same honors in the American League.) Harper, though, viewed other things as more important than individual prizes. "Getting on base for all these guys, just getting on base and letting them get those RBIs and whatnot, and get those Ws," he said. "As long as we get those Ws at the end of the night, that's all that matters to me. And as we get deep into October, that's huge."

Then on September 20, the Nationals clinched the first playoff appearance by a major league team in D.C. since 1933 with a 4–1 victory against the Los Angeles Dodgers. Many players took a low-key approach to clinching at least a wild-card berth, but Werth served as the voice of reason. "I think there was some talk about not celebrating at all," he said. "And I kind of talked them out of that. So, that was good. Any time you get to the postseason, it's a huge accomplishment."

With its sights set on claiming the NL East crown, Washington didn't stop there. But a murderer's row of fringe playoff contenders (the Milwaukee Brewers, Philadelphia Phillies, Cardinals, and Dodgers) meant the Nats' magic number shrunk more deliberately than they would have liked. With three games left in the season, the Nationals held a three-game edge over the surging Braves for the NL East title. This was crunch time, and the Nationals were savoring every moment. "I mean, it's the best position you can be in," Zimmerman said. "I think we've put ourselves in a good position all year. I remember when we first started talking about this a month or a month-and-a-half ago. We did everything we could to give ourselves a chance and now we're to the ultimate position where we've given ourselves the best chance."

Although the actual game that clinched the National League may not have been pretty—a 2–0 loss to the Phillies that did not matter once the

Braves lost to the Pittsburgh Pirates—the Nationals' accomplishments were not lost on anyone, as the announcement of the division crown sent the Nationals Park faithful and the team into delirium. "We've been through some ups and downs this year, and a lot of us have been through some ups and downs many years," Zimmerman said. "For us to stick together all year and be this team and for us to come out on top of this tough division—it's everything I could ask for and more."

No longer a laughingstock, the Nationals were now NL East champions. "We had our share of losing here. We know how that feels. That was a sour taste for us," Rizzo said. "And when we got these young kids from a player development that's second to none, these guys know how to play the game. Every guy that comes up here, they know how to win. They've got great makeup and character, and that's why we're celebrating tonight."

As the raucous celebration went into the clubhouse, back onto the field, and again into the clubhouse, where champagne and beer sprayed from all corners, there was a sense of reflection amid the joy. "Words can't describe it right now," Zimmerman said. "It means a lot. It's been a long season and a fun one, but it's just one step. This is such a team, I really haven't thought about anything for myself. It's more for these guys here. A lot of other guys have been here for a while, and this whole year was a huge group effort. Everyone came together and everyone did so many things to get us to where we're at now. I haven't even thought about me or myself or how long I've been here, because all these other guys deserve it as much as I do."

Typical of the Nats' climactic year, even the celebration wasn't without some small bit of drama. While the Nationals sprayed the bubbly and brew throughout the clubhouse, the underage Harper celebrated with Adam LaRoche's son, Drake, with cider. "We were pouring it on top of each other," Harper said. Eagle-eyed fans, however, saw Harper, who is also Mormon, holding a beer in his hand on the team's official Instagram site, ostensibly ready to spray fellow teammates, but it was perhaps a questionable call for a noted teetotaler.

There was one final matter to deal with in the season's last two games. The Nationals were in the hunt for MLB's best record, and with it home-field advantage throughout the playoffs. (But due to the wacky scheduling format introduced with the creation of the second wild-card, they would go on the road for the first two games of the playoffs.) Tied with the Reds on the final day of the season, Washington bested Philadelphia 5–1, while Cincinnati lost 1–0 to the Cardinals. That put an exclamation point on the mind-boggling season, as the Nats finished the year at an unthinkable 98–64, the best record in Expos/Nationals history and good enough for the top seed in the NL. "The sky's the limit for this team, not only this year but years to come," Werth said. "The main thing is just getting in. You've got to get in the playoffs…You've just got to get in. And we got in. Now all bets are off."

Mere months away from being wiped out of the record books, shuffled off to Washington, D.C., forced to flounder under MLB guidance, and treated as cannon fodder by the rest of the league, the Nationals' rise from pauper to power is a tale filled with daring choices, unlikely heroes, dumb luck, and transcendent talent, all thrown together and patiently stirred until the formula produced a team that will be reckoned with for years to come. "You have a manager that treats people like men and lets them be professionals," Santangelo said. "You have a great coaching staff together, a blend of veterans and young players, young players showing the vets how to play hard. Guys like DeRosa and Chad Tracy showing young players how to be bench players. You put all the pieces together, and it's one of those perfect storms."

It's one the Nationals plan on duplicating for years to come. Take it from the two players who helped change the face of a franchise. "I have fun playing baseball. I live with no regrets," Harper said. "I love this game like a little guy. Going in and playing every single day is a dream come true. It's a great time not only for us, but for D.C."

"We're not playing for one year," Strasburg said. "We're not going to try and win for one year and then jump ship."

18

ECSTASY AND AGONY

IN AN INTEREST TO BOOST EXCITEMENT FOR THE SECOND HALF of the season, Major League Baseball commissioner Bud Selig introduced a second wild-card playoff spot before the start of the 2012 season, giving more teams an opportunity to compete for the playoffs. The second wild-card proved to be a smashing success, with teams jockeying for position until the final day of the season. There, however, was one quirk in Selig's plan. In order to reduce the amount of travel days and prevent the World Series from stretching further into November, the winner of the wild-card play-in game would get to host the first two games of the National League Division Series—a curious edge that seemingly negated the benefit of winning your division. "I don't like to criticize Major League Baseball, but from an operational standpoint, to line up your pitching, it's very difficult," Nationals manager Davey Johnson said. "It's great for the fans, but, boy, for a manager, it's tough."

In the Nationals' case, the best record in baseball meant they would be headed on the road on short notice to face the winner of the contest between the two wild-cards, the St. Louis Cardinals and Atlanta Braves. The Nationals knew what they would be getting with the Braves, an NL East rival and a team ready to make one last run with retiring legend Chipper Jones. The Cardinals were the 2011 World Series champs, a team with a never-say-die attitude and one of the league's best offenses.

The wild-card matchup would not be without controversy. With St. Louis holding a 6–3 lead in the eighth inning, Atlanta looked to make one last charge, putting runners on first and second. Andrelton Simmons hit a pop fly to shallow left that fell in between Cardinals shortstop Pete Kozma and left fielder Matt Holliday, seemingly loading the bases.

But umpire Sam Holbrook signaled the infield fly rule was in effect, automatically making Simmons out, even though the ball landed well beyond the infield. Atlanta's fans expressed their displeasure by throwing beer cups and garbage on the field, forcing a delay in the action. The Braves never recovered from the controversial call, and the Cardinals won 6–3 and moved on to the NLDS against Washington. Through a quirk in the schedule, the Cardinals and Nationals played all seven of their games after August 29, with the Nats winning three of four in D.C., and St. Louis taking two of three during September 28–30.

The series would start with two games at Busch Stadium, one of the loudest and most partisan venues in the majors, a distinct advantage for a veteran, battle-tested Cardinals team. Before the series started, the Nationals' playoff inexperience was the major talking point. Only four of the 25 players on the D.C. roster had been to the postseason before—Jayson Werth, Edwin Jackson, Adam LaRoche, and Mike Gonzalez—compared to 19 players on the Cards' roster, many of whom were part of the team's World Series run in 2011.

In his typical confident fashion, Bryce Harper, the youngest National, suggested that postseason playing time would hardly make a difference in the series. "I think you guys are more nervous than we are," Harper said prior to Game 1 of the NLDS. "It's just another game, just another series. I'm excited, but I'm just going to look at it like it's another game and another place that we play and another team that we play. I guess, when you step in the box, it's going to be a lot different with the crowd and everything, but you can't look at it that way."

Johnson also said his young charges would be ready to handle the emotionally charged environment of playoff baseball. "The preparation that you have for a ballclub comes in 160 games in a regular season," he said. "You really don't do anything different. I don't want to act any different. It's going to be business as usual. We've got no trick plays we're running out there. [We are] going to try to miss some bats, and try to hit some pitches, and outscore them."

Game 1 saw Washington send its 21-game winner, Gio Gonzalez, to the hill to set the tone and steal a critical road game. But from the start, Gonzalez was off. Whether it was nerves or mechanics, the normally pinpoint Gonzalez was all over the place, spraying fastballs around the plate and looping curves either too high or down in the dirt. He walked five of the first nine Cardinals batters he saw, running up his pitching count and putting the Nationals in a 2–1 hole.

Washington had its chances against St. Louis starter Adam Wainwright but squandered several huge opportunities. Werth came up with the bases loaded twice, and the Nationals went home empty-handed both times. Werth, though, came up big in the field in the sixth inning, fighting the blinding sun to rob David Descalso of a two-run homer. Reliever Ryan Mattheus also did his part, coming in to a hair-raising situation in the seventh inning with the bases loaded and none out. But in just two pitches, Mattheus induced a force-out at the plate and a 5–4–3 double play to keep the score at 2–1.

Michael Morse reached on an error by Pete Kozma during the eighth, and Ian Desmond followed with a single to put runners on the corners. Danny Espinosa bunted to move Desmond to second, and Kurt Suzuki—who had driven in the Nats' only run of the game—struck out. Washington sent Chad Tracy to the plate to pinch-hit, but St. Louis countered with left-hander Marc Rzepczynksi, forcing Johnson to turn to Tyler Moore.

A 25-year-old outfielder with tons of power, Moore was selected by the Nationals in both the 2005 and 2006 amateur drafts, but he did not sign with the team. The Nats chose him again in the 16th round of the 2008 Draft, and this time he did sign. Moore was brought up by Washington during the same April series in Los Angeles, in which the team promoted Harper, leaving the rookie completely eclipsed by his more famous teammate. In 75 games, however, Moore proved his worth, hitting .263 with 10 home runs and 29 RBIs.

Still, this was a tough situation for any player, much less a rookie. But Moore proved ready for his shot, poking a 2–2 pitch by Rzepczynksi into right to score Morse and Desmond to give the Nationals a stunning 3–2 advantage. "I'm just glad to have the opportunity, because they didn't want to face Chad Tracy, which is our best pinch-hitter," Moore said. "I came in and talked to Mark DeRosa, and those guys have been great for me all year, because they sit on the bench with me and help me out, going through pitchers. They let me know what can happen. And I've failed a lot, too, during this thing, and it's helped me keep my heart rate down and just come up and try to put the ball in play."

Tyler Clippard and Drew Storen closed the game out for the Nationals, and Washington held a 1–0 advantage in the best-of-five series, snagging home-field advantage. The win was the first for a Washington franchise in the postseason since Game 3 of the 1933 World Series. "You know, I think there's going to be some new history in Washington from here on out," Desmond said.

GOING INTO GAME 2, the Nationals had a huge opportunity to put a stranglehold on the series before it returned to D.C. Jordan Zimmermann was scheduled to take the hill for Washington, and with his steady (some might say boring) demeanor, he appeared to be the ideal choice to handle a swing game. "He's had great presence on the mound," Johnson said. "He knows he's got good stuff and he attacks hitters. He's pitched arguably as good as any guy has all year. Sometimes when he's had too much rest, he's shown a tendency to kind of jump at the hitters, but I think he's overcome that tendency. I like where he's at."

So did the Cardinals, who jumped all over the righty to easily take control of the game. Zimmermann allowed four runs in the second inning and gave up a long home run to Allen Craig in the third, giving St. Louis a 5–1 lead. Although Gonzalez struggled with his control in Game 1, lead was simply too hittable. The Cardinals crushed pitches that offered little resistance, and Zimmermann was out of the game after three innings. "I wanted to go out there and go deep into the game and try to get out of here with two wins," Zimmermann said. "I didn't do my part."

The Nationals appeared to catch a break when Cardinals starter Jaime Garcia was forced to leave the game in the second inning with a shoulder injury, but the pressing Washington hitters weren't able to capitalize. Harper, who surprised many by returning to his collegiate look of having eye black smeared all over his visage (something the Nationals asked him to tone down after he was drafted), struggled mightily during the first two games of the series while fighting the flu. He struck out four times in Game 2, and his first hit of the playoffs would turn into a teaching lesson.

Harper hustled for a double in the seventh inning, but then with two on and no outs, Ryan Zimmerman hit a fly ball to left. Holliday's dribbling throw was terrible, allowing Werth to score from third, but Harper went for third base and was thrown out easily by Kozma, the Cardinals shortstop, helping to kill a rally in the eventual 12–4 loss. "Sometimes you've got to roll the dice," Harper said. Johnson wasn't quite as sanguine about Harper's base-running blunder. "Well, that's inexperience, too. We had a little rally going there, and he was in scoring position and he tried to get to third, and that kind of killed the rally we had going," Johnson said. "Again, that's just a little inexperience. He's overly aggressive there. He didn't tag up. He had to go back and tag up, and that was right. But it was wrong to try to go to third."

Harper, 1–of–10 in the series through two games, bristled when veteran *St. Louis Post-Dispatch* reporter Rick Hummel asked him whether he was overanxious at the plate. "You think so?" Harper snapped. "Maybe you should be the hitting coach."

Even though Game 2 was an ugly loss, the Nationals were heading home tied in the best-of-five series, which put them in good shape considering the challenging nature of the format. There was no panic with three straight games at what promised to be an electric Nationals Park. "We're 1–1. Maybe not the best-case scenario," Harper said, "but a good-case scenario to come in here and really play hard the next three games and just try to play the game we've been playing all year and just have some fun."

WITH AN OFF DAY BEFORE GAME 3, the Nationals returned home with the dreams of a city riding on nearly every pitch. "To bring a playoff game to D.C., something that's been a long time coming, they've been through a lot—a lot of tough years," Desmond said. "It's an exciting time in the Beltway."

Although St. Louis held a distinct edge in experience, the Nationals were counting on the peripatetic and playoff-tested Jackson, who had pitched in the World Series for both the Tampa Bay Rays and Cardinals, to provide them with a stabilizing start. "I think it definitely helps," Jackson said. "The thing about postseason baseball is the game can speed up real quick. You have to kind of control the pace and control the tempo, and having experience in that, it definitely helps when you get in those situations, being able to slow the game down and kind of take the crowd out of the equation and just think about concentrating on what you have to do."

Jackson had been up and down during his first season with Washington, posting a 10–11 mark with a 4.03 ERA in 31 starts. But he threw 189⅔ innings, which is exactly what the team had in mind when they signed him. If Jackson had a particular knock against him, it was that he was a slow starter, and teams would tag him in the first or second inning for some quick runs before he settled down. "Every inning you have to treat like it's the ninth inning," Jackson noted before Game 3. "You definitely want to come out and you want to get in a rhythm as early as possible and keep it rolling in a positive direction."

Sporting a ghastly 1–for–10 mark with six strikeouts heading into Game 3, Harper had not been his usual dynamic self during the first two games of the playoff series. But like the rest of the Nationals, he was looking forward to playing at home and turning the series in their favor. "I'm 1–for–10. It's two games," he said. "It's not the end of the world. I've got three more games left, and we're at home and hopefully I can get to raking. My six strikeouts, you know, I've gone 3–2 on pretty much every single one. I swung at six balls. It could go either way—strikeout or walk. My approach has been good, and my swings have been good. Sometimes you get in that little funk that you can't worry about. Wainwright threw great. They've got some tough guys in that bullpen, too. [Trevor] Rosenthal came in throwing 101 last night. That's absolute fuego. If any of you guys want to step into the box, you guys can go ahead, because that's pretty fun."

While Harper held court before an armada of assembled media, across the Nationals locker room, Stephen Strasburg sat quietly, going about his business and making small talk with several teammates. Although the Strasburg shutdown drama had receded, it was never far from public conscience, as TV broadcasts of the playoff games referenced general manager Mike Rizzo's decision and showed the pitcher watching from the dugout.

Strasburg tried to take the high road through much of the debate, but after being shut down, his angry remarks publicly confirmed what those who knew Strasburg suspected—that he was too much of a competitor to willingly take a backseat during this important stretch of the season. Now that the playoffs were in full swing, Strasburg somewhat reluctantly took on his role as spectator. "I don't think [watching the playoffs] is painful in any sense," he told *The Washington Times*. "It's hard being in the dugout, but at the same time it's exciting, and the atmosphere's great. I just can't wait for my opportunity."

Strasburg had a kindred spirit in Wainwright, who missed the Cardinals' World Series run in 2011 after undergoing Tommy John surgery. "During the time, I felt like I was a huge impact to that team," he said. "I'm not so sure I did anything. But I tricked myself into believing I was, you know, pretty important last year. I felt like I was there for anybody who needed me, at whatever level that was. Nothing else to do, right?"

Rizzo's decision to shut down Strasburg rankled many throughout baseball, and that enmity toward the franchise became clear when Bob Nightengale of *USA TODAY Sports* ran a column in which unnamed general managers of other teams had a scathing viewpoint of the Nationals' choice to close out their ace. "If we don't win the World Series, I don't care who does," one general manager told the paper, "as long as it's not those guys. They don't deserve to win it—not after what they did." Another GM added: "I hope they go down in flames. I hope it takes another 79 years before they get back to the playoffs. That's how strongly I feel about it."

Those were stunning words, considering that Rizzo is generally well-liked among other GMs in the league, given his background as a former player and scout. But the Strasburg decision hit home for a lot of teams and put the spotlight on how they handle their own pitchers, making plenty of other GMs uncomfortable.

For the people of D.C., however, that was a mere afterthought on the day of Game 3 as the city bathed in abundant sunshine for another afternoon start. A huge American flag and thousands of balloons greeted fans as they entered the centerfield gate at National Park, and the team handed out rally towels. The stadium and the surrounding areas were jumping with people eager to celebrate the return of playoff baseball to the nation's capital. "It doesn't go unnoticed," first baseman LaRoche said. "Until recently, it was almost more of a social gathering. 'Come out, nothing else to do, and we'll go hang out at the park.' Now, it's turned into some die-hard fans. People are probably skipping work and skipping school to come see the Nats. Our last few regular season home games were as close to playoff atmosphere as you can get. When you got fans getting up and getting into it in the second, third inning, I'm sure that's what it will be like, so it will be fun."

With an appearance by original Nationals manager Frank Robinson and a flyover by fighter jets, the crowd was whipped into a frenzy—only to see the Cardinals score a two-out run in the first inning and three more in the second. Light-hitting Kozma delivered the big blow with a three-run homer, making it 4–0. Just like that, the energy had been zapped out of the stadium. Hope was replaced with worry, as the Nationals fell flat in clutch situations time and again.

Even though it was just his fourth start of the year, Cardinals pitcher Chris Carpenter managed to work himself out of trouble, thanks to a timely pop-up or strikeout by pressing Nationals hitters, who went 0–for–8 with runners in scoring position. "We had him in some tough spots," Werth said. "We had him on the ropes a couple times. We were just one bloop away from a totally different ballgame."

But the Nationals never got that bloop or anything else, and when it was all said and done, St. Louis walked away with a dominating 8–0 triumph and a 2–1 lead in the series, putting Washington in a do-or-die situation for Game 4. "We are not out of this by a long shot," Johnson said. "Keep us in the ballgame tomorrow, get a few key hits, we're right back in it. Shoot, I've had my back to worse walls than this, but I like my ballclub, and I think we'll come out and play a good game tomorrow."

Were the Nats tight? To a man, they said no, but it definitely looked as if the playoff atmosphere was affecting them in ways that hadn't been seen by this group all year. "You could see it in some of their at-bats in big spots—trying too hard to make something big happen instead of just putting together a good, productive at-bat when that's all they needed," said longtime Nationals reporter Mark Zuckerman. "And you could see it from some of the pitchers, especially Gio Gonzalez, who in Game 1 was over-amped and got caught up in the moment. Whether that was being tight or just a case of these guys being far less experienced in postseason play than the Cardinals, it definitely was a noticeable difference between the two teams."

THE UNBRIDLED OPTIMISM OF GAME 3 had given way to a nervous energy in Game 4, as the Nationals faced a sudden and shocking elimination contest. Although Johnson planned on staying the course, a player who wasn't even on the playoff roster would make the most indelible impact on this game, stirring his teammates with words that held special meaning for this franchise.

During his 15-year career in the majors, Mark DeRosa had just about seen it all. The utility man was a steadying, veteran influence on the Nationals' young players, often taking one to the side for personal instruction or motivation. DeRosa hit just .188 in 48 games with Washington in 2012, but to a man, the Nats will say that his impact went way beyond numbers. And in the hours before Game 4, DeRosa used his veteran status to take the floor. He grabbed the clubhouse microphone and proceeded to passionately read a passage from Theodore Roosevelt's speech "The Man in the Arena," stopping teammates in their tracks and bringing others in from various parts of the clubhouse.

> *It is not the critic who counts; not the man who points out how the strong man stumbles, or where the doer of deeds could have done them better. The credit belongs to the man who is actually in the arena, whose face is marred by dust and sweat and blood; who strives valiantly; who errs, who comes short again and again, because there is no effort without error and shortcoming; but who does actually strive to do the deeds; who knows great enthusiasms, the great devotions; who spends himself in a worthy cause; who at the best knows in the end the triumph of high achievement, and who at the worst, if he fails, at least fails while daring greatly, so that his place shall never be with those cold and timid souls who neither know victory nor defeat.*

DeRosa, who had been using those words as motivation since his Ivy League days at the University of Pennsylvania, added his own personal flair to the speech, dropping a few choice profanities in the mix for good measure. He then delivered this bit of info for those who didn't realize the author of the passage. "You know who spoke these words?" he said. "Teddy *fucking* Roosevelt."

The legendary president, who had been reduced to a stumbling boob in the Nationals' mascot race—an unintended symbol of the team's futility—only to experience triumph during the team's last homestand, was more than just a big-headed diversion. He was a hero and a winner, and in DeRosa's view, the perfect inspiration for a team in dire need of a push in the right direction. "I actually know that speech real well," said Werth, who had pushed for Roosevelt to get a chance to win the Presidents Race. "It's a good one. It's kind of very parallel to the world we live in today—not only that, but the fact Teddy gets disrespected for however many years it was. When I did some research on Teddy last year, I ran across that and I found it to be a very powerful segment of that speech. So, when I heard D-Ro with some of that stuff I was like, 'Somebody *finally* is reading this aloud in our clubhouse.' I thought it was good."

Of course, playoff battles are not won with pregame speeches, and the Nationals were facing an uphill battle against Cardinals starter Kyle Lohse, who was the Cardinals' best pitcher all year. The Nationals were countering with Ross Detwiler, the man who edged out John Lannan for the No. 5 spot in the rotation and a complete stranger to such a pressure-packed environment.

But Detwiler threw the kind of game the Nationals had been hoping for all series from their starting pitchers. Unfazed by the atmosphere, Detwiler challenged Cardinals hitters and threw six stellar innings. His only hiccup came in the third, when Kozma walked, moved to second on a sacrifice bunt, went to third on an error by Desmond, and scored on a sacrifice fly. That run, though, merely tied the score, as Washington had touched Lohse for a run in the second on a titanic shot over the wall in dead center by LaRoche.

After that, it was a pitcher's duel. Johnson said that he'd turn to the starter Zimmermann on short rest, and he did, giving the ball to the pitcher in the seventh. Zimmermann responded by striking out the side in a dominant inning. Clippard pitched the eighth and also struck out the side, pumping his fist with pure, raw emotion after recording the final out. Storen came on for the ninth and struck out his first two batters before Desmond closed out the frame with a tumbling catch of a pop-up in short left field.

The Nationals had relied on dominant pitching all year, and this was the first time in the playoffs where their arms completely overmatched St. Louis. "It was electric. It's been that way most of the year. But in both cases," Johnson said, "they rose to the occasion. All of them were throwing harder than I've seen them throw."

The Cardinals matched the Nationals out for out. Lohse went seven innings and allowed just two hits. Mitchell Boggs pitched the eighth with little problem, and to open the ninth, St. Louis skipper Mike Matheny went with hard-throwing righty Lance Lynn instead of his normal closer, Jason Motte.

What followed was one of the great at-bats in playoff history, and one that will forever be etched in the annals of Nationals lore. The matchup itself was an interesting sight—the burly, hirsute Lynn going up against his doppelganger in the terrifically bearded Werth, who, while once a power hitter, had shifted his game to suit the Nationals' needs, hitting at the top of the lineup and seeing some of his strength drained by a troublesome wrist injury.

With the crowd anticipating and hoping for something to break their team's way, the at-bat began. The first pitch was a blistering fastball from Lynn that Werth took for a strike, and rightfully so, given that it was a 95 mph heater at the knees, a practically unhittable offering.

Lynn followed with another strike, a 94 mph seed that was arguably better than his first pitch, and in a flash, Werth was in an 0–2 hole. But the steely veteran did not panic or flinch when Lynn offered a curve that skidded far away from the plate—a waste pitch in the truest sense of the word. Now the count stood at 1–2. Lynn came back with another fastball, a 96 mph blaze of heat, which was just up and out of the strike zone—a tough pitch to take, but one that a batter with Werth's discerning eye can spot. Now it was 2–2.

Then the battle truly began.

Lynn's 2–2 offering was a running fastball that Werth fought off. The sixth pitch had the velocity at 97 but not the location. Still, Werth, late on the fastball over the middle, fouled it away. Pitch seven was another 97 mph fastball, and Werth again went foul with a defensive swing. Werth fouled *another* fastball off on the eighth pitch, but this was the one that came closest to ending the at-bat. The pop-up barely drifted into foul territory, and St. Louis' Allen Craig ran out of the room at the rail of the Nationals dugout. The ball fortuitously fell into a sea of Washington players.

Undaunted, Lynn uncorked a picture perfect curve for pitch No. 9, and Werth barely got the bat on the ball as it tumbled out of the strike zone. The fans of the sellout crowd, realizing the great standoff they were witnessing, were on their feet with every pitch, cheering every foul ball like it was a game-winning hit. The 10th pitch of the Lynn-Werth battle was another rising fastball, which likely would have clipped the top corner of the strike zone, so Werth fouled it off yet again.

Having consistently attacked Werth with fastballs, Lynn upped the ante in the chess game by breaking off another excellent curve on the 11th pitch that missed by *this* much. Perhaps if Cardinals catcher Yadier Molina hadn't dropped the ball, it would have been called a strike. But the count finally moved, going to 3–2.

On the 12th pitch, Lynn went back to his bread and butter, throwing another rising fastball to the upper end of the strike zone, and again, Werth did what he could, fouling it off. At this point the stalemate had reached a baker's dozen, and someone had to blink. In this case, it was Lynn. After painting the corners of the strike zone for the entire at-bat, he made a mistake on what would turn out to be the final offering of the game, delivering a 96 mph fastball right down the heart of the plate.

Werth didn't miss this one, crushing the ball into the stands above the St. Louis bullpen, pointing to his Nationals teammates as he rounded first and sending the sellout crowd into hysterics. By the time he reached home, where he went airborne to touch home plate, the game—and the at-bat—had become an instant classic. Washington won 2–1 to even the series and force a decisive Game 5. "That's the way that game should have ended," Johnson said. "Jayson Werth hitting a home run. He has not hit that many this year. What was it, a 13, 14-pitch at-bat, something like that? It was unbelievable."

For the combatants in the epic duel, it was simply baseball. "[A] 3–2 heater," Lynn said. "He beat me. Everyone in the stadium knew what I was throwing there. Tip your cap to him. The guy can play, and he beat me."

"He's tough," Werth said. "We've faced him a lot over September and in the series. So, I knew what he had. But I think he threw a hook, 2–2 to get to 3–2, and I figured from then I wasn't going to get off the heater. [I] fouled a couple more off and finally got one to hit. You know, I can't even remember any of the other [big hits] right now. This one's pretty fresh. This is, given the situation, definitely pretty big."

In the press box, veteran scribes with thousands of games under their belts could hardly fathom what they had just witnessed. "Epic doesn't even begin to describe it. It's probably the greatest single at-bat I've ever seen in person, certainly given the circumstances. He just kept fouling off pitch after pitch," Zuckerman said. "At some point I asked the guy sitting next to me in the press box how many pitches he had seen in the at-bat, and we realized it was 12. The 13th pitch, of course, was the one he hit out. The explosion, inside the ballpark at that moment, was unbelievable. Things had been building up since about the seventh inning, when Jordan Zimmermann came out of the bullpen and struck out the side, and it just crescendoed when Werth hit the home run.

"One of my immediate thoughts was, *It doesn't matter what happens in Game 5…D.C. just became a baseball town.*"

RIDING THE EMOTIONAL HIGH of the previous night's heroics, the Nationals took the field for Game 5 feeling good about their chances. Gonzalez was back on the hill, and surely the 21-game winner would be sharper than he was in Game 1, when he labored through his start. "It was my first postseason game, no excuses, but the way I see it is playing in someone else's house, it's pretty rowdy," he said. "It's pretty exciting. You catch yourself at the moment, take a step back, and take a deep breath, and try to find it again."

Against Wainwright, Washington showed it clearly was energized by the events of Game 4 and began the decisive contest with a rousing start. Werth picked up where he left off, lacing a double to left field to start the bottom of the first, and Harper made his first real positive impact in the playoffs, driving a ball deep to the wall in left-center for a triple, scoring Werth and giving Washington a 1–0 lead.

The teenager—he would turn 20 in a few days—had been struggling mightily entering the game, going 1–for–18 through the first four games, but he still became the first teen to ever hit a three-bagger in a postseason game. Zimmerman would cap the inning by blasting a two-run homer just over the wall in right, and before everyone was in their seats, it was 3–0 Nationals.

Harper opened the third inning by crushing a Wainwright pitch into the seats for a homer to make it 4–0, and the Nationals continued to pour it on. Zimmerman doubled, and Morse followed with a two-run shot to put the Nats up 6–0 and seemingly on their way to the National League Championship Series.

But St. Louis began to peck away. Gonzalez began nibbling around the plate, and in the fourth, the Cardinals got on the board with a Holliday double that scored Carlos Beltran to make it 6–1. Gonzalez's control betrayed him again in the fifth, as a wild pitch and a bases-loaded walk scored two runs to close the gap to 6–3. But with each passing out, the Cardinals' chances seemed to grow slimmer.

There were, however, several moments that, in hindsight, could be second-guessed.

After Gonzalez's five-inning stint, Johnson turned to bullpen stalwarts Craig Stammen and Sean Burnett to work the sixth, which they did effectively. Now, the Nationals bullpen was set up perfectly to close out the final three innings. But instead of going with right-handed reliever Mattheus, Johnson turned to Jackson, the Game 3 starter, on short rest to pitch a pressure-packed seventh inning. Given the righty's penchant for slow starts, that was not his strong suit.

Jackson walked Jon Jay to start the inning and then allowed a double to Beltran to give St. Louis a golden scoring opportunity. Holliday hit an RBI ground-out to shortstop to make it 6–4, and even though Jackson would strike out two of the next three hitters, it was another chip in the Nats' armor, and one of the few times Johnson's acumen in handling his staff would be called into question. "Well, I just felt like Jackson was the best choice I had to get through that part of that lineup," Johnson said. "He did the job for me. He gave up a run, but he did what we needed to do to get to the people we needed to get to."

While the Nats' bats had gone silent, St. Louis remained relentless in its pursuit. In the eighth, Johnson turned to Clippard, who had excelled for the most part as the team's closer in the absence of the injured Storen. But Clippard began to struggle down the stretch, forcing Johnson to return the hard-thrower to an eighth-inning role. Here, nursing a 6–4 advantage, Clippard's job was to throw strikes against the less-than-fearsome part of the Cardinals lineup. But light-hitting Descalso poked a Clippard fastball just over the wall in right to close the deficit to 6–5 and officially put the more than 45,000 in attendance at Nationals Park on high alert.

But with the ship sinking, Washington made what appeared to be a game-saving charge in the bottom of the eighth, as LaRoche and Morse opened the frame with back-to-back singles. After Desmond's fielder's choice moved LaRoche to third, Espinosa popped out, leaving it up to

Suzuki to drive in a critical insurance run. Suzuki did just that, hitting a line drive to center to give Washington a 7–5 lead, putting the Nats three outs away from a series win.

Storen came out for the ninth to face the heart of the Cardinals lineup, and Beltran led off the inning with a stinging double to center. But Storen bounced back to get Holliday to ground to third and struck out Craig, leaving the Nationals just one out away. Perhaps realizing the magnitude of the situation, though, Storen got too careful with his pitches. Twice, he was one strike away from closing out the game and just missed with borderline pitches. Instead it resulted in consecutive walks to Molina and David Freese to load the bases.

With little margin for error, Descalso came up and ripped a hot shot up the middle that ticked off Desmond's glove and dribbled into center, allowing the Cardinals to tie the score at 7–7, an unthinkable scenario just a few innings earlier. "He hit it good," Desmond said. "I did the best I could to get my glove on it. I didn't get it."

Storen wasn't out of the woods yet. Descalso stole second to put runners on second and third, and Kozma followed by chipping a single into shallow right to score both runners and give St. Louis a stunning 9–7 lead.

Down to their last strike, the Cardinals would not go away. With one strike left to get, the Nationals could not seal the deal.

Three quick outs later, the dream season was over in nightmare fashion, as the Cardinals celebrated in front of a stunned gathering of fans, players, and media. "You know, I've been on the other end of the stick where [you] just [get] one out, and you move on," Johnson said. "We couldn't get it. We had the right people there—just got a little too cautious."

It's easy to blame Storen, but there were other reasons for the loss as well. "I really think it started with Gio Gonzalez being unable to give them more than five innings and not being able to take a 6–0 lead and quash any hope of a comeback," Zuckerman said. "Things were already starting to go downhill, when Jackson entered for the seventh. Ultimately, the biggest pitching mistake I think Davey made was not using Ryan Mattheus at some point in that game. The guy had been one of his most-trusted relievers all season, and he was brilliant pitching out of a bases-loaded jam in Game 1. How he didn't somehow find his way into Game 5 is still a mystery to me. Of course, if Drew Storen throws one more strike in the ninth inning, all of this is moot."

In the funereal Nationals locker room, the reality of what happened and the finality of the season was setting in. "We're all in the same boat right now," Clippard said. "Obviously Drew feels bad. I feel bad. We're all pretty devastated right now."

"This is not how I wanted my year to end," Harper said. "I definitely wanted to play deeper into the postseason. I'm not ready to go home and take off that uniform." But the wild ride had come to a crashing halt—just one strike away from the finish line. It was an amazing season, but that meant little to the collection of crushed men in the silent clubhouse. "Surreal. That's the best way I can describe the scene in the clubhouse after the game," Zuckerman said. "They didn't have enough time to tear down all the champagne-proof plastic and carpet, so some of it was still up. The room was dead silent, except for the slapping sound of players hugging each other.

"I don't think anyone was able to process what exactly had just happened. I'm sure in that moment—and probably for several weeks after—it took away from the season as a whole. But ultimately, I think they'll all realize what a success the season actually was. To go 98–64, after never having had even a winning season before, was no small feat. If someone said on Opening Day they would win the NL East and then lose in the first round of the playoffs, there probably wouldn't have been two people in that room who wouldn't have been satisfied with that."

And that's what their venerable skipper, who had been through the ups and downs of many a postseason as both a player and manager, told his shell-shocked team. "It was nothing to hang your head about. It was a great year," Johnson said. "We overcame a lot of problems. We proved our worth and we just need to let this be a lesson and learn from it, have more resolve, come back, and carry it a lot farther."

EPILOGUE

IN THE AFTERMATH OF THE WASHINGTON NATIONALS' BITTER defeat at the hands of the St. Louis Cardinals in the National League Division Series, the pain of the loss slowly gave way, and the realization of what the team and its remarkable young players had accomplished moved to the forefront. "Everyone knows this was the first of what should be several postseason trips for the franchise," NatsInsider.com founder Mark Zuckerman said. "Obviously there's no guarantee of anything, but the Nationals are as well-positioned as any team in baseball to make it back in 2013 and for several more years after that."

A franchise that had a cumulative record of 492–640 put together the best record in baseball. A manager, whom many thought the game had passed by, was named NL Manager of the Year. A player considered an expensive bust remade himself and delivered the biggest hit in team history. The first baseman, who couldn't even swing the bat in 2011 due to a debilitating shoulder injury, became an offensive force and won a Gold Glove. A pitcher who had the weight of the world on his rebuilt arm continued to mature and dominate, even in the face of swirling debate on how to handle his pitch limit. And a teenager, thought by many to be the epitome of what's wrong with the game, proved his critics wrong with his unflagging hustle and unyielding desire to win.

The team that no one wanted around now had an ownership group ready to ensure success for years to come. "You can see this product on the field, and the fact that these guys are locked in for a long time," principal owner Mark Lerner said. "We're going to continue to try and keep our young players as part of the organization, hopefully for their entire careers."

The Washington Nationals of the past are no more. Now, and seemingly into the future, these Nationals are on the verge of being the new beasts of the NL East, with Stephen Strasburg and Bryce Harper leading a talented collection of players, and the top farm system in the majors eager to make its mark on the baseball world. "You're going to see some great baseball in the next couple of years," pitcher Gio Gonzalez said. "We have such a great future for every single one of these guys. I think what we have done this year is shock the world, and you know what? I think we are going to continue to try to play Nationals baseball, and we are going to continue to try to make adjustments. I think what we gave you guys is a taste of what's coming for the next couple years."

What's coming for Stephen Strasburg in 2013 will be a year just about pitching, and the young ace will be grateful for that. Without the circus of Strasmas and the controversy of the shutdown taking away from his focus, the right-hander simply will focus on striking out hitters, the task at which he's best. A full season lies ahead for the pitcher, and with it the opportunity to silence critics about innings limits and arm strength and give the Nationals what they need—a fireballing young arm entering the prime of his career.

Despite being far from even reaching his prime, Harper, at 19, put together one of the most statistically impressive seasons by a young player in baseball history, especially considering the amount of scrutiny he faced in every big league town. Harper's 254 total bases and 57 extra base hits were the most ever for a player under age 20, and his 22 home runs, 98 runs scored, .340 on-base percentage, .447 slugging percentage, and .817 on-base-plus-slugging were the best regular season totals for a teenager in the past 45 years.

Harper won the NL Rookie of the Year Award, becoming the first teenager to do so since New York Mets pitcher Dwight Gooden in 1984 and the youngest position player to ever receive it. "It's a great award, and I'm so excited and proud of it, but my biggest thing is I want to win a World Series," Harper told *USA TODAY Sports*. "I want to put that ring on my finger and I want to give that to the town and city of D.C."

With a year under his belt and an offseason of intense study and conditioning, the 20-year-old will once again be making waves in the heart of the Nationals lineup. "I don't like to look ahead," Harper said, "but if you play the right way, do it the right way, then good things will happen." While Harper won the NL rookie award, his friend and former Scottsdale Scorpions teammate from the Arizona Fall League, Mike Trout won the AL version. The two young outfielders will inexorably be mentioned together and compared.

The Nationals made several moves in the offseason to solidify and bolster the team going forward, most notably re-signing first baseman Adam LaRoche to a two-year contract, waiting patiently for the player to test his worth on the free agent market while letting him know all along they wanted him back in the fold. Washington also got the speedy center fielder and leadoff man it had been looking to acquire for several years, working out a trade with the Minnesota Twins to get Denard Span, giving up hard-throwing pitcher Alex Meyer for the chance to set up their outfielder.

Then, late in the offseason, the Nationals surprised many by adding veteran closer Rafael Soriano to an already loaded bullpen at the cost of $28 million over two years and the team's first-round (No. 29) draft pick—a clear sign that the team is taking a win-at-all-costs approach. It's something that manager Davey Johnson, who is retiring after the 2013 season, appreciates. "Next year is going to be my last year, and I'm going to go out with my fourth World Series ring," the always forthright manager said.

Despite his connection to Trout, Harper will be more linked to another player. Strasburg and Harper were the No. 1 overall picks of the 2009 and 2010 MLB Drafts, respectively, and having both earned their first All-Star nods during 2012, the dynamic duo stand as the pillars of the Washington Nationals franchise and as forces to be reckoned with for years to come. "We're not playing for one year," Strasburg said. "We're trying to take over the NL East."

APPENDIX

Stephen Strasburg MLB Pitching Stats

Year	Tm	W	L	W-L%	ERA	G	GS	IP	R	ER	HR	BB	SO	WP	WHIP
2010	WSN	5	3	.625	2.91	12	12	68.0	25	22	5	17	92	2	1.074
2011	WSN	1	1	.500	1.50	5	5	24.0	5	4	0	2	24	0	0.708
2012	WSN	15	6	.714	3.16	28	28	159.1	62	56	15	48	197	5	1.155
3 Yrs		21	10	.677	2.94	45	45	251.1	92	82	20	67	313	7	1.090
162 Game Avg.		16	8	.677	2.94	34	34	190	70	62	15	51	236	5	1.090

Stephen Strasburg Minor League Pitching Stats

Year	Tm	Lev	W	L	W-L%	ERA	G	GS	CG	SHO	IP	H	R	ER	HR	BB	SO	WHIP
2010	2 Teams	AAA-AA	7	2	.778	1.30	11	11	0	0	55.1	31	14	8	1	13	65	0.795
2010	Harrisburg	AA	3	1	.750	1.64	5	5	0	0	22.0	13	9	4	0	6	27	0.864
2010	Syracuse	AAA	4	1	.800	1.08	6	6	0	0	33.1	18	5	4	1	7	38	0.750
2011	4 Teams	A-AA-AAA-A+	1	1	.500	3.54	6	6	0	0	20.1	14	9	8	1	3	29	0.836
2011	Hagerstown	A	0	1	.000	9.95	3	3	0	0	6.1	9	8	7	1	3	13	1.895
2011	Potomac	A+	0	0		0.00	1	1	0	0	3.0	2	0	0	0	0	5	0.667
2011	Harrisburg	AA	1	0	1.000	0.00	1	1	0	0	6.0	1	0	0	0	0	4	0.167
2011	Syracuse	AAA	0	0		1.80	1	1	0	0	5.0	2	1	1	0	0	7	0.400
2 Seasons			8	3	.727	1.90	17	17	0	0	75.2	45	23	16	2	16	94	0.806
AA (2 seasons)		AA	4	1	.800	1.29	6	6	0	0	28.0	14	9	4	0	6	31	0.714
AAA (2 seasons)		AAA	4	1	.800	1.17	7	7	0	0	38.1	20	6	5	1	7	45	0.704
A (1 season)		A	0	1	.000	9.95	3	3	0	0	6.1	9	8	7	1	3	13	1.895
A+ (1 season)		A+	0	0		0.00	1	1	0	0	3.0	2	0	0	0	0	5	0.667

Bryce Harper MLB Batting Stats

Year	Tm	G	AB	R	H	2B	3B	HR	RBI	SB	BB	SO	BA	OBP	SLG	OPS
2012	WSN	139	533	98	144	26	9	22	59	18	56	120	.270	.340	.477	.817
1 Yr		139	533	98	144	26	9	22	59	18	56	120	.270	.340	.477	.817

Bryce Harper Minor League Stats

Year	Tm	Lev	G	AB	R	H	2B	3B	HR	RBI	SB	BB	SO	BA	OBP	SLG
2011	2 Teams	A-AA	109	387	63	115	24	2	17	58	26	59	87	.297	.392	.501
2011	Hagerstown	A	72	258	49	82	17		14	46	19	44	61	.318	.423	.554
2011	Harrisburg	AA	37	129	14	33	7		3	12	7	15	26	.256	.329	.395
2012	Syracuse	AAA	21	74	8	18	4		1	3	1	9	14	.243	.325	.365
2 Seasons			130	461	71	133	28	3	18	61	27	68	101	.289	.382	.479

Montreal Expos/Washington Nationals Franchise History

Year	Tm	Lg	G	W	L	Ties	W-L%	Finish	Managers
1969	Montreal Expos	NL East	162	52	110	0	.321	6th of 6	Gene Mauch (52-110)
1970	Montreal Expos	NL East	162	73	89	0	.451	6th of 6	Gene Mauch (73-89)
1971	Montreal Expos	NL East	162	71	90	1	.441	5th of 6	Gene Mauch (71-90)
1972	Montreal Expos	NL East	156	70	86	0	.449	5th of 6	Gene Mauch (70-86)
1973	Montreal Expos	NL East	162	79	83	0	.488	4th of 6	Gene Mauch (79-83)
1974	Montreal Expos	NL East	161	79	82	0	.491	4th of 6	Gene Mauch (79-82)
1975	Montreal Expos	NL East	162	75	87	0	.463	5th of 6	Gene Mauch (75-87)
1976	Montreal Expos	NL East	162	55	107	0	.340	6th of 6	Karl Kuehl (43-85) and Charlie Fox (12-22)
1977	Montreal Expos	NL East	162	75	87	0	.463	5th of 6	Dick Williams (75-87)
1978	Montreal Expos	NL East	162	76	86	0	.469	4th of 6	Dick Williams (76-86)
1979	Montreal Expos	NL East	160	95	65	0	.594	2nd of 6	Dick Williams (95-65)
1980	Montreal Expos	NL East	162	90	72	0	.556	2nd of 6	Dick Williams (90-72)
1981	Montreal Expos	NL East	108	60	48	0	.556	2nd of 6	Dick Williams (44-37) and Jim Fanning (16-11)
1982	Montreal Expos	NL East	162	86	76	0	.531	3rd of 6	Jim Fanning (86-76)
1983	Montreal Expos	NL East	163	82	80	1	.506	3rd of 6	Bill Virdon (82-80)
1984	Montreal Expos	NL East	161	78	83	0	.484	5th of 6	Bill Virdon (64-67) and Jim Fanning (14-16)
1985	Montreal Expos	NL East	161	84	77	0	.522	3rd of 6	Buck Rodgers (84-77)
1986	Montreal Expos	NL East	161	78	83	0	.484	4th of 6	Buck Rodgers (78-83)
1987	Montreal Expos	NL East	162	91	71	0	.562	3rd of 6	Buck Rodgers (91-71)
1988	Montreal Expos	NL East	163	81	81	1	.500	3rd of 6	Buck Rodgers (81-81)
1989	Montreal Expos	NL East	162	81	81	0	.500	4th of 6	Buck Rodgers (81-81)

Year	Tm	Lg	G	W	L	Ties	W-L%	Finish	Managers
1990	Montreal Expos	NL East	162	85	77	0	.525	3rd of 6	Buck Rodgers (85-77)
1991	Montreal Expos	NL East	161	71	90	0	.441	6th of 6	Buck Rodgers (20-29) and Tom Runnells (51-61)
1992	Montreal Expos	NL East	162	87	75	0	.537	2nd of 6	Tom Runnells (17-20) and Felipe Alou (70-55)
1993	Montreal Expos	NL East	163	94	68	1	.580	2nd of 7	Felipe Alou (94-68)
1994	Montreal Expos	NL East	114	74	40	0	.649	1st of 5	Felipe Alou (74-40)
1995	Montreal Expos	NL East	144	66	78	0	.458	5th of 5	Felipe Alou (66-78)
1996	Montreal Expos	NL East	162	88	74	0	.543	2nd of 5	Felipe Alou (88-74)
1997	Montreal Expos	NL East	162	78	84	0	.481	4th of 5	Felipe Alou (78-84)
1998	Montreal Expos	NL East	162	65	97	0	.401	4th of 5	Felipe Alou (65-97)
1999	Montreal Expos	NL East	162	68	94	0	.420	4th of 5	Felipe Alou (68-94)
2000	Montreal Expos	NL East	162	67	95	0	.414	4th of 5	Felipe Alou (67-95)
2001	Montreal Expos	NL East	162	68	94	0	.420	5th of 5	Felipe Alou (21-32) and Jeff Torborg (47-62)
2002	Montreal Expos	NL East	162	83	79	0	.512	2nd of 5	Frank Robinson (83-79)
2003	Montreal Expos	NL East	162	83	79	0	.512	4th of 5	Frank Robinson (83-79)
2004	Montreal Expos	NL East	162	67	95	0	.414	5th of 5	Frank Robinson (67-95)
2005	Washington Nationals	NL East	162	81	81	0	.500	5th of 5	Frank Robinson (81-81)
2006	Washington Nationals	NL East	162	71	91	0	.438	5th of 5	Frank Robinson (71-91)
2007	Washington Nationals	NL East	162	73	89	0	.451	4th of 5	Manny Acta (73-89)
2008	Washington Nationals	NL East	161	59	102	0	.366	5th of 5	Manny Acta (59-102)
2009	Washington Nationals	NL East	162	59	103	0	.364	5th of 5	Manny Acta (26-61) and Jim Riggleman (33-42)
2010	Washington Nationals	NL East	162	69	93	0	.426	5th of 5	Jim Riggleman (69-93)
2011	Washington Nationals	NL East	161	80	81	0	.497	3rd of 5	Jim Riggleman (38-37), John McLaren (2-1), and Davey Johnson (40-43)
2012	Washington Nationals	NL East	162	98	64	0	.605	1st of 5	Davey Johnson (98-64)

2012 Nationals Batting Stats

Pos	Player	Age	G	AB	R	H	2B	3B	HR	RBI	SB	BB	SO	BA	OBP	SLG	OPS
C	Jesus Flores	27	83	277	22	59	12	1	6	26	1	13	59	.213	.248	.329	.577
1B	Adam LaRoche	32	154	571	76	155	35	1	33	100	1	67	138	.271	.343	.510	.853
2B	Danny Espinosa	25	160	594	82	147	37	2	17	56	20	46	189	.247	.315	.402	.717
SS	Ian Desmond	26	130	513	72	150	33	2	25	73	21	30	113	.292	.335	.511	.845
3B	Ryan Zimmerman	27	145	578	93	163	36	1	25	95	5	57	116	.282	.346	.478	.824
LF	Mike Morse	30	102	406	53	118	17	1	18	62	0	16	97	.291	.321	.470	.791
CF	Bryce Harper	19	139	533	98	144	26	9	22	59	18	56	120	.270	.340	.477	.817
RF	Jayson Werth	33	81	300	42	90	21	3	5	31	8	42	57	.300	.387	.440	.827
UT	Steve Lombardozzi	23	126	384	40	105	16	3	3	27	5	19	46	.273	.317	.354	.671
OF	Roger Bernadina	28	129	227	25	66	11	0	5	25	15	28	53	.291	.372	.405	.777
LF	Tyler Moore	25	75	156	20	41	9	0	10	29	3	14	46	.263	.327	.513	.840
CF	Rick Ankiel	32	68	158	15	36	10	2	5	15	1	12	59	.228	.282	.411	.694
C	Kurt Suzuki	28	43	146	17	39	5	0	5	25	1	11	20	.267	.321	.404	.725
OF	Xavier Nady	33	40	102	6	16	3	0	3	6	1	7	24	.157	.211	.275	.486
CI	Chad Tracy	32	73	93	7	25	7	0	3	14	0	10	15	.269	.343	.441	.784
UT	Mark DeRosa	37	48	85	13	16	5	0	0	6	1	14	18	.188	.300	.247	.547
C	Wilson Ramos	24	25	83	11	22	2	0	3	10	0	12	19	.265	.354	.398	.752
C	Jhonatan Solano	26	12	35	6	11	3	0	2	6	1	2	5	.314	.351	.571	.923
C	Sandy Leon	23	12	30	2	8	2	0	0	2	0	4	11	.267	.389	.333	.722
OF	Corey Brown	26	19	25	4	5	2	0	1	3	0	1	9	.200	.231	.400	.631
C	Carlos Maldonado	33	4	9	0	0	0	0	0	1	0	2	4	.000	.182	.000	.182

Pos	Player	Age	G	AB	R	H	2B	3B	HR	RBI	SB	BB	SO	BA	OBP	SLG	OPS
OF	Eury Perez	22	13	5	3	1	0	0	0	0	3	0	0	.200	.200	.200	.400
IF	Cesar Izturis	32	5	4	4	2	1	0	0	0	0	0	0	.500	.500	.750	1.250
CF	Brett Carroll	29	5	2	2	0	0	0	0	0	0	0	0	.000	.000	.000	.000
P	Gio Gonzalez	26	32	64	2	6	1	0	1	4	0	1	25	.094	.106	.156	.262
P	Jordan Zimmermann	26	32	57	5	11	2	0	1	4	0	4	13	.193	.246	.281	.527
P	Edwin Jackson	28	34	57	6	13	0	0	0	0	0	3	21	.228	.267	.228	.495
P	Stephen Strasburg	23	28	47	4	13	4	0	1	7	0	3	13	.277	.333	.426	.759
P	Ross Detwiler	26	33	45	0	2	0	0	0	1	0	1	22	.044	.065	.044	.110
P	John Lannan	27	6	9	0	1	0	0	0	0	0	1	4	.111	.200	.111	.311
P	Craig Stammen	28	59	6	0	0	0	0	0	0	0	0	4	.000	.000	.000	.000
P	Tom Gorzelanny	29	45	6	0	2	0	0	0	1	0	1	1	.333	.429	.333	.762
P	Chien-Ming Wang	32	10	6	1	1	1	0	0	0	0	1	3	.167	.286	.333	.619
P	Zach Duke	29	8	1	0	0	0	0	0	0	0	0	0	.000	.000	.000	.000
P	Ryan Mattheus	28	66	1	0	0	0	0	0	0	0	0	1	.000	.000	.000	.000
P	Sean Burnett	29	70	0	0	0	0	0	0	0	0	1	0		1.000		
P	Tyler Clippard	27	74	0	0	0	0	0	0	0	0	0	0				
P	Ryan Perry	25	7	0	0	0	0	0	0	0	0	0	0				
P	Mike Gonzalez	34	47	0	0	0	0	0	0	0	0	0	0				
P	Drew Storen	24	37	0	0	0	0	0	0	0	0	0	0				
P	Henry Rodriguez	25	35	0	0	0	0	0	0	0	0	0	0				
P	Brad Lidge	35	11	0	0	0	0	0	0	0	0	0	0				
P	Christian Garcia	26	13	0	0	0	0	0	0	0	0	0	0				
	Team Totals	27.1	162	5615	731	1468	301	25	194	688	105	479	1325	.261	.322	.428	.750

2012 Nationals Pitching Stats

Player	Age	W	L	W-L%	ERA	G	GS	CG	SHO	SV	IP	H	R	ER	HR	BB	SO	WHIP
Gio Gonzalez	26	21	8	.724	2.89	32	32	2	1	0	199.1	149	69	64	9	76	207	1.129
Jordan Zimmermann	26	12	8	.600	2.94	32	32	0	0	0	195.2	186	69	64	18	43	153	1.170
Edwin Jackson	28	10	11	.476	4.03	31	31	1	0	0	189.2	173	90	85	23	58	168	1.218
Ross Detwiler	26	10	8	.556	3.40	33	27	0	0	0	164.1	149	75	62	15	52	105	1.223
Stephen Strasburg	23	15	6	.714	3.16	28	28	0	0	0	159.1	136	62	56	15	48	197	1.155
Tyler Clippard	27	2	6	.250	3.72	74	0	0	0	32	72.2	55	32	30	7	29	84	1.156
Craig Stammen	28	6	1	.857	2.34	59	0	0	0	1	88.1	70	27	23	7	36	87	1.200
Ryan Mattheus	28	5	3	.625	2.85	66	0	0	0	0	66.1	57	22	21	8	19	41	1.146
Sean Burnett	29	1	2	.333	2.38	70	0	0	0	2	56.2	58	16	15	4	12	57	1.235
Mike Gonzalez	34	0	0		3.03	47	0	0	0	0	35.2	31	14	12	2	16	39	1.318
Tom Gorzelanny	29	4	2	.667	2.88	45	1	0	0	1	72.0	65	27	23	7	30	62	1.319
John Lannan	27	4	1	.800	4.13	6	6	0	0	0	32.2	33	15	15	0	14	17	1.439
Chien-Ming Wang	32	2	3	.400	6.68	10	5	0	0	0	32.1	50	24	24	5	15	15	2.010
Drew Storen	24	3	1	.750	2.37	37	0	0	0	4	30.1	22	8	8	0	8	24	0.989
Henry Rodriguez	25	1	3	.250	5.83	35	0	0	0	9	29.1	19	20	19	4	22	31	1.398
Zach Duke	29	1	0	1.000	1.32	8	0	0	0	0	13.2	11	2	2	0	4	10	1.098
Christian Garcia	26	0	0		2.13	13	0	0	0	0	12.2	8	3	3	2	2	15	0.789
Brad Lidge	35	0	1	.000	9.64	11	0	0	0	2	9.1	12	10	10	1	11	10	2.464
Ryan Perry	25	1	0	1.000	10.13	7	0	0	0	0	8.0	12	9	9	2	2	3	1.750
Team Totals	26.8	98	64	.605	3.34	162	162	3	1	51	1468.1	1296	594	543	129	497	1325	1.221

ACKNOWLEDGMENTS

The author would like to thank everyone who assisted with this project. Your insights, thoughts, and honest opinions are much appreciated. There are a lot of great reporters who cover the Nationals, and I am thankful for their help in providing background information and quotes, especially my old college friend Mark Zuckerman, who does a fantastic job with his Nats Insider website.

SOURCES

Prologue

"We believe..."

http://www.usatoday.com/sports/baseball/nl/nationals/2010-06-08-nationals-harper-first-pick_N.htm

"He pitched..."

http://scores.espn.go.com/mlb/recap?gameId=300608120

Chapter 1

"This is another..."

http://washington.nationals.mlb.com/news/article.jsp?ymd=20041203&content_id=918287&vkey=news_was&fext=.jsp&c_id=was

"What a day..."

http://sports.espn.go.com/mlb/news/story?id=2432187

"We believe..."

http://mlb.mlb.com/news/article.jsp?ymd=20021120&content_id=179701&vkey=news_mlb&fext=.jsp&c_id=null

"I'll tell you why we..."

http://www.startribune.com/templates/Print_This_Story?sid=95430139

Ted Williams info and quotes:

http://sportsillustrated.cnn.com/vault/article/magazine/MAG1082138/index.htm

Smiley Gonzalez info: http://sportsillustrated.cnn.com/2009/baseball/mlb/02/17/nats.gonzalez/index.html

Sidebar

"If he's going to play..."

http://sports.espn.go.com/mlb/news/story?id=2377395

Chapter 2

"It was a total..."

http://washington.nationals.mlb.com/news/article.jsp?ymd=20080929&content_id=3572650&vkey=news_was&fext=.jsp&c_id=was

Bedard info: http://blog.thenewstribune.com/mariners/2010/11/05/the-erik-bedard-timeline/

"There were never any…"
http://seattletimes.com/html/thehotstoneleague/2015383260_ackley_arrival_could_make_losi.
html

Chapter 3
"I was going to find…"
http://sportsillustrated.cnn.com/2009/writers/lee_jenkins/03/25/stephen.strasburg/1.html
"I had to get tougher…"
http://washington.nationals.mlb.com/news/article.jsp?ymd=20090609&content_
id=5226364&vkey=draft2009&fext=.jsp
"I just never really…"
http://mlb.mlb.com/news/article.jsp?ymd=20090610&content_
id=5248502&vkey=draft2009&fext=.jsp
"I had never seen…"
http://www.stack.com/2010/09/01/stephen-strasburgs-path-to-the-pros/
"He didn't understand…"
http://washington.nationals.mlb.com/news/print.
jsp?ymd=20120710&content_id=34808700&c_id=was
"He was in my mix…"
http://www.southcoasttoday.com/apps/pbcs.dll/article?AID=/20090524/SPORTS/90523002/-1/
sports0713
"He was on our radar…"
http://www.baseballamerica.com/today/majors/international-affairs/2008/266532.html
"It's been a strain…"
http://www.usatoday.com/sports/baseball/2009-04-09-strasburg_N.htm
"I've had numerous requests…"
http://www.cbssports.com/mlb/story/11688928
"He reminds me…"
http://www.cbssports.com/mlb/story/11688928
"I was giving…"
http://mlb.mlb.com/news/article.jsp?ymd=20090509&content_id=4636418&vkey=news_
mlb&fext=.jsp&c_id=mlb
"I was pretty excited…"
http://sports.espn.go.com/ncaa/news/story?id=4216074
"I didn't do much…"
http://washington.nationals.mlb.com/news/print.
jsp?ymd=20120710&content_id=34808700&c_id=was
"Washington is going to draft…"
http://mlb.mlb.com/news/article.jsp?ymd=20090430&content_id=4501732&vkey=news_
mlb&fext=.jsp&c_id=mlb

Chapter 4
"We are thrilled…"
http://mlb.mlb.com/news/article.jsp?ymd=20090609&content_
id=5230046&vkey=draft2009&fext=.jsp
"It was an amazing feeling…"
http://washington.nationals.mlb.com/news/article.jsp?ymd=20090610&content_
id=5248502&vkey=draft2009&fext=.jsp
"The best thing to…"
http://www.nytimes.com/2000/12/13/sports/baseball-the-modern-master-in-the-art-of-the-deal.
html?pagewanted=2&src=pm

"I fired Scott Boras…"
http://www.sportsonearth.com/article/39979646
Mark Appel info:
http://sports.yahoo.com/news/appel-fails-sign-no-teams-003100670--mlb.html
"We intend to be…"
http://www.washingtonpost.com/wp-dyn/content/article/2009/06/08/AR2009060803123.html
Aaron Crow info:
http://washington.nationals.mlb.com/news/article.jsp?ymd=20080816&content_
    id=3319888&vkey=news_was&fext=.jsp&c_id=was
"It feels awesome…"
http://sports.espn.go.com/mlb/news/story?id=4403920
"I believe Stephen…"
http://mlb.mlb.com/video/play.jsp?content_id=7174113&topic_id=8048958&c_id=mlb
"I definitely was…"
http://sports.espn.go.com/mlb/news/story?id=5075808
"Why is he…"
http://www.washingtonpost.com/wp-dyn/content/article/2010/06/03/AR2010060304607.html
"He's exceptionally prepared…"
http://www.washingtonpost.com/wp-dyn/content/article/2010/06/03/AR2010060304607.html
"We believe he is…"
http://sports.espn.go.com/mlb/news/story?id=5236853

Chapter 5
"It was an uphill slog…"
http://www.washingtonian.com/blogs/capitalcomment/sports/former-mayor-anthony-williams-
    recalls-the-struggle-to-get-baseball-back-in-washington.php
"The attention rivals…"
http://www.washingtonpost.com/wp-dyn/content/article/2010/06/08/AR2010060805223_2.
    html?sid=ST2010060900179
Debut revenue figures:
http://www.cnbc.com/id/37571281?__source=RSS*blog*&par=RSS
"The most amazing thing…"
http://washington.nationals.mlb.com/news/article.jsp?ymd=20100608&content_
    id=10944784&vkey=news_mlb&fext=.jsp&c_id=mlb
"The only thing…"
http://www.natsinsider.com/2010/06/event-to-cherish-forever.html
"I think he's very…"
http://mlb.mlb.com/news/article.jsp?c_id=mlb&content_id=11836040&fext=.
    jsp&vkey=news_mlb&ymd=20100702
"I really didn't feel…"
http://content.usatoday.com/communities/dailypitch/post/2010/07/strasburg-on-all-star-game-i-
    wasnt-qualified/1#.UGvWSE3A-So

Chapter 6
"I thank the Nationals…"
http://sports.espn.go.com/mlb/news/story?id=4323256
"We had recently…"
http://www.csnwashington.com/06/20/11/A-minor-trade-that-paid-major-dividends/landing.
    html?blockID=536158&feedID=9656
"I don't see a mass…"
http://www.washingtontimes.com/news/2009/oct/6/nats-want-a-lot-from-a-little/?page=1

Chapter 7
"Be in the Hall…"
http://sportsillustrated.cnn.com/vault/article/magazine/MAG1156215/3/index.htm
"Bryce had a…"
http://www.lvrj.com/sports/harper-lifts-csn-to-junior-college-world-series-94686519.html
"He felt terrible…"
http://www.lvrj.com/sports/bryce-harper-s-ferry-to-sail-today-95753119.html
"It's what I've…"
http://sports.espn.go.com/mlb/news/story?id=5262217

Chapter 8
"If he doesn't…"
http://sports.espn.go.com/mlb/news/story?id=5466181
"He deserves it…"
http://sports.yahoo.com/mlb/news?slug=ti-harpersigns081610
"Why can't it be realistic?"
http://www.csnwashington.com/03/12/11/Zuckerman-Harper-impressed-but-has-much-/
    landing.html?blockID=439449&feedID=287
"I hate to bring…"
http://sports.espn.go.com/mlb/news/story?id=6634378
Harper contact lens info:
http://www.washingtonpost.com/sports/now-seeing-in-hd-bryce-harper-lays-waste-to-sally-
    league-pitching/2011/05/12/AF60aG1G_story.html

Chapter 9
"They're talking every…"
http://voices.washingtonpost.com/nationalsjournal/2010/07/
    stephen_strasburg_headed_to_di.html
Strasburg press conference:
http://voices.washingtonpost.com/nationalsjournal/2010/08/
    stephen_strasburg_addresses_hi.html
"We're going to take…"
http://www.csnwashington.com/08/27/10/Zuckerman-Strasburg-Likely-Needs-Tommy-J/
    landing_v3.html?blockID=298830&feedID=5685
"He already throws…"
http://www.bloomberg.com/news/2010-08-27/stephen-strasburg-s-likely-elbow-surgery-
    means-a-busy-day-for-tommy-john.html

Chapter 10
"It's a step…"
http://diamondbacks.scout.com/2/550182.html
"I do believe…"
http://www.csnwashington.com/10/19/10/Nationals-Ink-Rizzo-To-5-Year-Extension/
    landing_v3.html?blockID=334445&feedID=5685
"I sleep like…"
http://www.natsinsider.com/2010/12/highlights-from-jayson-werth.html
"Jim told me pregame…"
http://sports.espn.go.com/mlb/news/story?id=6697463
"For us, there's…"
http://www.natsinsider.com/2011/09/turning-point-for-this-franchise.html

"I see both…"
http://www.masnsports.com/the_goessling_game/2011/06/player-reactions.html
"[He was] a good headsy hitter…"
http://www.federalbaseball.com/2012/10/29/3573066/
    washington-nationals-managers-davey-johnson-and-frank-robinson-on-the
"He was able to seemingly…"
http://www.nytimes.com/2012/07/19/sports/baseball/davey-johnson-baseballs-oldest-manager-
    leading-washingtons-youth-movement.html?pagewanted=all
"Oh, Marge was something…"
http://espn.go.com/mlb/story/_/id/8383480/
    davey-johnson-brings-lifetime-baseball-wisdom-washington-nationals
Davis quote and fine info:
http://www.washingtonpost.com/wp-srv/sports/orioles/longterm/memories/davey/articles/
    poorcomm.htm
"I love baseball…"
http://www.nytimes.com/2012/07/19/sports/baseball/davey-johnson-baseballs-oldest-manager-
    leading-washingtons-youth-movement.html?pagewanted=all
"He's been around the…"
The Associated Press, October 5

Sidebar
"Let's say it's Teddy…"
http://www.washingtonpost.com/blogs/nationals-journal/post/jayson-werth-takes-washington-
    nationals-president-races-into-his-own-hands/2011/09/24/gIQAYqcOuK_blog.html
"I guess it marks…"
http://www.natsinsider.com/2012/10/teddy-wins.html#more

Chapter 11
"It's hard…"
http://www.natsinsider.com/2010/12/strasburg-rehab-update.html
"I went out there…"
http://www.csnwashington.com/08/07/11/Strasburg-tops-out-at-98-mph-in-debut/landing.
    html?blockID=546582&feedID=9656
"It's good to go…"
http://www.csnwashington.com/08/17/11/Strasburg-roughed-up/landing_v3.html?blockID=55
    0470&feedID=5685
"I wasn't surprised…"
http://www.syracuse.com/poliquin/index.ssf/2011/08/poliquin_stephen_strasburg_was.html
"The one thing you…"
http://www.csnwashington.com/sportsnetWashington/search/v/45717137/nats-pitching-coach-
    mccatty-from-everything-i-ve-seen-strasburg-is-fine-9-2.htm
Postgame quotes:
http://www.csnwashington.com/09/06/11/Strasburg-dominates-in-return-from-Tommy/
    landing_nationals_loud3r.html?blockID=560214&feedID=9656

Sidebar
"What they did…"
http://latino.foxnews.com/latino/news/2011/11/17/
    eight-arrested-in-wilson-ramos-kidnapping/#ixzz1e0jmDCxH

"The truth is I'm…"
http://latino.foxnews.com/latino/news/2011/11/17/
    eight-arrested-in-wilson-ramos-kidnapping/#ixzz1e0jmDCxH
Rescue info:
http://sportsillustrated.cnn.com/vault/article/magazine/MAG1194466/1/index.htm

Chapter 12
"He brings a presence…"
http://espn.go.com/mlb/story/_/id/7385033/oakland-trade-gio-gonzalez-washington-nationals
"We saw an opportunity…"
http://washington.nationals.mlb.com/news/article.
    jsp?ymd=20120202&content_id=26551880&vkey=news_was&c_id=was
"I've always been…"
http://www.natsinsider.com/2012/02/zim-its-where-ive-always-wanted-to-be.html
"It sucks…"
http://www.washingtonpost.com/blogs/nationals-journal/post/nationals-option-bryce-harper-to-
    aaa-syracuse/2012/03/18/gIQA7wgBLS_blog.html
Tim Kurkjian prediction:
http://espn.go.com/mlb/preview12/story/_/id/7734460/
    previewing-national-league-east-teams#nationals
Tom Verducci prediction:
http://sportsillustrated.cnn.com/video/mlb/2012/03/26/verducci_nationals.SportsIllustrated/

Chapter 13
"If you didn't…"
http://www.natsinsider.com/2012/04/april-win-with-october-vibe.html
"If you develop properly…"
http://espn.go.com/mlb/story/_/id/7863831/
    phenom-bryce-harper-recalled-washington-nationals
"I really didn't have…"
http://espn.go.com/mlb/recap?gameId=320428119
"He thinks he's sending…"
http://www.washingtonpost.com/blogs/nationals-journal/post/mike-rizzo-calls-cole-hamels-
    fake-tough-calls-for-suspension-after-classless-gutless-act/2012/05/07/gIQAZPO07T_blog.
    html
"He's come a long way."
Associated Press, October 5
"I just got caught…"
http://www.washingtonpost.com/sports/nationals/nationals-vs-reds-gio-gonzalez-cruises-to-
    win-after-offense-provides-rare-first-inning-outburst/2012/05/11/gIQA9mMLJU_story.html
"I've got no words…"
http://www.washingtonpost.com/sports/nationals/nationals-vs-padres-bryce-harpers-first-home-run-
    helps-washington-overcome-sandy-leons-injury/2012/05/14/gIQAbj92PU_story.html
"He's a man-child…"
http://espn.go.com/mlb/recap?gameId=320605120
Clown question beer info:
http://www.washingtonpost.com/blogs/nationals-journal/post/bryce-harper-uses-clown-
    question-bro-beer-to-raise-money-for-fallen-policewoman-in-denver/2012/06/28/
    gJQArErc9V_blog.html

"This is probably his first…"
http://mlb.mlb.com/news/article.
    jsp?ymd=20120616&content_id=33423380&vkey=news_mlb&c_id=mlb
"I texted him last night…"
http://atlanta.braves.mlb.com/news/article.
    jsp?ymd=20120702&content_id=34333078&vkey=news_mlb&c_id=mlb

Chapter 14
"Harp's a good guy…"
http://sportsillustrated.cnn.com/2012/writers/ben_reiter/04/26/washington.nationals/1.html
"You've got a bunch…"
http://www.washingtonpost.com/sports/nationals/bryce-harper-loves-washington-and-says-he-
    wants-to-play-his-entire-career-there/2012/06/29/gJQAnc5OBW_story_2.html
"I love the challenge…"
http://www.natsinsider.com/2012/07/eventful-all-star-win-for-nats.html
"It didn't hit me…"
http://www.natsinsider.com/2012/07/eventful-all-star-win-for-nats.html
"Being able to sit there…"
http://espn.go.com/mlb/allstar12/story/_/id/8155668/
    mlb-all-star-game-brings-chipper-jones-bryce-harper-mike-trout-together

Chapter 15
"Ozzie complained that…"
http://mlb.mlb.com/news/article.
    jsp?ymd=20120715&content_id=35003412&vkey=news_mlb&c_id=mlb
"Nothing, I was just telling him…"
http://mlb.mlb.com/news/article.
    jsp?ymd=20120715&content_id=35003412&vkey=news_mlb&c_id=mlb
"I told [Guillen] it was…"
http://articles.sun-sentinel.com/2012-07-16/sports/fl-miami-marlins-notes-
    preview-0717-20120716_1_marlins-manager-ozzie-guillen-pine-tar-bryce-harper
Maddon-Johnson war of words:
http://espn.go.com/mlb/story/_/id/8078765/
    washington-nationals-manager-davey-johnson-tells-joe-maddon-read-rulebook
"I told him, 'Don't worry…'"
http://network.yardbarker.com/mlb/article_external/bryce_harper_shatters_bat_over_home_
    plate_but_fails_to_match_catcher_john_bucks_feat_video/11387065
"He's a great manager…"
http://www.natsinsider.com/2012/07/guillen-lashes-out-at-harper-over-pine.html
"He's just a 100 percenter…"
http://www.washingtonpost.com/blogs/nationals-journal/post/bryce-harper-ejected-for-first-
    time-nationals-address-his-frustrations-i-just-need-to-grow-up-in-that-mentality-a-little-
    bit/2012/08/30/26cad5dc-f286-11e1-892d-bc92fee603a7_blog.html
"I just need to stop…"
http://www.washingtonpost.com/blogs/nationals-journal/post/bryce-harper-ejected-for-first-
    time-nationals-address-his-frustrations-i-just-need-to-grow-up-in-that-mentality-a-little-
    bit/2012/08/30/26cad5dc-f286-11e1-892d-bc92fee603a7_blog.html

Chapter 16
"You take the best…"
http://usatoday30.usatoday.com/sports/baseball/nl/nationals/story/2012-08-13/
    stephen-strasburg-shutdown/57042340/1
"I'm definitely happy…"
http://www.washingtonpost.com/blogs/nationals-journal/post/before-stephen-strasburgs-
    innings-limit-the-nationals-shut-down-jordan-zimmermann/2012/07/17/gJQA15kIqW_
    blog.html
"I think that all depends"
http://dc.sbnation.com/washington-nationals/2012/7/9/3146993/pudge-rodriguez-stephen-
    strasburg-bryce-harper-washington-nationals-mlb-all-star-game-2012
"I don't make the…"
http://www.washingtonpost.com/blogs/nationals-journal/post/scott-boras-on-his-nationals-
    influence-and-stephen-strasburgs-innings-limit/2012/08/23/39c4c3f2-ed61-11e1-9ddc-
    340d5efb1e9c_blog.html
"Everybody knows he wants…"
http://bigstory.ap.org/article/nationals-strasburg-shutdown-dcs-big-debate
"The guy's a big strong…"
http://bigstory.ap.org/article/nationals-strasburg-shutdown-dcs-big-debate
"Should we follow…"
http://www.cbssports.com/mlb/blog/jon-heyman/19824561/
    agent-scott-boras-slams-tommy-john-on-his-stephen-strasburg-opinion
"When we feel that he's…"
http://espn.go.com/mlb/recap?gameId=320902120
"He's had a great year."
http://www.washingtontimes.com/blog/nationals-watch/2012/sep/8/
    davey-johnson-his-decision-shut-down-stephen-stras/
"I don't know…"
http://espn.go.com/mlb/story/_/id/8351235/
    stephen-strasburg-washington-nationals-not-too-happy-decision-shut-down
"We've come a long…"
http://www.csnwashington.com/baseball-washington-nationals/
    nationals-talk/82-wins-for-Nats--and-still-counting?blockID=767405&feedID=10376
Tommy John pitcher info:
http://sportsillustrated.cnn.com/2012/writers/tom_verducci/09/04/stephen-strasburg-shut-
    down-mike-rizzo/index.html

Sidebar
"I understand the…"
http://espn.go.com/mlb/recap?gameId=320803220

Chapter 17
"It's very satisfying…"
http://hamptonroads.com/2012/10/long-shot-pays-nationals-zimmerman
"I guess it's never…"
http://washington.nationals.mlb.com/mlb/gameday/index.
    jsp?gid=2012_09_27_wasmlb_phimlb_1&mode=recap_away&c_id=was
"Getting on base…"

http://mlb.mlb.com/news/article.jsp?ymd=20120927&content_id=39103068&notebook_
    id=39122608&vkey=notebook_was&c_id=was
"I mean, it's the best…"
http://www.csnwashington.com/baseball-washington-nationals/nationals-talk/
    Nationals-go-extras-to-beat-Cardinals?blockID=781415&feedID=10376

Chapter 18
"I don't like…"
http://www.washingtonpost.com/blogs/nationals-journal/wp/2012/09/24/
    davey-johnson-concerned-about-planning-with-new-mlb-playoff-system/
"I think you guys…"
http://www.washingtontimes.com/news/2012/oct/6/
    nationals-cardinals-nlds-postseason-experience-not/?page=all
"I wanted to go…"
http://www.csnwashington.com/baseball-washington-nationals/talk/
    cardinals-get-zimmermann-nats
"I actually know that speech…"
http://www.natsinsider.com/2012/10/from-teddys-mouth-to-nats-ears.html
"He hit it good…"
http://www.natsinsider.com/2012/10/from-ecstasy-to-agony.html

Appendix
http://www.baseball-reference.com/teams/WSN/

ABOUT THE AUTHOR

Elliott Smith is a freelance writer/editor in the Washington, D.C. area who has covered the Nationals for the *The Washington Times,* Associated Press, and MLB.com. He also has contributed to the *Washington Post Express*, CBSSports.com, and *USA TODAY.* Additionally, he spent six years covering the Seattle Mariners and Seattle Seahawks for *The Olympian*.